# THE RESURRECTION OF PHILOSOPHY

Intercultural Research Series of Anthropography No. 3

# THE RESURRECTION OF PHILOSOPHY

KEVIN SHEPHERD

Anthropographia Publications
Cambridge

First published in 1989
by Anthropographia Publications,
P.O. Box 13, Cambridge CB4 1EZ,
England.

ISBN 0 9508680 3 5

Printed and bound in Great Britain by
Redwood Burn Limited, Trowbridge, Wiltshire.

CONTENTS

# PREFACE

This book is a complement to my *Meaning in Anthropos*, and extends the philosophical horizons of polymathic anthropography, which is my term for an interdisciplinary science of culture.

Though the present book is intended as a work of philosophy, scholarly considerations are not neglected, particularly in the last chapter, where scholarship is particularly applicable in the history of philosophy.

Some have wondered why I used the academic style in my first book *Psychology in Science*, since I am not an academic. The extreme of this query tends to the view that I should not write like an academic if I am not one, and even that I have no right to do so. But if members of the public are deterred from increasing their education, then what can be the possible fate of the public at educational level? Is all research invalid if it is not undertaken by an academic?

Happily, this more hostile attitude represents only a minority of the academic response (or at least I hope so). Other academics have been very much fairer in their estimation.

This book is as readable as I can make it, though there may occasionally be complexities which are not easily simplified. I do not believe that philosophy requires formal credentials, though it does have firm requirements.

Kevin R.D. Shepherd

Cambridge

March 1985

# CHAPTER ONE

## THE ESSENCE OF PHILOSOPHY

In this book I intend to cut across static ideas of what philosophy is. In the Western world, philosophy is usually taken to mean the vehicle of modern Western thought that came into being with Francis Bacon and Rene Descartes. It is often associated with ancient Greek thought, but in a much more indirect manner, particularly on the part of those who tend to regard anything ancient with supercilious contempt.

It is obvious to many that philosophy is not the scholastic method, though some philosophers have been good scholars. It is also obvious to many that philosophy is not reducible to the scientific method of experimentation, though some philosophers have been very scientifically oriented. It is much less obvious that philosophy is not reducible to academic philosophy, although this is one of my contentions. It has become increasingly and habitually difficult for many academics to appreciate non-academic philosophy. In part I sympathize with this difficulty, since "popular" philosophy is a very mixed source of thinking abilities. But not all non-academic philosophy is popular. Further, non-academics and "amateurs" have left their mark upon the modern philosophy that is studied in the academic curriculum, and hence the demarcators are that much less rigidly drawn in reality than is often facilely supposed.

I maintain that the essence of philosophy is not academic philosophy, though it has at times deteriorated into this more circumferential exercise. This does not mean that it is a useless expedient to pick over the arguments of academic philosophers like Kant, Hegel, Bertrand Russell, and Wittgenstein. This I myself have done elsewhere, and I meant it very seriously. This does of course contradict some popular notions that it is totally a waste of time to sample academic philosophy. Even many academic scientists converge with these latter notions.

The reason why empirical scientists frequently express disdain for philosophy is because it is considered speculative. Yet the scientist, in seeking to extend his work, is frequently exasperated to find that he is becoming a philosopher. If he is sufficiently venturesome, he will build theories, which may or may not prove viable. Theories often read like philosophy, but theories are not the essence of philosophy.

In the opposite camp, popular interests frequently denigrate discursive philosophy because it does not sound sensational enough to compete with the latest fad for ESP or spacemen. In these avenues, philosophy is almost invariably deemed equivalent to logic, and therefore irrelevant. Now if philosophy were only equivalent to logic, this judgment would perhaps be substantially relevant. But the essence of philosophy is not logic, though competent logic is increasingly necessary in both academic and popular sectors.

One reason why it is not useless to study arguments in academic philosophy is that a sufficiently complex focus of attention can be a prelude to a flexibility and acuity of mind which is not always present in those who never study anything. However, contentment with the mere study of arguments, however extensive, does not comprise the essence of philosophy.

There has been a great deal of confusion in the priorities of thinking caused by fixation upon the inductive and deductive methods in science. Philosophers are often regarded as exhibiting the deductive method of reasoning. In very many cases this is doubtless true, but the deductive method does not comprise the essence of philosophy.

Nevertheless, there are certain components of the deductive method which have extensions in a very important perspective. Some philosophers have believed (and do believe) that it is possible to know things (or to know about things) in advance of scientific discoveries, and irrespective of whether science is ever able to verify these things. The average scientist finds this difficult to acknowledge in principle, though exceptional scientists have concurred with this view.

Now, if such a perspective has any deep validity, some philosophers are justified in standing aloof from matters of scientific verification, particularly since it is now widely acknowledged that science can achieve only a probabilistic accuracy, and not a total accuracy in knowledge. But in terms of reality, such aloofness would only be accurately grounded if it is the essence of philosophy that has been encountered. Circumferential philosophy, or secondary philosophy, may not achieve anything like an intrinsic stance of perception and knowledge, no matter how vaunted the claim to aloofness from empirical considerations. At this juncture, the contention of substantial differences in perception and knowledge amongst philosophers is likely to arouse criticism, but as with demarcations in the standards of scientific (empirical) knowledge, quantitative differences in apprehension and data loom large. This leads to the vexed question of qualitative differences also, though that much more difficult to chart in empirical terminologies.

Qualitative differences imply, at the least, a deeper philosophy amongst some exponents than amongst others. One could, for sheer convenience, describe this as depth philosophy, providing it is also stipulated that there are many layers of depth, with some of these possessing only a surface value. The deepest layer can then be conveniently described as the most ramifying, the most accurate, the most essential, the most real, if liable to poetic surfeits of description. Academic philosophy does not recognize such divisions, which may be one reason for its currently notorious sterility. Circumferential aptitudes will not know where the centre is, since by nature they are not at the centre. But it is also necessary to bear in mind that a person somewhere in between the circumference and the centre may wrongly assume that he has gained the ultimately central vision.

It is an increasing matter of scientific intuition and logic that the factor of consciousness is too closely implicated in matters of scientific reality for this factor to be ignored. Experts in physics, for example, are beginning to seriously postulate human consciousness as a determining factor in the apprehension of physical realities. This causes some physicists to increasingly wish to become psychologists, and this is no trifling development in modern science. Consciousness looms as a factor that can conceivably be measured (however approximately), and hence now more than ever, gradations and variations in consciousness are likely to become units of scientific calculus.

Academic philosophy is likely to have to take its cue from improved science in deeper matters than are currently focussed upon, but the depth philosopher is not necessarily limited by scientific rates of discovery any more than he is by academic norms of philosophy and psychology. Psychology, for instance, is still a very inchoate science. (In deference to current specialist appetites, I will deal with psychology more specifically in the next chapter, but I myself regard it as an integral part of the present chapter). It is arguable that only a new thinking breed of philosopher-psychologists will be able to sort out the anomalies affecting the academic study of psychology, since, e.g., Freudian, Jungian, and cognitive contrasts are still amorphous in general thinking, and cognitivism is itself beset by anachronistic experimental attitudes of the "old science."

Depth philosophy may be said to be rooted in *both* intuitive capacities and the discriminative network of the alert mind. In terms of verbalism, the former often seems unintelligible without the ballast of the latter. But verbalization capacity and mere conjecture do not constitute either quality (i.e. discrimination and intuition). Verbalism and conjecture tend to be the common stuff of both academic and popular trends in philosophy.

The two fundamental modes of human mentation (currently implicated in brain research) are sometimes currently described in terms of the analytic/holistic polarity. More well known terms are rational/intuitive, though these have disadvantages owing to loose usage. Various philosophers and scientists have attempted to define these modes in different ways. For my own part I am unhappy with "rational," and consider that "discrimination" has advantages over "analytic" in respect of the more advanced perspectives of the relevant mode of thought. Also, discrimination has an implicit affinity with intuition, helping to offset the rather rigid dichotomy that is often deduced to exist between the two modes. Further, it is my view that the higher forms of enlightened discrimination cannot occur without an impulse from intuitive batteries of the mind. Yet intuitive impulses are incomplete without discriminative feedback in mentation complement.

In tabulated form, some of the salients in these modes can be expressed as follows:

| ANALYTIC | HOLISTIC |
|---|---|
| discrimination, corrector to diffuse holistic, scientific exactitude, disposition for specifics, linear logic, verbal finish, some forms of concentration, willpower, some forms of emotion. | intuition, corrector to linear logic, some forms of meditation, disposition for unbroken contours, feeling, instinct, creative and non-creative art, spatial skills. |

Academic philosophy in general assumes that the analytic mode is *the* priority. But academic philosophy in general does not accumulate a depth focus in discriminative wisdom, and is effectively insulated from a great deal of the potential ballast in the holistic mode. On the other hand, popular philosophy is frequently addicted to what I have elsewhere termed the diffuse holistic deficiency, i.e., intuitive proclivities exercised at an insufficient pitch for any deep accuracy, and frequently distorting in their operation. The disadvantages in this sector of diffuse holistic deficiency generally pass unsuspected, resulting in many errors and false claims that are not infrequently amusing.

The position of both philosophic and scientific thinking without holistic mode complement is a painful one, though in general inadequately evaluated. The attempt at pinning down specifics is usually attended by various angles of a linear logic that may or may not prove accurate and creative. A stylized verbal finish is no proof of success, and the inbuilt facility of a corrector to diffuse holistic tendencies is frequently taken to excess, resulting in amplified linear errors and a narrow exactitude.

The two major modes of mentation are sometimes said to be mirrored in the ancient Chinese classic known as the *Yi-Ching*, which was subject to much popular treatment. In very recent times, popular versions of these two-mode concepts have certainly been widespread, but neglect finer points. There has been much academic interest also, facilitated by concrete brain research, but a *modus operandi* for an experiential axis has so far not been accommodated into academic philosophy.

The overall problem with many visible and vestigial ideas on these two modes in philosophical, religious, and psychological formats is that they are obliquely expressed, poorly correlated, and inadequately evaluated. Many unbiased opinions concede truth in this matter; the open question is exactly how the human mind operates and how these two modes can be used to maximal advantage in learning and lifestyle.

I do not presume to give a nutshell answer to this open question, but I will attempt to formulate some points for due consideration.

Persons committed to the holistic mode frequently affirm that "only intuition" counts in the assessment of reality. But their lack of discrimination is not infrequently sadly apparent even in relatively mundane and simple matters. Some say that all words are useless, which one suspects is often an excuse to avoid reading and having to think hard. Yet from the perspective of intrinsics, silence is noble in the face of inane chatter and customary excuses; the problem is that the intrinsic is rare, and that in cultural communication some verbalization is advisable, particularly in cultures fixated upon verbalism.

The holistic mode is often unduly idealized, as if there were no drawbacks to its function. But it would seem that bad moods and other negative manifestations arise from complexities of feeling in this mode. This mode is not only the province of intuition, but also of emotion (though by no means exclusively), a component which varies greatly in its value and manifestation, to say the least. There is refined emotion and savage emotion, love and hate, and other sharp contrasts. Emotion is of course implicated in the analytic mode also, but with very much less capacity for extension. One will expect that control of emotion is not easy for the would-be intuitive, who is frequently the product of instinct rather than anything more exaltedly autonomous.

One mammoth difficulty in the interpretation of these modes has been the extent of their functional specialization in isolation from the other. Some have urged that both these modes are automatically in operation in human thinking as an integral feature which it is erroneous to bifurcate in theory. Others (myself included) deem this an extremely weak argument, since it omits all possibilities of magnification and accumulator strength in respect of a predominance at any given time of a particular mode in an individual mind. Academic education very largely awards magnification to the analytic mode, with a corresponding attenuation of holistic mode accumulation-potential. Hence the holistic mode tends to be assigned to the vague subdomain of manual work by conventional thinkers, who are still very largely following nineteenth century prescriptions for mental scope. It is more accurate to view spatial skills as the common denominator of this misunderstood mode, sometimes typified as "minor" by those biased towards innovations in creativity.

Though creative art may be said to be an holistic mode magnification, it should not be taken as the apogee of achievement in this mode, which is not limited to aesthetic standards or considerations.

At levels of increased magnification, the two modes are not in balance in the individual consciousness. It can be considered a very rare achievement for an intensive balance in focus to occur. Lesser degrees of balance here are not an ideal. Many people are not of course concerned with such matters, including those who decry attendant possibilities in learning and education while deeming themselves to be intuitive superstars. Individual capacity and application varies pronouncedly, and with due consequences.

When discussing integrative matters in this subject, the conventional interpretation is only dealing with the factor of an automatic generalized function in which the two modes are represented only very vestigially. Neither developed discrimination nor hyper-intuition exists at this micro-level. The potential for these achievements exists in the rate of magnification and due correlation of mode characteristics. The fully integrative interplay of advanced mode characteristics is not something to be taken for granted in the facile manner that is too often indulged in.

The disadvantages of working perpetually under virtually exclusive analytic mode influences are quite apparent to some conscientious (and not merely lazy) academic philosophers. A good example is that of Ludwig Wittgenstein, who deferred his Ph.D for many years, and who retreated to remote rural places in Europe rather than work in Cambridge with the Bertrand Russells. He even built himself a solitary hut in Norway where he could live in complete seclusion for a while. He was evidently trying hard to clear his mind of debris such as he had accumulated from his tutor Bertrand Russell. A worthwhile respite from analytic influences does not mean living in a mental vacuum; it does not mean a skiing holiday or a pub crawl.

Self-professed intuitives often carp at "rational" criticism. There is some justification for this stance in respect of destructive criticism, but constructive criticism is an attribute of a valid discriminative faculty that enhances the analytic mode. In the field of actual wisdom, "let go" philosophies are liable to come under heavy fire. These "let go" philosophies are proclaimedly intuition-based (and "spiritual") and denigrate all characteristics of the analytic mode. They are rampant in the free and easy world of gestaltmania, and taper their own intuitive bases to an extraordinary and unenviable extent, with the result that the mind=body equation is sometimes exposited as a naive extrapolation from anti-Cartesian materialist thought.

The analytic/holistic modes are sometimes described as masculine and feminine, an interpretation that appears to have been based in large part upon the rather enigmatic *Yi-Ching*. This may be partly appropriate in a metaphorical sense, but in practice both men and women mentally function with these modes, and hence the stylism is misleading if too literally construed.

Important though the subject of mentation modes is (and too many attempt to modify it and explain it out of existence), it does not in itself comprise the essence of philosophy. Or to be more precise from the anthropographic point of view, the essence of philosophy is conjunct with a maximal achievement of integrative discrimination and intuition, but cannot be limited to this verbal abbreviation without danger of misrepresentation. This is because there are rather numerous factors attendant upon this maximal achievement which are not readily the province even of an enlightened depth philosophy. In straining for accuracy in expressing scope, one is led to the minimal stipulation that an extra-depth philosophy awaits those in transit to the central axis of wisdom from the circumference of academic and popular zones of philosophy and error.

Some will of course object that this proposition sounds far too mystical. This is a common accusation made against perspectives which exercise more faculties than are necessary for physical survival. I cannot help noticing that not a few undergraduates seem to feel that everything would be so much easier for everyone concerned if it were only a B.Sc. that was required for a career in science. They have a point of course, but seniors do not have to agree with them for that reason, even if the former happen to sympathize with the junior contention.

The essence of philosophy is not reducible to the conscientious conduct of one's life in accordance with the theoretical principles of one's philosophy. This can still represent a pronouncedly relativistic situation. The essence of philosophy is, more accurately, the fulfilment of a conscientious objective to penetrate the significance of being and to express this in some way for the benefit of the (or a) human community. This is still a very minimal definition, but one sufficient to demarcate its implications from much current philosophy.

The problem with talking about significances is whether or not these are operationally valid as significance in a total context of reality. I am referring to the question of whether all philosophers who exposit the significance of being have encountered the same reality. In my view the answer is pronouncedly in the negative; the significance of being is not truly significant unless it is ultimately real. If an unalterable standard of significance exists (because of the very nature of reality), then this is likely to recur in sufficiently adjusted human events and their expression. Logical justification of this principle means that the essence of philosophy will be encountered in more than one ethnic guise and in more than one chronological era. But this process is extremely unlikely to be at all uniform; statistics are likely to vary enormously from sector to sector. This does not equate with a "perennial philosophy" as it has been simplistically promoted by various exponents. (For more on this subject, see chapter nine).

Some will perceive that there is an explicit difference in the level of objectivity signified in what I have chosen to conveniently and broadly refer to as depth- and extra depth-faculties of philosophy. Significances may therefore differ in scope without being invalidated, though gradations do exist, and always bearing in mind the transitory nature of verbal vogues.

Some of the ancient Greeks (and Romans) conceived of philosophy as a quest; this concept is largely in abeyance today. Some of them at least did not mean this rhetorically. It was not merely the quest for order in the sense that science envisages, but the quest for "wisdom." This ideal was differently interpreted, but the ancient meaning of the word philosophy (or *philosophia*) frequently had more subtle connotations than it does today. Plotinus, for instance, would not have seen eye to eye with the modern academic perspective of "doing philosophy," but then Plotinus is frequently derided by moderns as being antiquated and mystical in tone. Yet it is difficult to see of what positive use was the negative attitude of Bertrand Russell in denying any intrinsic quest for a wisdom more significant than that of sceptical commonsense. Valuable though this scepticism often is in applicable contexts (I hope I would be amongst the last to deny this), it does not successfully negotiate such facts of life as the supercession of Russell's "logical atomism" by current scientific perspectives which have exploded atomistic horizons.

It is strongly arguable that modern academic philosophy has tended to blanket finer points – ironically enough, in much the same way as theology has done. The meaning of the word philosophy requires a resurrection, not in the pedantic sense of the definitions of words, but in terms of essential aptitudes and objectives.

Some are concerned about the relationship of philosophy to "mysticism," since the latter is frequently not theological. Here there appear to be many misunderstandings. Some think that philosophy has no mystical content, and affirm that modern Western philosophy cannot be considered mystical. However true this may be in general, the crux of this issue appears to be argument over a word that is singularly loosely defined and effectively blank in many inventories. There are some people who make a mystical issue out of even their most trivial dreams, and even motorcycles are mystical media for some contemporary connoisseurs. I would go so far as to say that Plato and Plotinus should not be confused with the latest novels of mystical science fiction which go well with a bottle of beer or an incapacity to do anything other than be entertained by whimsy. I extend the same benefit of the doubt to Gautama Buddha without hesitation, despite the existence of many Western enthusiasts of the "Alan Watts zen" idiom of nihilism.

An unusually sane thinker of seventeenth century Europe was Baruch Spinoza, classified as a philosopher, but in whom some think there to have been a strong mystical streak that is elusive of definition by numerous conventional standards. Even today his example is often favourably acknowledged even by those who cannot feel very much affinity with his writings. Spinoza turned his back upon academic honours and instead earned his livelihood as a craftsman, living a simple external life that did not prevent him from writing. There is every reason to believe that he lived up to his written observation that the undue acquisition of wealth, sense pleasure, and fame are a hindrance in the philosophical quest for the "true good."[1]

It is generally assumed that the philosopher is only a specimen of the analytic mode, hence paralleling the oft-depicted trend of exclusively holistic mode mystics. It is arguable that this is simplistic folklore when sweepingly applied to the categories in question. Yet it remains true that many mystical types are not philosophers, and that many philosophers are pseudo-, unfledged, or otherwise partially skilled. Unfortunately, many philosophers do mislead with a facile logic, just as many shallow and fake mystics easily attract adulation by the means of sensational claims and entertaining ventures such as those of the current "workshop" vogue.

For the benefit of those unaccustomed to this method of analysis, one can state the following points:

1. Depth philosophy is not mysticism as commonly understood.
2. Mysticism is often shallow philosophy, but not invariably.
3. Depth philosophy has mystical aspects, but until shallow philosophy and shallow mysticism are better understood, it is optimistic to assume a common working knowledge of subtleties.

If philosophy does not fundamentally affect the philosopher's mental orientation, even leaving aside problems of lifestyle, it is as superficial as any other pastime. The "philosopher" may deteriorate into a barren theorist because he has not in fact been "doing philosophy" but merely writing essays and taking exams. The result of over-stressing logical propensities in incomplete curricula is enough to produce numerous barren theorists. A logical acumen is necessary however; those lacking basic requirements often become the worst mystics.

Without implying any dogmatic aversion to mysticism, it is obvious that self-proclaimed mystics can and do dupe admirers. The uninformed person is potentially at a grave loss in this respect. Many persons do of course prefer the "exciting" approach to matters of depth, though some pay very heavily for it. Many current "workshops," for instance, are big business venues for the promoters and a respite from tv for the other participants. Clearly, some gauge is needed in such matters; the philosopher ought to be able to contribute here. But it is necessary to remember that only the shallow mystical types come under simplistic categories. The more complex mystical types require a different evaluation, not least because some complex "mystics" have been philosophers.

It is evident that scientists quite often have an affinity with mystical attitudes. One reason for this is that empirical events and discoveries often cause scientists to mistrust chains of formal reasoning, which frequently do not yield logically expected results. However, there is also the type of scientist who tends to an extreme transit in mental orientation, with the consequence that he can mistake a simplistic mystical attitude for a complex one. Empirical verification of depth matters is not amenable to an inadequate investigation at experimental level. No experiment is likely to yield inspiring results in a fool's paradise, and accuracy will be even more at a premium.

In fundamentals, it is an experiential, and not a conceptual, philosophy that is being discussed here. The concept of an experiential philosophy is apt to be strange to Western canons, and is often extremely lop-sided in Eastern presentations. To some extent of course, the conceptual level is an experiential one, but this is a crude equation. There is a great difference between the Cartesian *cogito ergo sum* ("I think, therefore I am") and the action of less mechanical profundities. Conceptual views are often nonplussed by concepts denoting an unknown experiential range, and will frequently repudiate the latter. For instance, what are the stock reactions to such statements as the following, duly improvised here: exceptional philosophers may have abilities and perspectives which they do not expound to inappropriate audiences, or even to any audience at all.

Philosophers of science have tended to miss the point of deeper implications in philosophy. Methodology has become an embarassing question for some scientists, which has prompted at least one major academic philosopher to disrupt the theoretical bases of methodological commitment.[2] But the methodology of experimental science is not that of intrinsic philosophy, the psychology of which is oriented at depth levels to psycho-constants which are not part of the fluctuations of empirical investigations in the physical sciences (and nor the existing methodologies of social science). It can be affirmed here that there is a methodology involved in the route to the essence of philosophy, but to master it requires the discernment of psychovariables for what they are, including those which amount to constants in terms of aggregates.

A philosophy without an adequate methodological rudder is prone to shipwreck in the squalls of nihilism, relativism, phenomenology, existentialism, scientific materialism, and several other variants of ideology. Some or all of these may have their own form of methodology. There is perhaps no logic which will indisputably prove which type of philosophy is the most viable; only the empirical testing of the methodology in its experiential extensions (however blunted) can convey a direct knowledge of whether it is *terra firma* or a volcano that one's vessel has lodged in. But the tyro may be in jeopardy for a considerable length of time before realizing that there is anything amiss with his field of experience.

Merely to refute the bases of any specific philosophy or methodology is not necessarily any proof of disconfirmation,[3] though it may reveal in the case of the more shallow methodologies that it is not worth spending one's time laboriously accumulating a lifelong heritage of ignorance.

There is a sense then in which the depth philosopher is even more scientific than the experimental scientist, particularly since the essence of philosophy concerns a definite knowledge of reality that does not have to be indefinitely concealed by ignorance. An experiment, even if totally successful in its results, may be acutely limited in range.

To assert that a definite knowledge of reality does exist is, of course, no proof that it does. Some will merely believe that such an assertion is sheer optimism, while some will concur owing to prior convictions that may or may not be thorough. One might therefore concede that a more appropriate phrase is viable knowledge of reality, though a great many convinced people believe that their conviction is the most viable. In view of the diversity of convictions, they cannot all be right, which is a more definite judgment.

There is no reason why the essence of philosophy should not extend into other fields of expertise. in fact, the philosopher should be able to clarify (at least some) social and psychological matters. If not, then he may be as limited by current paradigm-thinking as are the more standard aptitudes in the disciplines of sociology and psychology.

Accuracy in scholarship is generally considered to be a specialist activity for which philosophers are non-equipped. History proves otherwise, even though absolutely accurate data may be lacking. The history of philosophy is often written badly, particularly when divided up between very local frameworks. In my view, it is better for a Westerner to study Eastern philosophy rather than Western in order to counteract ethnocentric tendencies, but more desirable it is to study both with accuracy. The philosopher's method of scholarship may differ from conventional exercises in data array, but it should be comparatively more accurate in depicting what actually happened or is happening.

In the history of Western philosophy, Rene Descartes looms large as a primary influence at a critical juncture in time. Intersecting the Renaissance and the Scientific Revolution, his method of logic gained a widespread influence that now results in some regarding him as a source of metaphysical distraction and others regarding him as a scientific reductionist who went too far. Descartes did view the basis of philosophy as metaphysics, but his version of this was piecemeal and more on the lines of a revised Christian theology than the metaphysical standards of the Greek philosophers. His conviction that he was divinely guided is no proof of his philosophical depth, though he was an ingenious thinker. A polymath he was, but not nearly so thoroughgoing as some of his predecessors in the Islamic world. His preoccupation with mathematics and his belief in the certainty of scientific knowledge do not make him a depth philosopher, but a clever mathematician and an influential theorist of experimental science. It is as a philosopher of science that he should be rated, and not as one familiar with the essence of philosophy. (This does not of course mean that a philosopher of science cannot also be a depth philosopher, but the latter will be careful to distinguish priorities relating to the essence of philosophy).

The psychological theory of Descartes is notorious for its rigid separation of mind and body. Unlike some critics, I do not think he was wrong to make a distinction between mind and body, but I do think that he used a hopelessly inadequate method of interpretation in psychology that wielded fatal consequences.

The philosopher need not be a polymath, but in the educational field he ought to be. But the essence of philosophy is not polymathy, though the priorities of an enlightened polymathy should point in the direction of a complete philosophy.

A mere display of words or vocational trappings does not prove acquaintance with a complete philosophy. In verbal media, a minimal requirement for polymathic priorities should be the recognition of a gradient in accuracy: natural science affords only a probabilistic accuracy in knowledge; greater accuracy can be achieved in a science of culture; a comparatively absolute accuracy and certainty is experientially possible via the essence of philosophy, though words might fail it.

# CHAPTER TWO

# THE PHILOSOPHY OF PSYCHOLOGY

The philosophy of psychology does not necessarily tally with accepted findings and norms of the conventional science of the mind. The function of the former is to extend the latter in a productive manner. The former takes account of the experimental reservations of modern psychology, but does not give these reservations precedence owing to the contant need to avoid being outdated. In psychology, anachronisms can be particularly lethal obstructions.

There are different forms of modern psychology, sometimes mutually conflicting. I propose to treat here briefly of some different aspects of approach in psychology, and attempt to pinpoint some salients and alternatives. Undue digression will not be necessary for reasons of coming to the point.

Despite a great deal of psychoanalytic talk about the subconscious mind, even many professional psychologists are still not clear as to exactly what it means and entails. It is not difficult to concede that the subconscious exists, but very difficult to do anything about it in common experience. Yet the main purpose of a science of the mind should be to control the mind (though not in the sense of conditioning it). In this respect, psychology is an integral science, and one may overlook the various branch distinctions insisted upon by departmentalists.

There is remarkably little achieved in pursuit of this control owing to the prevalent cognitivist view that "more needs to be discovered" in order to understand the complex neural machinery and other factors of componency addressed under mind or brain (the two are often treated as synonymous).

Control of the mind, in our present context, should not be confused with manipulation of the mind by official entities or organizations such as is now envisaged by extremist scientific materialism. I am instead referring to a control of the mind achievable by an individual within his own experiential pattern.

One drawback to empirical discovery is that it may occur in too fragmentary a series to catch up with overall implications of empirical dimensions until it is too late to stop cultural anomalies from wrecking the culture.

Recent implications in brain research have tended to be constricted in the official narrowing down approach of prevalent scientific materialism. Some specialists have even relegated certain important empirical matters to the realm of philosophy (deeming this a gesture of contempt, not realizing that they have lost anchorage in a viable empirical philosophy).

The discoveries in styles of information-processing relating to the two hemispheres of the brain have received differing assessments. For long it has been a custom of conventional science to designate the left hemisphere of the brain as "major" and the right hemisphere as "minor." This abundantly reflects the bias of preference for the capacities of verbalism that have been located in the left hemisphere. The right hemisphere has been customarily devaluated, a trend which continues in current neuroscience and cognitive psychology.

The research of the medical scientist Roger Sperry gained a very empirical edge in his work involving "split-brain" patients, i.e., persons who had been surgically treated for disabilities by the disconnection of the brain hemispheres. This controversial practice and resulting data led to the empirical conclusion of Sperry that there are effectively two streams of consciousness in the brain, channelled via the two hemispheres. The data uprated right hemisphere function. Although the left hemisphere is the predominant (but not exclusive) focus for speech and verbalism, the right hemisphere focus gains its own "autonomy" in conscious processes, a discovery that disrupts conventional ideas.

One objection frequently voiced against this new data is that the experimental cases involved abnormal cerebral functioning imposed by surgery. But many controlled experiments with normal human subjects have also attested a wide variety of processing complexities in the asymmetrical (or specialized) function of the two hemispheres that is not easily explained away by those wishing to revert to customary standards. Ironically enough, scientific reductionists prefer to neglect empirical findings and implications in favour of *a priori* ideas of "major" and "minor" hemisphere function.

There is a further twist to developments. Sperry has adopted a mentalist view in which the priority of mind over matter is stressed.[4] This is in contrast to the principles of scientific materialism, which are normally construed as the imperatives in brain research, as with other departments of experimental science.

In my essay *Psychology in Science*[5] I presented a version of mentalism that attempted to pick out some of the neglected details in the connection between a science of the mind and scientific aptitudes in general. It was deliberately presented in a kaleidoscopic format of short compass for philosophical reasons. I will attempt here to round off some of the arguments explicit and implicit in that treatment. I should add that my version of mentalism differs from that of Sperry, though I accept the validity of his model of causal potencies of mental events in the brain.

A degree of convergence appears to have recently occurred betwen Sperry and John C. Eccles, another leading neuroscientist who has been amongst the most unrelenting opponents of an uprating of the "minor" right hemisphere. Eccles has been obliged to modify his extreme denial of self-conscious properties in the spurned hemisphere, but has firmly clung to his relegation of that hemisphere to minor and peripheral status.[6] Another irony here is that Eccles is committed to a (sophisticated) theological interpretation, but his perspective on the brain is equivalent in its basic extrapolations to those of the materialist reductionists.

An early complexity in the focus of interpretation was pioneered by Robert Ornstein, a medical psychologist of California who has received much criticism from the reductionists owing to his emphasis upon an "intuitive mode of consciousness" which he linked with the right hemisphere. Ornstein's thesis advocated a switch in values to this intuitive mode from the over-analytical mental set of conventional science; he focussed upon Eastern "esoteric traditions," meditation exercises, and emerging Western psychotherapies.[7] This approach was considered extremist by many of Ornstein's colleagues, but it is possible to modify it and to see its application in terms of a very feasible enlargement of right hemisphere function. Ornsteinian "extremism" did not advocate an abandonment of left hemisphere function as more popular enthusiasts have done, though Ornstein's version failed to elaborate a finer context of function for the left hemisphere in the necessary correlation with the "intuitive mode."

The prevalent reaction of conventional researchers has been to cast strong doubts upon the extension of the information-processing of the right hemisphere into an "intuitive mode" of consciousness. This conventional position is not without its acute difficulties, both scientifically and philosophically. The conventional neuroscientific argument tends to be that although the two hemispheres have been proven to have different and contrasting styles of information-processing (i.e. analytic/holistic), there is no proof that the "minor" hemisphere has its own mode of consciousness. But this introduces an extremely arbitrary assumption of conscious processes for the left hemisphere only, which would seem in the nature of a biological (or rather psychobiological) failing. The standard recourse employed in materialist interpretation to surmount this problem is to assert that the hemispheres are integrative in their function, and therefore the question of "separate" modes of consciousness does not really arise. This is rather like saying that two people can have a good conversation, but that only one of them can do the talking.

It is obvious enough to clear-thinking reflection that the two hemispheres must employ a substantial degree of integrative function. But it does not follow that such integrative function is pervasive at all levels of mentation. The potentials for higher mental functions are primarily the focus here. This matter is lent accentuation by the fact that many higher mental functions are virtually impossible to pin down in the variety of ingenious experiments currently employed in neuroscience in relation to the brain hemispheres.

A factor not commonly envisaged is that two modes of consciousness which answer to, and complement, the basic styles of information-processing operative in the two hemispheres, are not separate "physical" entities but intersecting accumulators of experiential coding which may influence the subject (or personality) in a way that is logically supported by the very existence of separate processing styles. It is logical that these intersecting modes can achieve a great variety of both integrative and specialized orientations. It can be maintained here that it is illogical and impractical to divorce "holistic" information-processing from holistic experiential patterns of intake and response. The problem is the unknown for conventionalists: if the "minor" hemisphere is an equal in potential and fact, then too much may need to be changed in both practice and theory.

It is here that I have to disagree with the academic philosopher Roland Puccetti, who early urged a "two self" context for the hemisphere specializations.[8] Puccetti's argument is sophisticated, but can tend to cause misunderstandings in the orientation of the two modes of consciousness. Just as each hemisphere deals with the same information as its partner, but from a different angle of mentation, so is the same self reflected at different angles in each of its subfields of consciousness.

It can also be urged here that cognitive function via the lateralization of the brain can change in both range and cohesion according to the dispositional training of the "self" constituting the human being. The adaptation of the self to different integrative and specialized orientations of bimodal consciousness is a subject not included in current educational curricula to any intensive degree, and therefore it is arguably premature to dispense with the possibilities of an advanced potential in both modes of information-processing and consciousness. Mere information-processing reduces human capacities to that of machines, which is a convenient hook for the computer specialists. Consciousness is not reducible to simplistic styles of information-processing unless horizons are restricted to, and fixated upon, such styles.

Psychologist Marcel Kinsbourne has concluded that the biasing effect of lateralization "becomes of less consequence as the further sophistication of the brain corrects for these adaptively irrelevant biases."[9] This is a reference to the asymmetries of hemispheric specialization that are often more detectable in children than in adults, but at this level, the evidence is of a comparatively physical nature insufficient to mesh with complexities in higher mental functions. I once heard of an eccentric Cambridge professor who was in the habit of taking refuge in his wardrobe whenever a visitor came to his abode while he was engaged in complex ruminations. New stresses of specialization at points of concentrated attention seem fairly common in intelligent types, though not always with such pronouncedly eccentric manifestation; that many adults do not concentrate intensively, or for very long, is not to be considered a proof of intellectual maturity.

The tendency to focus upon simplicities has been particularly marked in the trend of allocating specific skills exclusively to one or other of the brain hemispheres. Music, for instance, has often been assumed to be only a right hemisphere manifestation, though expert musicians themselves appear to use analytic-mode characteristics in their vocation. Yet the identification of music with the holistic mode still seems accurate enough in respect of general appreciation. The associations attendant upon emotional energy are similarly prone to simplistic classification. Depression and anxiety can legitimately be related to the analytic mode, but disorders of mood are strongly attributable to the holistic mode. There is the overall complexity of the existence of emotion in both hemispheres being both subcortical and cortical in wavelength, and hence varying pronouncedly in componency and quality. My own view is that a balance of emotional tendencies at an *advanced* integrative pitch can completely alter the structure of emotional disposition at a cruder integrative pitch, though various permutations in specialized (non-integrative) experiences are likely to be required to effect such patterns of transmutation.

The refusal to accept styles of information-processing as separate and interacting modes of consciousness is perhaps a limitation of the researcher committed to physical test procedures. That many researchers have favoured the Ecclesian view of left hemisphere priority against the Sperry research has doubtless enabled them to retain conventional ballast, though it may yet transpire to be a scientifically insane exclusion of actualities and possibilities. Those discovering the less verbal complexities of intelligence and creativity do not have to wear the same strait-jacket.

Breakthroughs of discovery are customarily shelved by both science and theology. Philosophy does not have to acquiesce, since it is not limited to a plethora of contradictory experiments and nor to dogmatism. According to conventional science and theology, we can all go to sleep again in respect of brain complexities. Some neuroscientific researchers have carped that the evidence for an "intuitive mode" does not come so much from scientific experimentation as from experiential self-examination. But a science of the mind is not limited to laboratories for those in possession of bigger minds. Psychology is very often what you make of it by dint of personal effort and commitment; those who rest content with being nearer the state of a cretin than to the experience of genius will conceivably argue that the effort is impossible.

There are some in the current category of mystical interests who carp at any "reductionist" analysis of the brain in terms of consciousness. They query: why seek intuition in relation to the brain? Of course, faculties of the mind will exist whether or not they are related to conventional science, but it is obscurantist for some to deny any such connection. The fundamental complementarity of styles and modes is often neglected and ignored by those claiming intuitive status, quite often for the simple reason that this neglect makes it easier for them to survive in uninformed sectors.

The total magnification of cerebral abilities may well amount to something much greater than the sum of its parts, i.e., a truly holistic phenomenon of consciousness which cannot ultimately be pinned down to physical constituents. But while holding this position on ultimates, one can remind the holistic enthusiasts and obscurantists that if the parts themselves reflect the pattern of the whole, then it is surely worthwhile to investigate the parts for those who have not yet achieved holistic totality.

One of the scientific critics of the "intuitive mode" was neuroscientist Colin Blakemore. He did not deny the existence of this mode of consciousness, unlike certain other critics, but he did firmly relegate it to the conventional status of a "minor" accompaniment to the "major" left hemisphere. This despite his affirmation that we should not pamper either hemisphere at the expense of the other. Recourse to the integrative emphasis logically breaks down at this disparity in status. Blakemore seems correct enough in deducing that intuitive thought is amongst those capacities that are not easily amenable to conventional education, but this is not necessarily any reason to ignore it or to deem it inferior to conventional education. Blakemore urges that left hemisphere powers of speech depend on factual knowledge and prolonged training, but it is arguable that intuitive thought also requires a prolonged training to mature, and that factual knowledge is not so readily to be dissociated from the holistic mode as some would have us believe. I can personally sympathize with Blakemore in defending the necessity of retaining the analytic mode in education, but his warning that an encouragement of the "minor" hemisphere at the expense of the left hemisphere "may produce deleterious consequences in behaviour" is equally applicable in reverse.[10] Elevation of the "major" hemisphere at the expense of the "minor" has for long caused its own crippling deficiencies in education and culture, not least of which was the Darwinian "survival of the fittest" syndrome. Blakemore writes like a staunch Darwinist (or neo-Darwinist), and Eastern matters have never been particularly favoured by this trend.

The astroscientist Carl Sagan set a fashion for an integrative interpretation of hemispheric function,[11] but this does not clarify the occurrence of magnification in either mode. A balanced view is indeed necessary to unwind the partisan perspectives of "anti-intuitive" and "anti-rational," but it is not truly balanced if one hemisphere effectively remains a "minor" appendage rather vaguely tacked on to speech proclivities via spatial mobility and control.

A recent academic analysis establishes the working concept of "left brain, right brain," affording a useful review of experimental data, but without venturing to extend horizons of the subject any further than an endorsement of Sagan's interpretation.[12] Hence magnifications of mode experience are effectively redundant in official investigation.

Turning to more popular versions, an influential interpretation comes from the well known writer Colin Wilson, who has arrived at the conclusion that the "right brain" is equivalent to the unconscious specified by psychoanalysis.[13] I can agree with this in part only, since in my view a valid "unconscious" necessarily pertains to both hemispheres.

The subject of brain hemispheres has recently been assimilated by Jungian psychotherapy, which tends to represent the "Western tradition" in the more esoteric quarters of interpretation. Unlike some others, Anthony Stevens has concluded that the "unconscious" cannot be too rigidly associated with the right hemisphere,[14] but his interpretation does not go far enough in the analysis of mode magnifications, particularly in respect of the left hemisphere.

It is my contention that the achievement of an advanced form of analytic mode discernment and discrimination will eradicate the tendencies to despise holistic mode assets and will, at the minimum, commence to utilize holistic mode assets in a way that jettisons diffuse holistic deficiencies in information-processing and consciousness. Many "holistic" enthusiasts are encumbered by holistic deficiencies in programming, and very often misuse their analytic mode potential.

The vexed subject of the "unconscious" is rather similar to that of the brain hemispheres in that it has been variously defined by diverse parties to no unanimous satisfaction. Some critics have outrightly denied the validity of the Jungian "unconscious." It is not on this account to be considered without foundation, though it requires to be defined with a much greater precision if it is to gain an acceptance amongst non-Jungian brain theorists and experimenters.

It is well known in the annals of psychoanalysis that Carl Gustav Jung seceded from Sigmund Freud on the matter of the unconscious. Freud only saw in the "unconscious" an aspect of the personal entity containing thoughts forgotten or repressed, or elements that had never been conscious in any way. Freudians have accordingly seen in Jung's increased dimensions of the "unconscious" the survival of a remnant of Platonism, and dismiss it as the product of a mystical orientation.[15]

Freud's view has been described as tallying with that of the British philosopher John Locke (d.1704), who interpreted human development as being dependent upon the environment, and who believed that all human knowledge is based on sensory perception. In contrast to this, Jung concluded that the conscious mind of the individual did not come into being from the mere sense impressions accumulated from the time of birth, but instead grew from an unconscious psyche which predates physical birth. In the Jungian worldview, each individual has a personal unconscious and is connected to a collective unconscious. Lodged in this collective unconscious are archetypes, which represent possibilities of thought and action.

When it comes to a close definition of what archetypes are, Jung is unsatisfactory from both an empirical and a philosophical viewpoint. He referred to archetypes in a hereditary context, as patterns of instinctual behaviour.[16] As a liberal biologist has commented, it is very doubtful that anything with the properties of the archetypal forms could be chemically inherited in the structure of DNA molecules, or indeed in any other physical or chemical structure.[17] Nor would Jung's explanation meet the requirements of a non-geneticist philosophy. Hereditary archetypes might suffice for a mystical version of sociobiology, but not for those who desire a more scientific version of Platonism.

Jung himself claimed to be an empiricist and not a

philosopher. According to him, the philosopher "always takes it for granted that his own disposition and attitude are universal," and tends not to recognize "that his 'personal equation' conditions his philosophy."[18] This is standard empiricist denigration, and might suffice to correct the notion of Jung as some kind of Platonist. Jung himself was arguably as much subject to personal equations as other thinkers in physical and metaphysical areas. Only an experiential philosophy can be totally empirical.

Whatever might have been the status of opinions in an encounter between Jung and Plato, it is understandable enough that Jung was at loggerheads with Immanuel Kant (d.1804). According to Jung, it was Kant who was primarily responsible for destroying "in embryo every attempt to revive metaphysics in the old sense of the word." Much more difficult to agree with is that the Kantian doctrine of categories simultaneously prepared the way for "a rebirth of the Platonic spirit."[19] The nature of the Platonic spirit tends to differ with personal equations, and the variations here may even constitute the difference between the *a priori* structure of deductive reasoning and the intuitive mode.

The deductive cause-effect logic inherent in the genetic determinism of archetypes seems strangely contaminated with Darwinian reasoning in its more empirical overtones. Jung's individuation process consists of integrating the conscious and unconscious aspects of the individual psyche, and is specified as involving a confrontation with archetypes of the collective unconscious. But a liberation from genetic confines is not articulated, leaving one with the prospect of a universal repertory of myths and images in Darwinian dimensions. The Jungian objective is a new centre of personality, or the experience of the real self. This is a worthy aim, but the genetic reductionism of the archetypes seems an insufficient trigger for any such achievement. Nor is the presence of a therapist any guarantee in this direction, since the unconscious of the therapist is conceived as interacting with that of the patient, and the therapist is not relieved from the obligation of observing his own unconscious through such phenomena as dreams.

This whole matter seems more complex than in Jung's day, since some psychotherapists now hold workshops for enlightenment that go far beyond the psychiatrist-patient situation.

One would like to suggest that only a fully conscious person can grant enlightenment, and that the genetic lumber of archetypes represents the concepts of an inchoate Western mysticism in reaction to the Freudian Lockes.

I am not suggesting here that there was nothing of consequence in Jung's theories, as many do aver. On the contrary, it can be affirmed that he did latch on to something very important, but that this needs to be expressed much more accurately.

Jung's lack of precision does make it very easy for critics to dismiss his statements as flowery language. From the uniformity of brain structure, he deduced the premise that the collective unconscious in man "contains all the patterns of life and behaviour inherited from his ancestors." He described the collective unconscious as a "mighty deposit of ancestral experience accumulated over millions of years, the echo of prehistoric happenings."[20] This sounds to some like the akashic records of Western occultism.

A more subtly expressed alternative formulation was made many centuries ago, though this is very rarely given attention, and has been poorly reported in stray references. The Buddhist philosopher Asanga was active in India in the fourth century A.D.; one of his themes was *alayavijnana* or "storehouse consciousness," signifying a cosmic repository of impressions created by thoughts and actions. This repository is described as capable of being activated by the self-conscious mind (*manas*), which develops the individual consciousness of self. The repository itself is *not* conscious. This non-genetic formulation is every bit as coherent as the Jungian sequel, and makes more sense in its overall context than the Jungian version does. It differs crucially from Jungian conceptions in stressing that both tainted and untainted impressions are fed into the "storehouse consciousness" by individual minds. There is much in the "unconscious" that is not pure, contrary to Jungian notions of the uncontaminated collective unconscious. The Jungian version is very confused by intrinsic Buddhist standards, and gives only a partial and romantic picture of the phenomenon. Jungians stress the collective unconscious as influencing human mentation, and as being entirely beneficial in this influence. But ancient Buddhist philosophers viewed this "unconscious" in a twofold sense of contamination by *manas* and causal influence upon *manas*.[21] The Buddhist version seems that much more realistic.

The Buddhist model contrasts strongly with the Jungian in emphasizing that perfect enlightenment emanates a pure ideation which purifies tainted components of the "storehouse consciousness."

The Buddhist model makes no mention of the dream situation which plays such a strong part in the Jungian version. Jung interpreted dreams in relation to both the personal *and* collective unconscious. Jung was concerned to extend the limited horizons of Freud, who insisted upon regarding dreams in terms of distorted wish-fulfilment. But the Jungian trend tends to make the contents of all dreams unduly symbolic, and the standardization of symbols and meanings is not convincing and nor in accord with other "esoteric" traditions. Jung himself did recognize that the meaning of a dream should be linked up to the dreamer's state of consciousness (rather than be interpreted automatically), but in practice this requires a much more flexible perception than is afforded by Jungian dream theory.

Popular Jungianism is usually anything but flexible. Synchronicity can give some people a sense of drama and significance in whatever they do. I once knew a Jungian enthusiast who was in the habit of carrying about with him a couple of large books by Jung, as if to give the impression of knowledge; I am not sure that he ever read more than a few pages of these books, since he insisted upon recounting his dreams and interpreting them literally. Of course, one cannot criticize such people – it merely transpires that the critic is believed not to understand mystical matters.

The persistent infantilism of some dreamers is matched by that of Freudians who rigidly insist upon values of distortion and the infantile status of all mysticism.

As for the deductions that the unconscious is to be equated

with "right brain" assets, I believe it is much more accurate to assert that the unconscious is part of the collateral of both the analytic and the holistic modes of mentation, whether one is talking in terms of the personal or the collective unconscious. Further, a viable control of "unconscious" (or subconscious) contents requires a fully conscious leverage to be of any practical significance. In respect of metaphysical extensions, one could even assert that, since time-centredness is a characteristic of the "left brain," then any "universal mind" would require a sequence-operator even more than an expansive present-centredness focus (which is a feature of the "right brain").

It is now being widely declared that parapsychology is unlikely to be proven in the laboratory. The reason for this is that laboratory conditions do not accurately reflect the conditions under which parapsychological phenomena operate. To a philosopher, this disparity does not (or should not) seem strange, since gods of the laboratory refuse to grow bigger in thought than their environment. But while parapsychology is popularly assumed to be another commercial vehicle, it is as well to remind that there are gods outside the laboratory who will similarly remain dwarfs.

A problem with popular psychotherapy is that it is sometimes mistaken for something else. The therapist-patient relationship has sometimes been confused with the teacher-pupil relationship for which Eastern mysticism is noted. The disparity here needs to be pointed out. Psychotherapy involves the reduction of stress and anxiety, and is often successful in this direction, however temporarily. However closely the teacher-pupil relationship in Eastern traditions frequently amounts to this pattern, psychotherapy is not the fundamental intention of "esoteric" instruction in traditional annals. In view of continuing misunderstandings, some Easterners now feel that the only polite comment they can make on this matter is to the effect of: psychotherapy is a Western materialist recourse (favoured by some nominal Eastern gurus) for release from stress in order to get on with the materialist life. The corollary to this is that the psychotherapist who prematurely becomes a guru is merely a pedlar in esoteric dope.

Some Western esoteric enthusiasts nowadays favour ideas emanating from the forms of therapy known as Reichian and neo-Reichian. These have an express commitment to open up the horizons of sexuality, and aim at an uninhibited expression of erotic desires. What is known as the orgasm reflex is cultivated; this is not specifically a sexual form of expression, but it is closely related to the over-arching objective of sexual fulfilment. Closely associated with this are ideas of the institution of marriage being redundant in the desired termination of the "patriarchal" society. While sex therapy may help some people with the kindred disposition to find an aim in life, it is arguably not the great panacea for all ills that it is often claimed to be. This form of psychotherapy was founded by Wilhelm Reich, and there may be an apt lesson in the observation that: "He (Reich) put his faith first in sexuality, then in orgone energy, and the result in his personal life was tragic."[22]

While sexuality can be considered a secondary aspect of function occurring in the holistic mode repertory, its elevation to cosmic status will correspondingly obscure features of orientation that are capable of cultivation in both the major modes, whether it is men or women who are the victims of sexual indoctrination and mass media aggrandisement. There is such an accompaniment to sexual activity as debility.

Descartes is often an understandable target for anti-rationalist aspersions, but not in all respects. Certain epistles reveal how Descartes hoped that psychosomatic medicine would become an instrument aiding people to self-mastery, an instrument that should companion intelligently selected values. As part of this route to self-mastery, Descartes thought that the virtuous person should study the mind-body relation.[23] The discrepancy in modern counter-practice seems both amusing and tragic. In some ways at least, alternative medicine actually derives from this scorned gentlemanly amateur. Descartes did not want the passions to become tyrannical in the human body, whereas many modern therapists thrive on this predicament. The tyrannical stratagem is abetted by the fashionable neo-Reichian policy of assuming the total identity of the mind and body, an equation which can only gratify scientific materialism, which tends to view the mind-body relation as an exercise in casuistry having nothing to do with a self. In short, there can be no self-mastery when only the body is recognized and gratified.

In my essay on psychology, I proferred the postulate that "the traditional element of psychology is a limitation."[24] My phrase of "traditional psychologies" was meant in amiable contradistinction to Professor Ornstein's "traditional esoteric psychologies" in his well known book *The Psychology of Consciousness*. Ornstein was referring specifically to Eastern traditions, but my phrase had a much broader connotation. I do not believe that all Eastern traditions reputed to have an esoteric value actually contain such value, since it is very often only nominal values that are represented. The esoteric is, far more more often than not, a highly extroverted exercise in advertisement, gimmicks, and reliance upon hoary associations yoked to simplistic or erroneous belief. It then has no more "spiritual" validity than Freudian psychoanalysis, Marxism, Cartesian methodology, or Darwinian theory. All these are traditional psychologies, which frequently tend to dogmatism. What constitutes a traditional esoteric psychology is likely to remain a subject for disagreement amongst various parties, but one might venture to suggest that it would be invisible and unobtrusive by comparison with less esoteric manifestations of great secrets and prerogatives.

In respect of Eastern traditions, it is surely well known that many intelligent Easterners who believe in the existence of genuine "esoteric" traditions are accustomed to the coexistence of more anomalous events of proclaimed spiritual import. These intelligent Easterners perceive that traditional elements and trappings of mysticism are easily exploited by diverse profiteers, megalomaniacs, and simpletons. But this perception does not cause them to disavow all traditional values and emphases, which are often surprisingly modern in application when they are presented competently. The deeper traditional values of many Eastern countries do contain much of worth that is lacking in current Western perspectives, including the perspectives of many so-called esoteric enthusiasts and mystical experts.

In many Western minds, disillusionment with flotsam is a trigger for wholesale rejection of deeper traditional values that might be encountered. Some of the critics merely study a pile of the latest paperbacks (at least 95% of which will probably be extremely mediocre rehash), while others forage further afield in the initial hope of enlightenment and/or diversion. Whether tourist or researcher, the investigation is often felt to be a blank.

One of the critics who made a journey to India and Japan was the well known writer and novelist Arthur Koestler. "I came back impoverished rather than enriched," he writes. More drastic was his verdict that: "One is reluctantly brought to the conclusion that neither Yoga, Zen, nor any other Asian form of mysticism has any significant advice to offer."[25]

One wonders what depth of approach had actually existed in Koestler's pilgrimage to result in his return to the West in a mood of feeling "rather proud of being a European." One is even more suspicious to find that his disillusioned mood stresses the "unique history" of Europe, Koestler's native continent. He expresses pride at Europe's power of self-regeneration from stagnation, and affirms that Europe had provided the link between mysticism and logic. He urges that the notion of the crude materialism of the West is fallacious, and finds that a balance of desirable qualities occurred in European thought but not in Eastern thought. The East preferred intuition to reason, symbols to concepts, self-realization via ego-demise to self-realization via the unfolding of individuality; but Europe synthesized these contrasts, we are told. Examples of this unique achievement are stated to be the Dionysian and Apollonian principles; the materialism of the Ionian philosophers and the mysticism of the Eleatics; the negation of the world of the senses by Plato, Plotinus, and Augustine, and the reassertion of this world by Aristotle, Albertus Magnus, and Aquinas; the pessimism of Schopenhauer in confrontation with the superman of Nietzche; Jung's psychology of archetypes which contrasted with Adler's psychology of power. Koestler gaily affirms such unique polarities in a *yin-yang* context, but one is led to wonder if he had actually read much else of Eastern thought other than tourist guides and newspapers. One could, in a spirit of goodwill, mildly criticize such inventiveness with the observation that it reveals the error of ethnocentric attitudes.

This disillusioned pilgrim did not stop at a jettisoning of Indian and Japanese philosophical and other achievements. According to Koestler, the period of nearly five centuries during which the Arabs and Jews had been the sole guardians of Greek learning was a period that "remained barren." Yet, we are told with pride, as soon as the Hellenic heritage was grafted back onto the Latin culture of Europe, it exerted an immediate reviving effect. The touching conclusion is drawn that Europe has an individuality of its own. "It may be a somewhat parochial pride, but it is not smug."[26] Doubtless not if we are told so, but it is grossly inaccurate, insulting, and proof of the incompetence in research and observation that has marked so many European minds for so long.

One might or might not be despairing of such European airs of superiority as are reflected in Koestler's affirmation that Mahatma Gandhi's efforts on behalf of the untouchables, and Vinoba Bhave's efforts for the landless, were modern developments under Western influence. Koestler does not neglect to emphasize that Gandhi himself acknowledged that he was inspired by Christianity, Tolstoy, Ruskin, and Thoreau. But Koestler fails to mention that Gandhi also acknowledged the dominant inspiration of the *Bhagavad-Gita* and the not insignificant appeal of Swami Vivekananda, who in turn acknowledged the inspiration of Ramakrishna Paramhamsa of Dakshineswar, the Upanishadic sages, and Gautama Buddha.[27]

In the face of the formidable determination to be unique, thee is perhaps very little one can do about it except to point out where it leads. In a later bestselling book, Koestler proffered the hypothesis that the explosive growth of the human brain resulted in a faulty coordination between ancient and modern brain structures, involving a division between instinct/emotion and reason. Intuition is notably missing in this paradigm of the split mind, or rather, it is conflated with instinct in the fashion set by Bertrand Russell. In this instance, the recourse of European reason is to heal the split by very artificial, if unique, means of manipulation. Koestler is not without his redeeming features of individuality in the relapse into stagnation, since he makes an applicable criticism of Aldous Huxley for having advocated the use of mescalin and other psychedelic drugs in the pursuit of mystical enlightenment and artistic creativity. But Koestler could offer no saner alternative to this stagnation than to advocate the control of the mind by the chemical agents of psychopharmacology. He approvingly described the range of tranquillisers, barbiturates, stimulants, and anti-depressants as "merely a first step towards a more sophisticated range of aids" which he describes as leading to "a stage of dynamic equilibrium in which thought and emotion are reunited."[28] So much for the defeatism of Reason, or rather the bankruptcy of intuition in Europe. A novelistic salvation in the laboratory at the hands of molecular chemistry is no more creative a prospect than American LSD koans. Others would prefer the Stoics (detested by Koestler) to either European novelists or psychedelic ghosts in the wake of Huxley.

The "dissonance between the reactions of neocortex and limbic system" in the brains of a species producing paranoid maniacs will not be cured by maniacal procedures pioneered by those who do not understand brain-potential.

Are the psychedelics of Huxley and the psychopharmacology of Koestler one more of the *yin-yang* polarities in the unique history of the West in which mysticism and logic are so effectively sundered?

In the Koestlerian affirmations of European *yin-yang* verities, one perhaps has the answer as to why the new and more tangible "left brain, right brain" data is in general treated with only a modicum of perception. If, for instance, the Schopenhauer-Nietzche polarity is taken at face value, it is evident that Schopenhauer pessimistically misinterpreted Indian philosophy, while Nietzche became insane. Which one had viable discrimination and which one had viable intuition?

As to the allegations against Arabs and Jews in the

history of logical thought, why should intelligent contemporary Eastern sufi types – including diplomats, scientists, and university professors – consent to advertise their presence in tourist brochures in order to meet every European traveller eager to assert his cultural superiority at the first available opportunity? They are logically more likely to let such pilgrims vent their spleen on the local exhibitionists.

My inclusion of sufi psychology in *Psychology in Science* meets with disapproval in some quarters. The critics think that sufi psychology cannot be considered at all scientific. But in rather a large number of cases, the critics have not researched sufi history. They tend to work on the simple assumption that sufi = Muslim fanatic, which means a prescientific phenomenon. To the contrary, I take the view that it is unscientific to omit the Islamic era of science and psychology from the history of science, which is still the general academic recourse in the West. The same kind of ethnocentric barrier is to be encountered in respect of Indian and Chinese science, for instance. Some Westerners still render themselves ignorant of Joseph Needham's researches into Chinese technology and alchemy, while India commonly fares even worse in this respect. I had the temerity to include two well known Hindu thinkers – who can be considered avant garde psychologists – in the abovementioned essay. It is only barely possible to justify (to the critics) Vivekananda's inclusion in a philosophical context owing to the fact that he was early influenced by Herbert Spencer (though he subsequently diverged from the British evolutionist). But Gandhi is felt (by the critics) to be of impossible location in a history of science. One feels that social science must at least fit into the Gandhian situation somewhere. I do not believe that the British empirical tradition should so neglect working concepts that were so tangible in practice. I fail to understand the scientific breadth of mind that has become so incredibly narrow in some quarters.

Many Westerners still prefer to think that systematic psychology should be conceived of as originating in nineteenth century Europe and America. However, preference is not necessarily truth; it does not constitute cultural uniqueness, except perhaps in the more derogatory sense. An Iranian psychologist has recently made certain observations that should not be ignored. Reza-Arasteh refers to the experience of creative vision in the "transcendental psychology" of Persian culture, an experience in which philosophers, scientists, (sufi) poets, and others participated and to which they were able to relate their particular skills. Both Islamic and pre-Islamic Persian savants in all fields of thought are affirmed to have ultimately arrived at matters of cosmology and the search for meaning, ultimates best represented in sufi tradition. Illiterate persons also participated in the essential matters of experience. Persons failing to make sufficient preparation have in some cases resorted to the counterfeit medium of hashish.

This experience of the "creative moment" is not as simplistic a concept as might at first appear from a comparison with the present-centredness of Gestalt therapy known in the West. The thirteenth century sufi exemplar Jalaluddin Rumi affirmed that it is necessary to always remember that each experience of this "creative moment (*an*)" is only one rung of a ladder, and that it is a failing to remain upon any single rung. These rungs are only transitional states of experience.[29] The factor of sequence transforms an otherwise static condition, since *an* is of an instantaneous nature, an intuitive flash which only the foolish will rely upon as a permanent achievement. One can view this matter as an exercise in the correlated function of the analytic and holistic modes of consciousness. A training in mere present-centredness is a hindrance, since it conditions the receptive mind to only part of consciousness potential, and can create serious complications in the assessment of life and the quality of experience.

Nowadays, such experiential concepts are widely misused and flaunted by commercializing interests. A common fate of Eastern traditional disciplines is currently their execrable employment by Western gurus and pop-psychologists. Whether it is antique Chinese wisdom, Buddhist lore, Yoga, Sufism, or whatever, the alert critic should take most of it with the proverbial pinch of salt, while not denying a basis in more authentic practice for the more viable ingredients of such traditional psychology.

One faculty of a mature science of the mind should be that of being able to distinguish between the authentic and the spurious, and not to lump-categorize in either direction. The ratio will often favour the spurious, but mathematical accuracy should nevertheless be an objective of evaluation.

Many psychologists still erroneously make lump-classifications in respect of Western mentalism. Nineteenth century Western psychology was largely dominated by an extremely inadequate format of mentalism. Academic psychologists used a highly impractical method of "introspection" that justifiably causes amusement and ridicule on the part of behaviourists. To analyze the contents of personal consciousness only is a good warm-up procedure, but no more than that. Nineteenth century psychology went stone cold, but much twentieth century psychology merits a similar verdict. The new cognitive mentalism associated with Sperry's emergent-interactionism need not face the black tunnel proclivities of introspectionism unless something similar is imposed by blinkered agencies. In other words, the new mentalism will require opening up as distinct from closing down. This measure will not be greatly facilitated unless more psychologists become scientists of the mind and not mere scientists of the body.

# CHAPTER THREE

# THE PHILOSOPHY OF EDUCATION

The philosophy of education requires to be unusually practical. I have heard of eminent lecturers who speak on the problem of education and end lamely by saying something equivalent to a confession of failure: they say they cannot even begin to chart so vast a subject in so short a time. In order to avoid this kind of detour, I wrote an unconventional treatise of compact length in which numerous specialist subjects are dovetailed into a specific approach to education and learning. This approach I have chosen to call anthropography; it represents a science of culture that is both scientifically and philosophically motivated. It is uncompromisingly polymathic, since I believe that the only way out of current educational impasses and quandaries is by a broad-ranging and extremely flexible interdisciplinary policy.

My usage of the word anthropography is in radical extension from the definitions found in the best dictionaries. The *Oxford English Dictionary* states anthropography in terms of: "The branch of anthropology which treats of the geographical distribution of the races of mankind, and their local variations; ethnography."[30] This is supported by a quotation dated 1834, and is anachronistic in relation to my polymathic version of anthropography, which includes data drawn from anthropology, ethnography, *and* numerous other disciplines. I maintain that the insulation of these various disciplines is prejudicial to the interlocking of diverse types of data conducive to accuracy in the study of *anthropos*, i.e. man, or to be even less anachronistic, human, since males and females are signified in the new anthropographic terminology.

Polymathic anthropography is, in brief, the description of human intricacies in history, and the attempted charting of human evolutionary potential. In this respect, polymathic anthropography subsumes the second major dictionary definition, which originated with a statement by John Dee (who was borrowing from earlier sources) in a mathematical treatise dated 1570: "Anthropographie (*sic*) is the description of the Number, Measure, Weight, Figure, Situation, and Colour of every diverse thing, contained in the perfect body of Man."[31] This was a somewhat esoteric allusion to *anthropos*, which achieved a more literal stylization in a medical dictionary of 1839. In respect of brain complexities and attendant phenomena of *anthropos*, polymathic anthropography does include a description of anatomical and psychological structure (and also a radical revision of errors apparent in the work of Dee).

In *Meaning in Anthropos*, I have adopted the format of a research strategy for an exposition of polymathic anthropography (which I abbreviate for convenience to anthropography). I concur with usage of the term "research strategy," formulated by the anthropologist Marvin Harris. My approach is, however, diametrically opposed to that of Professor Harris, who represents a new form of scientific materialism in social science. Harris, the founder of cultural materialism, has effectively challenged those with anthropological interests to formulate a coherent and systematic exposition of their guiding principles of research and theory. I believe that it is a reasonable demand he has made of his academic colleagues, though whether he and/or they will accept the research of a "serious amateur" remains to be seen. However, anthropology is only one of the subjects encompassed by anthropography, and hence the acceptance of the latter in any quarter fundamentally depends upon broad-based educational interests and latitudes.

The treatise abovementioned covers evolutionary theory, medical science theory, anthropology, ethnography, the history and philosophy of science, the history of religion and mysticism, psychology, mind-brain metaphysics, the history of philosophy, and sociology or the "philosophy of history."[32] In deference to methodological considerations, I included a (purposely) brief epistemology in which the "rules" are deliberately non-ostentatious. This is because I concur with those views which deem inflexible rules in scientific curricula a disadvantageous basis for scientific prowess. The thesis goes on to outline some theoretical principles of my research strategy which are of use in coordinating the data contained in that thesis. These principles relate to the set of macro-theories outlined in the rest of the treatise, relating to various disciplines as abovementioned. The theories of a research strategy should be interprenetrating to maintain a useful coherence and explanatory power, and I believe that the interdisciplinary nature of the thesis justifies this arrangement of an interlocking framework of macro-theories.

The cultural materialist strategy emphasizes that a set of interpenetrating theories should be empirically testable, though conceding that a logical coherence is also a major consideration. In contrast, I maintain that the logical coherence of a set of interpenetrating *macro*-theories may far outweigh in relevance the immediate testable results in accuracy, and may better facilitate a knowledge of greater units of testability that empirically supercede unduly parsimonious units of logical coherence and testability.

The designation of anthropography signifies the interlocking of a diverse array of study disciplines that reflect upon human history (and prehistory) and human potential. Anthropology is generally taken to mean the inception of human communities in tribal and other groupings, and can relate to the most archaic vistas in palaeoanthropology. Whereas ethnography is now generally taken to mean the study of contemporary ethnic groups. Hence my stylism of anthropo-graphy can be regarded as signifying the bridging of this diachronic time arc represented at its extremities by anthropology and ethnography. But in between and adjacent are many other specialist fields of study which anthropography attempts to focus upon and coordinate in terms of essentials. It does not claim any total competence in this endeavour, only an incentive to do better than is very often found amongst both professionals and amateurs. Anthropography does claim that such an interdisciplinary science is a viable alternative to micro-focussed penchants for at least some serious temperaments, though it does not deny that micro-studies may be able to aid the macro-variety, and vice versa.

It was Bergson who urged that a man should apply

himself to one particular science only when he is no longer in need of studying all the others. In this perspective, the student might take longer to acquire knowledge (or credentials), but the actual advance of knowledge would be accelerated.[33] Bergson was a young man in his twenties at the time of these words, and he soon afterwards became a Professor of philosophy, whether inadvertently or no. Perhaps one could take the view that Bergson had concluded that philosophy was the best coordinator of studies, though the problem remains of determining which type of philosophy is the most conducive to knowledge.

In the perspective of anthropography, it is not mere polymathy that is important. A multi-faceted learning may simply prove an interesting encyclopaedia with little or no relevance to current issues, with little or no understanding of possibilities in education, and with little or no guide to the maximal horizons in specific branches of study and aptitude.

It is evident that, in the educational field, the question of empirical testability of specific theories involves more time than is readily available for crucially necessary decision-making. We may wait another century or two for clear-cut answers to certain parsimoniously formulated theories in natural and social science, but by that time most of the human race may have vanished. Unanimous concensus of opinion is not a general rule in current scientific studies, despite various empirical discoveries of undeniable importance, e.g., the complexities of quantum mechanics.

Viable educational contributions and research strategies must now take into philosophical consideration such necessary factors as: the visible deployment of different study aptitudes and dispositions in different parts of the globe, the decline of literacy in some Western countries, the ecological crisis, the need for a new type of researcher who will extensively correlate data in different fields and put the results to intelligible and publicly available use.

The problem at public level with the interpretation of significant research is acute in terms of the lack of communicability frequently apparent. Once while visiting a local Cambridge barber during an intensive session of study at CUL (Cambridge University Library), he asked me what my vocation was. Since many people are often puzzled by polymathic descriptions, I merely said that I was studying anthropology, thinking to make his reaction easier. He replied quite seriously, "What's that? Is it any use?" While it is easy for professionals to deride public ignorance and indifference, the increasing fragmentation of research sometimes confuses even the specialists when they have to find out what sources are where, and who is actually the most reliable authority.

In brief, anthropography seeks to chart essential contours in the social and human sciences, without neglecting the natural sciences. It takes particular account of the heritages of non-Western peoples. The European heritage is also covered, but not at the expense of Asiatic contributions. There is still widespread ignorance of the philosophical and polymathic heritages of the Islamic countries, Israel, India, and China, an ignorance that is actually furthered by the confusion wrought by some Western enthusiasts.

Even more fundamentally, anthropography attempts to indicate and outline the priorities that should govern a comprehensive curriculum that works a change for the better in individual and collective psychologies and their behavioural extensions.

Anthropography seeks to encompass the whole science of man, the *anthropos*, in a way that academic social science has often erroneously discounted. Anthropology bears one dictionary definition as the study of man as an animal, a retrogressive cliche acquired from nineteenth century Darwinism that still fetters a substantial amount of research and interpretation. Yet there have been other extremes in the twentieth century which are similarly unbalanced in emphasis. Probably the most famous anthropological name is that of the French structuralist Claude Levi-Strauss, whose many books have helped to stimulate ideas about an unfamiliar aspect of human existence. Yet his reliance upon concepts of the "unconscious" as a background feature of preliterate mentation is arguably both inadequate and confusing for much the same reasons as apply to conventional interpretations of the collective unconscious in psychology and alternative thought. There is much in the tribal "unconscious" that is as malformed and rudimentary as in the civilized equivalent.

The need to distinguish a "whole science of man," a science of culture, a viable philosophy, from less comprehensive definitions and formulations is imperative in the current climate of analytical assessment and the lack of it. For this reason I included much critique material in *Meaning in Anthropos*, since the construction of both theories and strategies is often inseparable from the repudiation of other theories and strategies considered (or found) to be inadequate. The comparative evaluation of different strategies and research penchants is now more relevant than ever in view of their proliferation in literate vogues. This fundamentally amounts to the evaluation of contrasting philosophies, or attempts at philosophy, which very often guide research more than is frequently realized or acknowledged.

Critique material was also incorporated in *Psychology in Science*, an essay employing a (deliberately) idiosyncratic variant of the academic format, complete with differing styles of discourse and a lack of sub-headings – since the essay was meant to be read *en bloc* and on different levels of impact. It was conceived as the most appropriate introduction to those subjects less in conformity with hard-nosed science. This propaedeutic essay reviews numerous subjects of scientific and scholarly interest, and fundamentally constitutes an unorthodox treatment of the history of science. I endeavoured, as discreetly as possible, to reaccentuate the cause of a "universal science" as proposed in the Latin West originally by Roger Bacon, a cause which has been rather variously treated over the centuries. Friar Bacon drew upon Arabic philosophical works for his inspiration in science, though these sources have been increasingly lost to view in medieval and modern annals of science and philosophy. Contrary to conventional books on the history of science, I attempted in this essay to indicate the Middle (and Near) Eastern contribution to the subject in terms of psychological evolution. This theme seems more likely to serve as a meeting-point between Western thinkers and those of the Islamic world than a purely Western scientific approach.

Yet rather than opt for more tenuous metaphysical matters in the propaedeutic essay under discussion, I attempted to tackle pragmatic issues which are currently the subject of much (heated) debate. For instance, I defended the Club of Rome's advocacy of an interdisciplinary approach to questions of brain and behaviour.[34] Because many people, even in the academic world, are still hazy on the important subject of brain hemispheres, I added a critical appendix which makes my position clear in relation to other perspectives which might otherwise have been confused with my own. For this reason also, I prefaced my semi-technical account of brain function with a disclaimer[35] of various cult tendencies (e.g., drug use) that are commonly thought to represent the viewpoint of non-academic thinkers in respect of social and psychological issues. I feel strongly that this mistaken idea (nurtured by many academics) should be corrected. In addition, a polemical excursus[36] attempted to point up the contrasts that the essay as a whole was methodologically avoiding. In this section a support for the Club of Rome was juxtaposed with a critique of both scientific materialism and relativism, here represented by two exceptional exponents respectively: the anthropologist Marvin Harris and the academic philosopher Paul Feyerabend. Both of these Professors are notable polemicists, but at opposite ends of the ideological spectrum.

My disagreement with both Harris and Feyerabend relates to the question of how the conduct of research is to be pursued. Harris displays an admirable concern with ecology, but in a very different perspective to that of the Club of Rome and their supporters, since he denies any primacy of mind over matter. Feyerabend displays an admirable concern with grassroots democracy, but his exposition is attended by an extremely disconcerting and explicit preference for aesthetic value judgments of a "Dadaist" idiom in which flippancy appears to be glorified beyond actual democratic safety level. Feyerabend is more likely to include anthropography in his world than Harris, but I am uncertain as to its fate in the milieux of Protagorean relativism (or rather the modern Dadaist version of this).

Since the arguments involved in the above confrontations are of increasing interest to readers, some of whom require the matter to be divested of its more abstract nuances, I will present the arguments here in greater detail, particularly since my essay assumed the reader's acquaintance with the sources specified.

Paul Feyerabend's well known and controversial book *Against Method* militated against rigid methodology in science, a contention with which I agree. Yet there are pronounced extensions to his argument that concern much more than experimental science, and this was what prompted my stiff literary response. This factor is explicit in Feyerabend's formulation that: "There is only *one* principle that can be defended under *all* circumstances and in *all* stages of human development. It is the principle: anything goes."[37] Note that it is human development specified here, and not merely scientific methodology (some readers have been slow to grasp this).

A few pages further on, Feyerabend warned his readers to remember that the "demonstrations and the rhetorics" used by him do not represent any deep convictions of his. "They merely show how easy it is to lead people by the nose in a rational way." Appended to this is a footnote which reports that the aesthetic Dadaist strategy not only had no programme, but was against all programmes – though "this does not exclude the skilful defence of programmes to show the chimerical character of any defence, however 'rational'." In another footnote, Feyerabend says he hopes "the reader will remember me as a flippant Dadaist and *not* as a serious anarchist," and further states that the Dadaist is "utterly unimpressed by any serious enterprise." Yet further, "a Dadaist is convinced that a worthwhile life will arise only when we start taking things lightly."[38] From the anthropographical point of view therefore, the purpose of criticizing Dadaism is to warn against flippancy being taken seriously. Furthermore, I feel that Feyerabend's supporters should not feel any loss by criticism, since they have been misled by the nose in a rational way.

In the same book, Feyerabend affirmed that his epistemological anarchism differs from both scepticism and political anarchism. He defined the sceptic as regarding every view as equally good or equally bad, or else abstaining from judgement altogether; in contrast, the epistemological anarchist "has no compunction to defend the most trite or the most outrageous statement." More definitively perhaps, "he is like the Dadaist." Quite unambiguous is the affirmation that the aims of the epistemological anarchist "remain stable, or change as a result of argument, or of boredom, or of a conversion experience, or to impress a mistress." In other words, anything goes, almost literally it would seem. The only qualification given is that this type of anarchist "opposes positively and absolutely . . . universal standards, universal laws, universal ideas such as 'Truth', 'Reason', 'Justice', 'Love'," and the attendant behaviour in their wake.[39] This sole pivot for fixity is evidently intended as a foil to dogmatism, but leaves nothing of definite value in its wake. In other words, the philosophical Dadaist can argue for or against anything, regardless of whether he believes in it or whether it is correct or injurious. This approach may prove latitude to some, but to others it will be evidence of indecision and sheer whim or caprice.

A Dadaist will not hurt a fly, affirms Feyerabend. Whether this is meant literally or seriously is difficult to say perhaps, though one can concede that this is true enough in Feyerabend's case. But some of those less sophisticated in democratic openhandedness are more than likely to take advantage of the lack of clauses, since any local standard of human development can apply in taking things lightly. Hence my conclusion that the advocacy of the principle "anything goes" is fraught with as much danger as more tightfisted constraints upon human development, and indeed, potentially even more so given a sufficient scope for flippancy in behaviour.

In the anthropographic view, the art of aesthetic judgments at democratic level does not amount to a viable philosophy for citizens of an enhanced democratic society, but to a flippant pastime for academic sophists.

Let me add here that much of Feyerabend's plea (whether

serious or no) for a grassroots democracy is commendable from a serious point of view. In this particular direction, I can seriously agree with much of what he says. His sequel book *Science in a Free Society* was more guarded than its predecessor, but still firmly in the relativistic style. The same latitude for "anything goes" was still discernible, though doubtless this can change. His deduction of "anything goes" for the situation of revisions in scientific methodology is valid up to a limited point in the history of natural and exact science, but there is a serious logical flaw implicit in the argument which I am totally unable to endorse, and which in my view threatens the related concept of a free society.

According to Feyerabend, one way of criticizing standards is to accomplish research that violates them, a research leading to formerly unspecified practice. The consequence is stated as "interesting research in the sciences (and, for that matter, in any field)," which frequently leads to an unpredictable revision of standards. Feyerabend's formula for such research is: anything goes, a judgment which he deems in conformity with currently accepted norms of scientific commitment to universal standards.[40]

The catchphrase "anything goes" is therefore applicable to "any field" of interesting research, which does of course extend to pseudoscience and mysticism, for which Feyerabend himself expresses partiality. But since the factor of violating methodological rules is not qualified by Feyerabend in the different kinds of sciences and fields of research (neither locally nor universally), this provokes the logical conclusion that the relativistic latitude will extend to the sadistic misdemeanours of persons like Aleister Crowley, who violated methodological rules in mystical and occult traditions. This sadistic "magician" therefore gains potentially flippant latitude for formerly unspecifiable practices in the relativistic sociology which does not clarify different standards of research. If such freewheeling practitioners are not made acquainted with the necessity for methodological rules (e.g. not to torture their wives, a rule which Crowley flouted), then "anything goes" is a disastrous deduction and catchphrase for a free society lacking universal standards to the contrary. "Anything goes" is itself a universal standard in the dimensions of the relativist argument, which is otherwise opposed to universal standards. Is the tapered science in the relativist free society to borrow elements from the Crowleys in order to revise its standards of research? As a member of the public, I very much hope not.

While an innovator like Paracelsus resorted to earlier ideas (some of them occult) in order to improve medicine,[41] he is not known to have committed any more serious a social misdemeanour other than drinking heavily. If a Crowley is likely to be mistaken in some research for a Paracelsus, then I urge that the standards of research require to be more discerningly differentiated and clarified in order to avoid undue mishap.

I therefore repudiate the assertion of Feyerabend that "anything goes" is the only way science can be understood by those committed to universal standards, even if Feyerabend is referring to the Popperian critical rationalists who have not yet grasped what (intrinsic) universal standards are – any more than relativists have done in more flippant equivalents. My remarks on the "open society"[42] were partly aimed at Popperians, since I hold that Feyerabend would merely replace that with another sociological fiasco. The "open society" version of anything goes has been violating standards in psychological and social life with the aid of scientific materialism – in such fields of interesting research as sexual permissiveness (rapists have been allowed to go scot free in law courts), the stimulation of juvenile delinquency by the media, the toll of drug addiction amongst the very young, the technological invention of video perversity, the power of terrorist methods. These are only a few of the new standards which the intelligent public are supposed to accept goodhumouredly as an inevitable appendage to the progress of scientific discovery. The public need to affirm that "anything goes" is a principle for lunatics, and the last principle to be sponsored either in the present or in the future – whether in science or aesthetics, in education or in religion, in fact or fantasy. Since Feyerabend makes no qualifications here, he is effectively advocating the "open society" principle as a "Free Society" principle. Ironically therefore (though some have been slow to see it), I am both agreeing and disagreeing with Feyerabend. But such arguments are dismissed as "moral" by relativists, since that is the most convenient recourse for them.

The answer to social problems is not merely to demote technological science, as some relativists think. Feyerabend is correct enough in insinuating that empirical science is incomplete in its perspectives at any given time. Yet it is not "anything goes" but rather unforeseen factors which revise purely scientific standards. It is my claim that the intelligent public do not want any science ruled by "anything goes" in a democratic society, but instead a social life (or rather psychocultural life) in harmony with the universal, ultimate truth – which does not fit the dwarf constraints of conventional empirical science. Feyerabend ignores value priorities just as scientific materialism does. Whether local or universal, standards of current relativism and scientific materialism have no viable values for the human community, since such values are disowned by "anything goes" and the close approximations of this principle.

Psychology and other fields of research cannot be subject to anything like a hyper-extreme violation of standards in a knowledgeable democracy geared to public benevolence. It can also be claimed that intrinsic traditional psychology, itself a science (however snubbed by moderns), has similarly not been in need of extreme violations – though these have occurred in cultic formats. The contrary inference would amount to equating all early Jewish Qabbalah with mountebanks like the so-called "Qabbalist" Aleister Crowley.

One can agree with Feyerabend that the general public display illiteracy in their choice between such alternatives as the space race and psycho-mystical perception.[43] The answer is to educate them, and not to confuse the public milieu even further by a tolerance towards all idiocies and social bruises and expenses. A flippancy in ideals is liable to land the public in the mire of four letter word occultism. A flippant relativistic liberalism would logically (and illogically) extend to such social abnormalities as that demonstrated by the Thug sect of India, who are on reliable record as having ritually murdered many thousands of their compatriots annually in the nineteenth century era of John Stuart Mill's essay *On Liberty*.

Other aspects of Feyerabend's educational deliberations (partly in alignment with Mill) make far more sense to informed members of the public. Freedom of speech is crucial, and the opportunity to intervene in some governmental decisions still sounds utopian. It is all the more regrettable therefore if academics sympathetic to public initiative tend, however inadvertently, to misrepresent the public in the aims and ideals of the latter. (I am sure that Feyerabend will not be dogmatic over the logical flaw in the catchphrase, and that there need be no acrimony between myself and he if the serious argument against the catchphrase is conceded to be at least as equally valid in the revision of standards).

Another academic with an avowed panhuman strategy, though from a very different angle of approach, is the anthropologist Marvin Harris. Contrary to Feyerabend, Harris is in full support of scientific positivism, or to be more accurate, the cultural materialist version of scientific materialism. Having reformulated the anthropology of Marx, Professor Harris is a formidable opponent of nonmaterialist (and materialist) strategies in anthropology and culture. In his book *Cultural Materialism*, he formulated the cultural materialist strategy, and also gave much space to systematically attacking and "knocking out" his opponents in verbal dimensions. His broadside at the structuralist Claude Levi-Strauss is controversial amongst anthropologists; some deem him to be fundamentally correct here, but unnecessarily harsh, and even crude. But perhaps the strongest antipathies of Harris are manifest in his repudiation of the "phenomenologists," whom he identifies in an unusually broad context, and whom he stigmatizes as obscurantists. Under this heading Harris manages to bring a diversity of Eastern and Western mystical traditions, modern counterculture, Wilhelm Reich, Feyerabendian relativism, the neo-Kantian philosophy of Edmund Husserl and Alfred Schutz, witchcraft, nationalism, ethnocentrism, the shamanistic books (or novels ?) of Carlos Castenada, and other trends. Harris defines obscurantism as something antiscientific rather than merely nonscientific. His bludgeoning tactics here can be accused of undue conflation in the wide variety of traditions which he lump-categorizes. Indeed, his own advocacy of modern scientific priorities can be considered phenomenological in that he does not distinguish between disparate traditions such as scientific evaluation requires. In this respect, it seems a little ominous to read the plea of Harris in his preface to the abovementioned critique "to strengthen the barrier against mystification and obscurantism in contemporary social science."[44] Does this mean new ramparts in academe against democratizers, or against all nonmaterialists?

In reaction to cultural materialist insistences as to what constitutes science, I included in *Psychology in Science* a pointed revision of the etic/emic clause much used by Harris. In brief, for Harris the etic represents the scientific materialist standard as ultimate referee of "observer" accuracy, while the emic represents the many ideologies, beliefs, and "participant" ideas which obscure scientific objectivity. There seem marked dangers of arbitrary distinctions in the extensive usage of these simple classifications, particularly when the dice are loaded for scientific materialism in the assumed event of there being any truth in the game of chance which the world is said to represent in scientific quarters.

To the credit of the cultural materialist approach, one can concede that it is neccessary to compare different strategies in order to assess priorities, though one would hope that strategies are compared accurately, or failing this, compared very briefly if there are not sound reasons for cudgelling them at brutal length.

A remarkable, and indeed a very commendable feature, in the tactic of Harris was the casting of his worldview in the format of a research strategy, designed to demonstrate its theoretical range and to establish its epistemological basis. Not only this however, he has challenged other claimants to anthropological perspectives to similarly demonstrate a scientific clarity by an equivalent formulatory procedure. It was to this demand for explicative principles that I responded with the anthropographic research strategy format.

Harris stresses that the uniqueness of (materialist) science as an ideal deserves to be defended. "No other way of knowing is based on a set of rules explicitly designed to transcend the prior belief systems of mutually antagonistic tribes, nations, classes, and ethnic and religious communities." Yet these premises can be logically disputed without denying the potential value of scientific discovery in the accepted sense. Materialist science is not unique in its idealism of establishing truth, or of recognizing truth, as a universal factor. Yet it may require some strength of purpose in order to meet the cultural (and scientific) materialist declaration that: "Those who doubt that science can do this must be made to show how some other tolerant and ecumenical alternative can do it better."[45] Note the phrase "must be made to show," which forcefully expresses the irritation with rivals. But if materialist science is culturally emphasized as a unique ideal, what chance do serious rivals actually have of proving their universal criteria of truth? In order to avoid laceration for not having complied with coercive demands, I have answered many aspects of materialist idealism in what is hopefully a more realistic research strategy format.

If scientific (and cultural) materialists dub all attempts to disprove the Western uniqueness of science as cultural relativism and a crime against humanity, then scientific (and cultural) materialism should be listed as obscurantist in terms of ethnocentric ideals.

It can be argued that Harris does not outline all the basics of a viable research strategy. This is because he adheres to the scientific materialist belief that it is not necessary to implicate mind as a causal factor in human events. The parsimonious worldview of scientific materialism therefore ignores the ranges of mind as an explanatory factor. For Harris and others, the environment is the answer to all problems and puzzles, which is one reason why they will never solve the important problems. Some scientific materialists prefer genetic solutions, but this is an even more restrictive paradigm.

The cultural materialist strategy is introduced in its definitive text by an outline of its philosophical pedigree. Francis Bacon's inductionism is apparently the genesis of ultimate revelation, but meets with due criticism for its limitations of experimental method. Looming much larger on the horizons of causality is David Hume, though Harris does state that: "I do not endorse the arrogant dismissal of non-scientific knowledge to which Hume seemed to be inclined."[46] Yet he is clearly deferential to Hume's strident anti-metaphysical credo. The ideal of Harris tends to emerge in terms of the contribution made by the twentieth century logical positivists of the Vienna Circle, whose worldview was constrained by an acutely mechanistic view of natural science in which anything contrasting with its logic was dismissed as metaphysical. This does in fact reflect the standpoint of scientific materialism in general, since despite the additions to scientific discovery since made in various disciplines, the worldview is basically unchanged and logical extensions are shirked.

It was the logical positivist Rudolf Carnap who affirmed that psychology is a branch of physics. Harris seems bent upon keeping as close as possible to this stifling view, and his incorporation of psychology is accordingly limited to the behaviourism chiefly associated with B.F. Skinner, in which what goes on inside the head is ignored in favour of visible behaviour. This is arguably no advantage for establishing the truth of causality, despite the frequently crucial importance of behaviour in human affairs. While Harris emphasizes the need for operationalism in the clarification of terms (with which I agree, though with different priorities), his operationalism is geared to excluding what goes on inside the head. In other words, he will only define environmental influences, since his strategy is committed to the parsimonious reduction of mind to visible matter. Now, it may be a lot easier (and at times more appropriate) to analyze only the latter as a causal factor, but it may be extremely unscientific to undertake this form of analysis as an invariable working habit.

The feature of non-behaviourist psychology to which Harris gives most credence is that of Freudian psychodynamics. This is not surprising in view of the cultural materialist preference for bio-psychological influences. According to Harris, Freud's causal arrows were pointing backwards in respect of the Oedipus complex.[47] But cultural materialism is still back to front in the excessive importance lent to biological features as distinct from psychological primaries. Hence both male and female mystics (and some philosophers) are regarded as aberrant, similar to the Freudian habit of regarding all "mystical experience" in terms of infantile traits of regression. Psychoanalysis and scientific materialism thus converge in this aversion to blanketed psychobiological primaries, possibly because consciousness is customarily identified only in terms of lump-aggregates which militate against the finer clarification of experiences and terminologies. Some forms of mysticism are arguably more liberating in the intellectual (and spiritual) sense than Freudian psychodynamics, scientific materialism, and NeoReichian Gestalt; each of these latter approaches have failed to distinguish between sensual ingredients and more intrinsically mentalist ingredients of experience.

I dare to suggest that an enlightened mysticism may be the only answer to unenlightened mysticism, egocentric mysticism, sensate mysticism, scientific dogmatism, scientific obscurantism, and psychoanalytic convenience.

Some of the more enlightened scientists have been strangely antiscientific in respect of materialist constraints with which they are confronted. Perhaps it all depends upon the wrong use of words and logic as to how much of the universal truth can be concealed to maximal social disadvantage.

Despite my strong differences with the cultural materialist strategy, I do not disagree with all the views of Marvin Harris. For instance, Harris has (in my view) justification for his criticism of certain forms of Western phenomenology which maintain that "truths are always relative and social," and which exhibit confusing ahistorical penchants. Harris understandably denies that the corpus of scientific theory necessarily differs from culture to culture. He defines obscurantism in terms of a strategy "whose aim is to subvert the possibility of achieving a science of human social life," and as possessing an aim orientation which "is to increase rather than decrease the semblance of disorder in the sociocultural realm."[48] Anthropography agrees that whoever subverts in this manner is worthy of the stigma of obscurantism, but cautions against applying the stigma in error. The tendency of cultural materialism is to apply this stigma not merely to the neo-Kantian phenomenology of the West, but to all Eastern systems of thought not professing scientific materialism. Harris himself may here be subverting a science of human social life in insisting upon a materialist semblance of constrained order. In ignoring the possibility of a transcultural community of scientific observers amongst non-behaviourist thinkers and mentalists, Harris can be accused of ascribing sole monopoly of truth to only one form of social science created in the image of the physical sciences. The reader uninformed about science might be misled into thinking that scientific contributions have only come from scientific materialists – despite the fact that many of the great names in scientific history have been of a different persuasion, e.g., Rhazes, Qutubuddin Shirazi, Roger Bacon, Johannes Kepler, Isaac Newton, Albert Einstein, to name only a few.

One error of scientific materialism and Western phenomenology alike is the inability to assess differences of quality in th variants of traditional psychologies. This flattening of perspective does not amount to an accurate semblance of order or a lived experience of depth, but instead amounts to an ahistorical obscurantism masking qualitative differences by the superimposition of myopic values and ideals.

## CHAPTER FOUR

# THE PHILOSOPHY OF ECOLOGY

The subject of ecology now merits its own form of philosophical approach. Despite its popularity, little is actually accomplished in the practical sense by many enthusiasts, and hence it is as well to be realistic. So realistic in fact that it seems unlikely that the global situation will be remedied in time to avert various forms of severe depletion of the environment.

One nowadays gets the impression that even if the most stunning ecological revelations were to become generally available at the actual time of discovery, they would excite no more profound an interest than that exhibited for the colourful pictures sometimes found in packets of cornflakes.

Since belief is a close companion of habit, it seems that most people do not want to change their ideas in case they have to act differently. Some of the most romantic visionaries in popular ecology are those most addicted to gadgetry and salary inflation. So artificial are some eco-drives becoming that everything is conceived as being definable by computers, as if the element of unpredictability did not exist in real life. But the point of no return can overtake even computer budgeting, and for this one does not require to invoke the "cataclysm" forecasts in psychic lore.

The boom in Artificial Intelligence is typically viewed by some as one more advance to the scientific credit of man. In some large libraries it does amount to being able to find a book that much quicker, but the expectation of instant aid is not necessarily amenable to the task of having to read the book once located. I dare say that soon all that will be needed to pass an exam in some forms of technology will be a photographed copy of the nearest textbook on the subject.

Creative imagination has long been in limbo in some sectors of thought. Desmond Morris aply pointed out that modern art creations are not superior to the artistic abilities of chimpanzees,[49] but the "naked ape" fashion of interpretation is a fatal thinking cul-de-sac tailor-made for behaviourist susceptibilities.[50] This fashion delights in dwelling upon the mechanical behaviour of humans with ape-like attributes and proclivities, little realizing perhaps that it is the worst human apes who continually stress such attributes at the expense of finer characteristics. The consequences of fashion do not always lead to good sense, even if it looks as though the increasing wreckage of finer characteristics will precipitate the "civilized" ape back to his natural environment – providing it is still there.

It is undeniable that some humans are worse brutes than any ape. The situation will not be remedied under the influence of inadequate and degenerate forms of education which do not understand human potential.

I have elsewhere devoted several pages to a coverage of an excellent review of current ecological problems written by Alexander King, a founder of the interdisciplinary scientific and humanist society known as the Club of Rome.[51] He ventures the conclusion that higher education and research will require fundamental reform in the interests of advancement, and that it is necessary to return to the universal concept of science, i.e., in the polymathic sense which does not leave all the bits and pieces in disarray. Unfortunately, some interpret the holistic view of science as an excuse for escapism and science fiction. Serious ecologists find it just as difficult to talk to some "holistic" enthusiasts as to those know-alls in the opposite camp who believe that there is nothing to worry about (since this would cause inconvenience).

It is well known amongst ecologists that the know-alls have not yet caught up with what the Club of Rome were saying over a decade ago, even though the situation is that much worse at the present moment. With something akin to desperation perhaps, Aurelio Peccei, President of the Club of Rome, wrote a book in which he stated: "The human race is hurtling towards disaster." He added that "humanity can emerge from this crisis and build almost literally the future it desires, if it can make intelligent use of its resources."[52] Yet this is a big *if* at the present time, particularly since the future that many desire is an increasing rise in the standards of living with no thought of the costs of tomorrow. One risks unpopularity if this latter theme is stressed pronouncedly, and since I have liberally taken this risk elsewhere, I will content myself here with a few points that might conceivably gain more credence.

In the sphere of ecological physics, a major problem is that chemical spraying in agriculture has increased the infestation of pests for every major crop in the world. Methods have been devised by the ecological physicist Glen Schaefer to reduce the dosage of chemical sprays to only one-tenth, but he says that this can only be effective in the short-term. He suggests that the only ultimate remedy is the influence of mind on insects, though he phrases this as a key question to which an answer is needed within a decade. He suggests that "nature is the image of man's thought," and that collective thought is somehow represented in material conditions.[53]

This concept at first sounds strange to some, but may become imperative to consider and clarify if material conditions affect natural resources more than is generally envisaged. Environmental disease has not been eliminated by the Green Revolution, and the ever-increasing supply of petrochemicals draining oil reserves is perhaps a slight problem by comparison. One does not have to be an "idealist" in the philosophical sense in order to realize that material conditions are seriously affected by the demand of the industrialized countries for an increasing rise in the standards of living.

One would hope that poetry still has a chance for survival in the material conditions imposed by technological thought. The word Gaia was applied by the ancient Greeks to the concept of the earth mother, which may not be quite the same as the more flippant Mother Earth of space age jargon. James Lovelock has significantly used the word Gaia as a shorthand for the hypothesis that the biosphere is a self-regulating entity with the capacity to maintain the planet in maximal health by controlling the chemical and physical environment. In brief, the suggestion is that the earth is a living organism, and a crucial unit of systems function that tends to make myth more actual.

The problem is that the Gaia concept is still apt to be

confused with the achievements of technological inventiveness such as the photographic reproduction of the earth's surface by the tv cameras of orbiting spacecraft. It has even been implied that the evolution of *homo sapiens*, abetted by his technological inventiveness, has "vastly increased Gaia's range of perception."[54] It is more likely that this is a facet of the prevalent science fiction, since Gaia has been rendered virtually blind by the poisonous leakage of man's ill-applied toys of inventiveness and destruction.

One fears that the Gaia concept is in danger of becoming truncated by the equation with technology in some quarters. The sooner the real situation is advertised, then even the concept of science might be freed from its mechanical constraints.

Some technologists are aware that a large proportion of the population in industrialized countries is disturbed by traffic noises, not to mention other forms of noise such as abnormally loud music often inflicted upon neighbours by morons. It has increasingly been recognized that noise is not only irritating, but also psychologically and physically harmful. The next step, scientifically at least, is to do something about it. Tests have shown that human beings react to noise with symptoms of excessively high blood pressure, a contraction of the arteries, and a bunching together of the red corpuscles. It is to be stressed that these symptoms are not necessarily accompanied by any obvious feeling of disturbance.[55] In other words, the process is much more subtle and insidious than might at first be thought.

While the pace of life is nowadays determined (even fatally) by how loudly a car radio (or cassette) functions at maximal speeds, it is not surprising if speed barriers are contravened and accidents are so plentiful even when the drivers are cold sober.

"Five minutes of solitude and we reach for the tv, a magazine, or organized entertainment."[56] This was one of the descriptions of current psychological standards by the Norwegian engineer Erik Dammann in his influential plea for a redressal of the wrongs suffered by the poor countries in the surfeit accruing to the Western countries. The response to his book (originally published in Norway in 1972) created the Scandinavian popular campaign of "The Future in Our Hands," which has served to show that many well-to-do Westerners are not nearly so happy with current affairs as others would like them to be.

Amongst Dammann's contentions was that Westerners should acquire a respect for other races and a knowledge of other cultures that were destroyed by the European colonialist and mercantile waves. Despite the prolific magazine material and tv fare, the Western public tends to be as illiterate as those lacking all such dubious amenities. How many Westerners stop to think of the effects upon Eastern society caused by such trends as the European opium trade? The British cultivation of opium caused a food shortage in parts of India owing to the annexation of the best agricultural areas for the favoured crop; this trend left a larger blot in the history of China, where the East India Company and other mercantile interests were ambitious in the cultivation of opium. Not only the British, but also the Portuguese, Dutch, and Americans created a market for opium amongst the Chinese, who had previously only used this commodity on a small scale for medicinal purposes. Physical and economic degeneration in China was thus inevitable well before the nineteenth century, when native attempts to stop the fatal process were met with an enforced peace agreement and the surrender of Hong Kong to the British. The United States declared that all resistance to the Western negotiations on the part of the Chinese would be treated as an act of war. The Chinese government had not only to accept the sale of opium by the foreigners, but also an increase in the slave-trade involving Chinese coolies, who were transported to other parts of the world in English and American ships.

Economic theories and market values tend to be taken as the rationale for current civilization. Dammann urges that an increased initiative in values from the ordinary citizen will disclose trends that cannot be explained by economic laws. Economists, marketing experts, and social planners would then have to reckon with the fact, however slight, that standards other than prices, wages, and competition for status, were determining human action. Even politicians would have a new reference point, contrary to their accustomed ignorance of any support for a halt in material growth.

Cultural conditioning seems a formidable obstacle for diverse types. While some "New age" enthusiasts tend to implement crass economic standards as criteria for motivation, Dammann was successfully able to point out how even distinguished men often chart forecasts of the future which amount to nothing more than a continuation of the luxurious living of the industrialized countries. One available report describes how in 1965, a group of scientists and writers imagined what world conditions would be like in 1984. There were more than a hundred forecasts, but they were so unrealistic on average that only four even mentioned the question of food for the starving millions, and only one who thought to predict any difficulties in this direction.[57]

A very different argument for evolution was expressed by C.D. Darlington, the Oxford professor of Botany. He justifies the European intrusion in Asian and African affairs by the conclusion that "what matters is the results." According to Darlington, Asia and Africa were effectively liberated from their former conditions imposed by religion, aristocracy, the Arab trade in black slaves, and the cannibalism of the Congo and remote islands. The results are here seen in terms of "the growth and the unity of all human understanding," though it is conceded that the European idea of progress also brought in its wake the unlimited exploitation of nature. More controversially, the same scientist interprets the evidence to mean that the non-Western world will not in general accept free speech, representative government, and human rights as known to Westerners. Unlike some commentators, Darlington does stress (to his credit) the need for ecological correction, but it is arguable that his general interpretation is unduly influenced by Darwinian concepts of evolution, concepts which tend to sanction the motive of self-interest. Professor Darlington observes that the teachings of Adam Smith, Thomas Malthus, Karl Marx, and Charles Darwin agree that: "the animal principle of the self-interest of individuals, often, as we know, enlightened and extended, is the only motive to be infallibly relied on in the conduct of human affairs."[58]

Is the infallibility of self-interest to be deified in colonialist ventures and heritages of wrongthinking? Anthropography urges that, at the very least, the most enlightened individuals merit a more detailed analysis in their contributions to the more essential growth and unity of human understanding. It ought to be more well known that Darwinian concepts require a drastic reappraisal, since otherwise they will continue to justify diverse crimes and follies of unfledged human understanding.

The Westerner ought by rights to conclude that there was very little self-interest evident in the enlightened social reform project of Swami Vivekananda (d.1902), an Indian who renounced the possibilities of a wealthy Europeanized career to become a mendicant monk. The fact of priests and maharajas did not prevent him from speaking in intelligent and non-dogmatic English during his travels in Europe and America during the 1890's, where he had difficulty in trying to correct the distorted Western conceptions of his compatriots as backward primitives who were desperately in need of conversion by the Christian missionaries (since the British Raj were too busy with affairs of colonialism to see to matters of social salvation). At the Parliament of Religions convened at Chicago in 1893, he criticized the policy of the Christian missionaries and affirmed that it was not religion but "bread that the suffering millions of burning India cry out for with parched throats."[59] This exemplar of free speech was a powerful advocate of human rights and the non-materialist values of Vedantic philosophy, both of these causes being endangered by the growing influence of Darwinist thought. It was not only the erstwhile dogmatism of orthodox religion with which he had to contend in both India and the West. It is perhaps no wonder that he died at the early age of thirty-nine, worn out from his labours, which were not sufficient to halt the retrogression and disunity of human understanding.

Why, one might pointedly ask, are not the Vivekanandas included in the conventional histories and "evolution" dissertations of the current milieu dominated by scientific materialism? Is it that the repressed vistas are too non-animal in principle for more pedestrian horizons of preferred fact and value?[60]

The cherished assumption that European Reason led to an adequate understanding of man and nature is reflected in the theories of the anthropologist Marvin Harris. Demonstrating the approach of cultural and scientific materialism, his ecological thesis *Cannibals and Kings* has been advertised as being as significant a book for the study of cultural development as Darwin's *Origin of Species* was for biological evolution. Certainly, there is a similar lack of scope for the importance of mind in human development evidenced in these two works. To do him credit, Professor Harris is unusually lucid in his concern to establish ecological (and demographic) factors as a pressing matter for attention and remedy. This aspect of his thesis is not at issue here. Nor is it necessary to disagree that the major transformations of human social life do not as a rule correspond to the consciously held objectives of the historical participants. But his version of cultural determinism makes a total insistence that "the thought and behaviour of individuals are always channelled by cultural and ecological restraints and opportunities."[61] The problem with the cultural materialist analysis of culture is that it excludes consideration of mental patterns inextricably connected with ecological restraints, ecological depletions, ecological catastrophes, and ecological rectifications. Those who already believe in the importance of ecological trends and responses are very often those most dissatisfied with a mechanistic model. To insist that people get down to brass tacks instead of irrelevant camouflaging antics is one thing; it is quite another to obscure the parallel train of cause-effect operative in psychological function and malfunction. Indeed, it is arguable that without due knowledge of the latter, it will never be possible to thoroughly achieve ecological solutions.

Explanations of cultural evolution in a Neo-Darwinian mould derive their rationale from the environment when the exponents perceive that geneticist models are inadequate. But nor will an environment-based philosophy (such as cultural materialism) come to grips with the deeper reasons for the deterioration and fall of cultures, since the mode of production (and reproduction, as specified by Harris) is only one of the macro-patterns selected and improvised by aggregate efforts. Were it not so, the survival of the fittest would logically be an evolutionary goal, and cultural vicissitudes like colonialism could logically be excused on the grounds that a new science of survival had gained circulation in an intercultural environment.

## CHAPTER FIVE

# AN UNORTHODOX NEW AGE PERSPECTIVE

In the attempt to extend educational horizons to maximal public benefit, anthropography does not hesitate to give attention to concerns broadly identifiable as "New age" thinking, in many respects representing a hybrid popular movement, though more critical thinkers are also associated with this focus.

The "New age" has become a blanket term for a variety of different approaches in "holistic" thinking, some of which have received much justifiable criticism. A major problem is that many proponents of "New age" perspectives now customarily reject criticism of flaws, and label even constructive criticism as "self-assertion." The disadvantages of this outlook are a loophole for the most severe criticism from non-partisans, since it is apparent that everyone can "do their own thing" without fear of any criticism at all within partisan ranks. I have attempted in *Psychology in Science* to point out some of the factors that need intelligent correcting from the more literate partisans of a new age. In this chapter I write as an unorthodox partisan. In deference to prevalent non-critical tastes in this sector, I will largely omit critique at personal level of contrasting viewpoints. What I hope to do is to clarify some basic issues that are of pressing interest to both academic and non-academic liberal thinkers.

The term "New age" popularly refers to the astronomical transition from the age of Pisces to that of Aquarius, part of the astronomical phenomenon of the precession of the equinoxes. The astrological beliefs associated with this sound very naive to critics, but the anticipated new age can also be taken as referring to the necessary transition in ecological tactics and thinking habits necessary for human survival and human progress.

There are some very different types of new age thinker, some alienated from the more vulgar idioms in vogue. The spectacle is one of ecologists versus gurus, anti-drug exponents versus drug advocates, the more reserved "academic" enthusiasts in contrast to the more extroverted accretions of the lunatic fringe. Superficially they are lumped together, but in reality there are some acute differences. Some (myself included) decline the "New age" label owing to the hybrid ingredients attaching to it. But those who take a new age most seriously are probably the most critical of the more juvenile tendencies of enthusiasm.

The commercial ASC (altered state of consciousness) and the unqualified "five minute" acupuncturist are among the more undesirable features of the uncritically qualified New age. One does not wish to unduly criticize a movement averse to criticism, but it is arguably some of the worst forms of self-assertion that masquerade as being in attunement with the Aquarian Age. It is a fact that close examination of astrological significations reveals a "Piscean" tendency in some New age approaches. Where is the true "Aquarian" spirit of objective appraisal?

It is now an irony of history to observe some "New age" approaches to alternative lifestyles: computers and gadgetry, slick sales talk and aids to big business meditations. Some of the New age superstars are perhaps amongst the least likely persons to adjust to the anticipated changeover in energy consumptions.

There are some commercial consultants who charge exorbitant fees for their other-worldly and this-worldly advice, and no doubt the commercial New age will be as expensive as the old one in the demand for an increase in the standards of living.

Meditation has become one of the most saleable wares in Western fashion. The various gimmicks and meditation masters are no reflection upon meditation itself. I have myself practiced meditation (privately) since the age of fourteen, prior to the hippy boom, and hence am not criticizing from thin air. In my view, there is no necessity for meditation masters, but a very great need for commonsense in the application of mental procedures made superfluously exotic by trendy know-alls. I must add that I do not envy those who never meditate, or who imagine that to cease talking is a terrifying experience. The most terrifying experience for a deep thinker is probably that of observing shallow thinkers at close range.

Now that samadhi is available on cassette and video, doubtless there will be more revelations of instant illumination than ever before.

The incredible margin for error in Western approaches to Eastern discipline has often fascinated me, and also eroded my sense of faith in Western commonsense. In one Buddhist ashram, I once encountered the case of a Western gent practising acupuncture on a hysterical young woman who was apparently thrilled at the mysterious touch of needles to her hands. The practitioner had read a book or two on acupuncture which he happened to think were interesting. He clearly liked the attention of young women prone to hysteria. It was my first introduction to amateur acupuncture, and I still doubt whether many cases go much further than that.

Detection of an acutely sloppy approach in such matters long ago led me to the realization that "anything goes" in popular acquisitions and imitations of hallowed practices and methodologies. I was perhaps more surprised to find this vagueness verbally encoded in the writings of a leading modern academic philosopher, namely Paul Feyerabend. Some New age enthusiasts have become interested in the relevant argument, and so I mention it here in a hopefully constructive context of criticism. Feyerabend is a much more intelligent philosopher than some of his contemporaries, and is so allusive in his style that even his fellow academics are not always certain what it is that he is saying. In replying to Feyerabend, one does not use the same tactic that one would with other contemporary philosophers, e.g., critical rationalists, since his style is that much more elastic. In my initial rendition of Feyerabend's "anything goes," I was not of course meaning that Feyerabend had literally stated all that I verbally decoded in the relevant section of my essay. Rather, it was the implications of the argument that were decoded, much as Feyerabend arrays the implications of the arguments of his opponents. For Feyerabend, "anything goes" appears to be the only solution for his opponents (e.g. the Popperians) in assessing complexities in the history and philosophy of science. But in avoiding an extension of deeper standards, Feyerabend leaves the potential of psychology and other sciences unclarified, and in peril from random interpretations. Since Feyerabend is sometimes associated with a form of New age concept, this open-handedness is of questionable value for more rigorous new age thinkers, particularly in psychology and ecology. I personally prefer less ambiguous arguments than Feyerabend offers on such points, though I must admit to being a member of the public and not an academic.

New age concepts have many worthwhile features in their inchoate representation, but if these concepts remain unclarified in terms of context and meaning, they will amount to another popular religion that ignores finer points of both metaphysic and social cohesion. True, heretics will be tolerated, but so will all the villains. The more thorough new age thinkers are not happy at the prospect of greater values being submerged by lesser ones. The ecologists of the broad trend designated have already been complaining that the attention given to dubious gurus and showmen has offset the drive needed for immediate global renovation.

The fundamental new age incentive was originally in reaction to technology. Yet some of the current exponents in the limelight are very technologically minded, and one suspects that a vast inventory of New Age patents will be required to cover all the New Age toys of technology. What happens to ideals when they become corrupted? Why do some New Age centres now require computers to keep check on their accounts and other proceedings?

The logical outcome of non-criticism of the "anything goes" mentality is that the New age universities (if there are any) will be teaching subjects like computer finance and voodoo alongside more intrinsic subjects, while equal scope will be given to those discoursing on the human being as a naked ape. I beg to be excused from this education; my response would be exactly the same as occurred in the Old age – I would want to leave school before any university syllabus is imposed upon me.

I do not think I will ever be able to understand why some

heroes of the more occult New Age think that Aleister Crowley was an "advanced yogi." A sadist he was, and that description is more accurate in terms of educational necessity.

It is a fact that some Eastern metaphysical teachers view Western perspectives on the occult with acute reserve. Tibetans, Hindus, and Muslims alike are often too polite as guests on Western soil to say very much about the incongruities of Western spiritual diets. This being so, it is up to Westerners to appropriately point out the Western precipices for those in both the old and new ages.

It is therefore to be hoped that unorthodox new age perspectives will gain an ascendancy in popular thinking, enabling more thinkers to create a united front against influences that will merely serve to weaken and cripple new trends before these have passed kindergarten stage.

The cluster of key concepts underlying the proposed new age is often surprisingly loosely defined. The time has come to sharpen the context and ascertain what the aims really are. If a new age philosophy is to prove viable, the clarification must be attempted, or else the prevalent vagueness and convenience will merely amount to one more deleted signpost from which creative thinkers will veer away. Owing to the disparities of "anything goes," I am prepared to incorporate clarified new age aptitudes in anthropography, but I am not prepared to subsume anthropography under New Age. At present the two are very distinct; a resurrected philosophy requires extra-clarity, not a loss in clarity, a loss which has been the fate of both conventional and unconventional philosophy in the modern era.

I frequently find myself in an atypical situation. I started my freethinking career as an (extremely) atypical drop-out who was not part of any drop-out movement. I was subsequently at acute loggerheads with the hippy movement whose ideals often resembled something like that of matchstick men in a nightmare of drug-taking and permissiveness. I have since been at pains to acquire a self-taught curriculum that I find to be uncommon amongst non-academics, though I am a complete outsider insofar as academic credentials are concerned. But I do not believe that rigorous perspectives of the self-taught are any more in error than the principles of "anything goes" or "only a fraction of human knowledge is to be specialized in."

I propose here to list key ideals of New age thinking, and to point out some of the deterioration that is already evident. I will also suggest extensions of the ideals in ways that allow for a working evaluation of contradictory and parasitic elements:

## 1. **Ecological balance**

The emphasis here is the rectification of ecological maladies; the planet itself is regarded as a living organism. The fundamental outlook seeks to bridge the gap in time between now and the anticipated changeover to new forms of energy use (if these do in fact become generally available). Hence existing technology is to be outmanoeuvred in both our mental horizons and the rectification of ecological depletions and anomalies. But a major discrepancy is that many of those nominally partisan to new age thought are in fact examples of almost complete dependence upon current technological assets. It is possible to find new age enthusiasts with electric toothbrushes, computers, supersonic hi-fi equipment, the latest streamlined model of tv, space age video equipment, de luxe telephones, telex machines, two or three cars per capita, private hovercraft, elaborate washing-machines in all-electric kitchens, elaborate forms of mechanical lawnmower, and indeed, most other technological contrivances barring the newly awaited battalions of robots for domestic help. Unless those concerned wish to merit the description of the most pampered breed of human yet to walk the globe, standards will clearly have to alter very substantially in order to adapt both to new age ideals and statistically inevitable drains upon current energy reserves.

The difference between hypocrisy and enthusiasm is often shadowy for those caught in the limelight of current affairs and preoccupations. It is of course very easy to *talk* about ecological rectifications, but the acid test of new age commitment is personal rectification of excess assets. Personal standards vary a great deal. At the moment it is unnecessary to go without electric light or heating, but the temperature in some centrally heated houses tends to be searingly tropical for indoor plants not reared in hothouse conditions. The minimal answer would seem to be that of minimizing upon superfluities, e.g., if one has to go a long way to work, one may need an economical car, but why keep a Rolls Royce as well? I recently heard of one new age enthusiast who was worried about moving to a "New age" centre in case their valuable antique furniture was over-exposed to bright sunlight.

In the current Western situation, it is as well to remember that the people who are trying to become idealists are amongst the greatest consumers of luxury goods and the greatest representatives of luxury attitudes. This being so, it is also necessary to become more realistic in the appraisal of what is actually being done. A materialistic New age looms large in some quarters, and it is increasingly relevant to define what is meant by blanket terms that are so glibly used by some as to be rendered absolutely meaningless.

## 2. **Self-supporting communities**

This is the logical extension of the ecological concern, in that a community can live in a suitable natural environment and produce all (or nearly all) of its food and domestic commodities. In practice, complete independence is difficult to achieve, but the main visible drawbacks to this idea have been the human ingredients of such situations. A major criticism is that the leadership of New Age centres is not of adequate standard. The fact is that well known New Age centres of Europe and America attempt to be self-supporting in a way that relies upon making substantial profits out of courses in psychotherapy and related interests. This recourse tends to rely upon the assumption that the practitioners involved are expert psychologists and spiritually accomplished entities. There have been complaints of narcissism and incompetence which cannot be ignored, however much the accused parties are averse to criticism. It is arguably not spirituality that is represented by the elite of such centres, but rather naive attempts and pretences at spirituality that are undermined by the preoccupation with psychotherapies like NeoReichian Gestalt. Popular Gestalt evidences an incapacity to distinguish between, e.g. Aleister Crowley and more altruistic entities, proof enough of a confusion in values, a confusion which has led to such an increase of popular interest in the socially harmful subject of magic and sorcery.

It is necessary for the relevant sections of the Western bourgeoisie (who predominantly comprise "New Age" fuel) to recognize the difference between spiritual self-development and the mundane distractions of occultism and commercial therapy. Otherwise their undiscerning appetite will be exploited, and they might even end up in a sadist cult of ritual magic, or as part of the Western vogue for "enlightenment intensives" which create megalomaniacs in need of social integration rather than an overdose of unskilled meditation.

### 3. Alternative medicine

The lunatic fringe have extensively exploited this ideal, often ludicrously, though not a few professional medics favour certain of the attendant health concepts. There are vast differences in expertise. It is possible for the milder critics to agree with the basic psychological ideas underlying this exploitable subject. It is obvious enough that surgical medicine does not always produce a favourable result, and an alternative emphasis is to allay the symptoms of malady before they even commence. There are many "overnight experts" administering remedies in this field, but few seem to grasp that it is up to the individual to provide his or her own form of "medicine" instead of being dependent upon the hit-or-miss therapist.

The vexed question of whether alternative medicine undermines professional medical services is best left to the experts in these departments.[62] However, it is surely well known that many ailments aired in front of doctors are imaginary, and conceivably the psycho-perspectives of alternative medicine could reduce the onerous waiting lists and pressing calls which confront doctors. On my own part, I once discovered how difficult it is to be self-monitoring healthwise and yet unavoidably linked to professional services. After undergoing eye tests with my optician as a result of eyestrain, a change in former statistics was apparent. As a result of my insistence, a new and stronger pair of spectacles was ordered for me, but these proved extremely painful, and I had to desist from wearing them. All this caused me much alarm, but I figured out for myself that intensive deskwork had caused a temporary change in my vision, and that the remedy was to temporarily relax the rate of work. I am glad to say that this decision was effective, and that I have since had no further trouble on this account. That I am dependent upon a professional optician for spectacles is undeniable, but there are some things only I can do for the preservation of health. I even came to the conclusion that I had "hypnotized" myself by a fixation upon the thought that I needed new spectacles after learning the change in vision data (that transpired to be temporary).

### 4. **Altered states of consciousness (ASC's)**

This is the aspect of New age thought which is the most subject to extravagant treatment, for which it receives due criticism amongst non-partisans (and unorthodox partisans). Since many trained scientists accept and exposit the possibilities in parapsychology, it is not possible to outrightly dismiss this subject as scientific materialists would wish. However, it is possible for partisans of parapsychology to cast doubts upon the accuracy of insubstantial reports, and to view with caution the claims of not a few persons who would elsewhere be classified as "lunatic fringe." The problem with this subject is that a great deal of cash flow is attendant upon sensational claims and limelight status; even some of the less critical pay that much less attention to so-and-so's visions once it is learnt how many dollars greet each new revelation. At least, this is what prudent attitudes will entail, but not everybody is even politely sceptical. I confess to being an inveterate critic of instant enlightenments, kundalini transports, reincarnations of Cleopatra, and numerous other more or less standard overtures of the occult. I once used to rant and rave at certain of these manifestations that I felt to be totally fake, but I found that it was of very little use to do this. A polite send-up wastes less energy, and is enough to give evidence that one is in disagreement. Those prone to be taken in by the exhibitionists generally have to find out for themselves what the priorities really are. Please note, however, that it is sometimes necessary to make a clear stand in relation to trends and entities with which one cannot agree; one reason is that you might otherwise be classified with your opposite number by those who assume that silence is proof of close affinity.

It is particularly difficult to separate the wheat from the chaff in New age ranks in a way that gains (orthodox) partisan credence, owing to the unfortunate convention of non-criticism left over from the hippy boom and its inarticulate psychedelic exponents who possessed no critical abilities whatsoever. This convention is also abetted by the "charitable Christian" approach which finds difficulty in distinguishing between different types of mysticism owing to an absence of taste. For these reasons, insidious salesmen of assorted wonders and miracles find it very easy to flourish in New age milieux, comparable perhaps to the delightful state of spirituality that might have ensued for the vendors of indulgences during the late medieval Christian era, if they had managed to silence Martin Luther.

### 5. **Non-ego**

To the best of my knowledge, this is very seldom lived up to, but it remains an excellent ideal. It is frequently contrasted with ego or personality, though the matter is not usually given much clarity by summarists (who are often, one suspects, merely copying what someone else has said). There are some highly amusing descriptions in print of various states of ego formulated by persons fixated upon simple renditions of complex Eastern teachings. This sort of simplicity tends to go amiably well with the discrepant situation of numerous New Age superstars and lesser celebrities all being active teachers of this or that spiritual speciality. The galaxy of workshops and rostrums can make one more than slightly dizzy. It is very difficult to believe that all the entities concerned have such stable accomplishments in spirituality (I may add that I do not believe anything of the sort, but then I am notoriously unorthodox).

### 6. **Holistic thinking**

This ideal implies focussing upon the whole rather than on parts. It is an ideal that is clearly accommodated to different wavelengths. At its most simplistic, there is a tendency to be vague in the extreme, with a total sacrifice of any analysis. Clearly, there is little use talking about the whole unless one knows something about the parts. It is true enough that to focus upon a part at the expense of the rest of the phenomenon is an unenviable vocation of thought, but there is such a thing as an incomplete whole viewed by a mind neglecting to take components into due consideration. There must be sufficient detail in holistic thinking for it to be a viable alternative to established norms. Unfortunately, many current twentieth century alternative vogues lag far behind the thirteenth century holistic ideal of a "universal science" as conceived by Roger Bacon (who was drawing upon Eastern concepts). One often finds brief references to this figure in "esoteric" literature, but little comprehension of his perspectives is actually evident. Ironically enough, Roger Bacon possessed an exceptionally critical mind that would have found New Age "non-critique" a stifling climate for freethinking. A premature Aquarian in a milieu of Piscean zombies? Bacon certainly knew about astrology, but he also knew about some of the strides in astronomy made by the Arabic-speaking world, and he was heir to several other scientific subjects also.

One drawback to some modern holistic thought is that it degenerates into the "anything goes" attitude of inclusion. This attitude is destructive of ideals at both theoretical and practical level. This tendency may, of course, appear in more conventional thinking in a different form, though the denominator is similarly one of ignorance.

In my remarks on "anything goes" in *Psychology in Science*, I deliberately focussed upon some aspects of an inchoate new age of divided attitudes and methods. Certain academic new agers have criticized me for interpreting Paul Feyerabend in this respect, affirming that he was merely referring to the history and philosophy of science in relation to his version of "anything goes." I find this a disappointing estimate of Feyerabend's talents, and even if he was being flippant, he might be disposed to flippantly concede that I have not given him undue credit for his incredible ingenuity at devising an exposition of an orthodox New age perspective in terms of academic philosophy.

### 7. **Female-Male Equality**

This ideal is still much needed on a global basis, but it must also be much more widely recognized that feminine liberation is prone to acutely commercialized emphases which actually result in losses to the intellectual status of women. If the female merely transits from being a domestic chattel to a sex queen, then she is merely gratifying the same masters, and conceivably more than ever. There appear to exist differences of opinion amongst feminists on such issues, and the final outcome is in their hands alone. Meanwhile, I am one of those who view "New Age workshops on sexuality" with a mixture of amusement and puzzlement at the preoccupation with biology that was such a feature of the Old Age.

It is now fairly common for the more permissive aspects of Women's Liberation to be blamed upon the early writings of Germaine Greer. But I am not persuaded that this represents anything of a fair judgment. Women have often been greatly influenced by men in their thinking, and it is perhaps more accurate to trace the over-enthusiastic excursions into permissiveness to the influence of such a famous philosopher as Bertrand Russell. Several decades ago, he was advocating a pre-hippy form of free love as part of his programme of separating metaphysics from philosophy. The result was materialist logic with a vengeance, from the consequences of which the Western world is still suffering in a variety of ways.

Much more demonstrative was the sex prophet Wilhelm Reich, whose extremely confused philosophy influenced many radicals prior to the hippy boom. The revolution in uninhibited sexuality is in large part traceable to the mental deficiencies of Reich, who appears to have been primarily reacting to his Freudian programming and also to his frustration with his formerly professed Marxism (though he retained the antipathy of Marx and Engels to the institution of the family). The more unthinking radicals have frequently been receptive to Reichian emphases without even knowing their origin. One has often to be very patient in attempting to educate otherwise unthinking radicals who do not realize how conditioned they have been to faulty doctrines acquired under stress from heterogenous ideologies.

## 8. **Non-violence**

This ideal is variously interpreted; some consider it to extend not only to physical manifestations of violence, but also to verbal manifestations concerning differences at personal and institutional levels. But extreme versions of verbal reticence would seem to mitigate the purpose of the ideal, particularly when new age standards are lowered in the process by those who find no regulations to cordon their every impulse.

Some Gandhian ideals are represented, though the Gandhian philosophy is very rarely understood satisfactorily. Some New age enthusiasts are not well conversant with the role of Mahatma Gandhi, and it was because of this that I specifically criticized in *Psychology in Science* a well-known guru who had expressed a sentiment against Mahatma Gandhi that had caused offence amongst Gandhians. However, I have nothing against the Rajneeshis (the followers of Bhagwan Shri Rajneesh), who have sometimes been very unfairly criticized by Christians.

Some of those who adhere in the neo-Reichian manner to

the ideal of non-violence do not appear to realize that the insidious innuendoes against the celibate life of monks amounts to a form of verbal violence. Many monks are amongst the most placid and harmless of men, for instance Father Thomas Merton (who was so notably in affinity with monks and ascetics of the Orient). It would be permissible to carp at the medieval misbehaviour of Dominicans, who were agents of the Inquisition, but celibates like Francis of Assisi are in a different category altogether.

Some supporters of Reichian and neo-Reichian interpretations do not yet appear to realize that recent discoveries of the extent of wife-beating and other crimes have disproven the theory that sexual repression is the cause of social maladies like fascism. Rather, it is a valid sociological and psychiatric conclusion that an unduly permissive and unrestrained milieu can encourage and facilitate widespread sexual abuses. The influence of alcohol in combination with current mass media is not conducive to decorous lifestyles of peace and cooperation.

Some Indian spiritualists have been perplexed by the classifications of Western occultists. The well known writer Colin Wilson described Aleister Crowley as an "advanced yogi,"[63] a designation which some Indians consider relevant to Gandhi. (I am sure that Colin Wilson would be willing to rectify this phraseology, since he often admits with great honesty that he does not know the answers.) Crowley was definitely not an incarnation of non-violence. Some (myself included) consider him to have been in the worst category of the practitioners of "left hand" tendencies, to use a phrase relating to the infamous *vamachara* Tantra as it is known in India. Such practitioners vary from libertinism to outright sadism, while adopting some mystical trappings. One of Crowley's reported misdemeanours was that of boasting of how he had suspended his pregnant wife by her thumbs in an attempt to produce a monster-child.

## 9. **Alternative lifestyles**

This concept relates to behaviour, and should in practice mean an improved life pattern. But a mere alternative is not necessarily a viable prospect. Since the time of the hippy boom in the 1960's, the less dynamic alternative thought has opted for a drug-taking habit pattern, frequently resulting in deteriorated life patterns that have proved fatal in too many cases. I am amongst those who are uncompromisingly opposed to the drug habit, and can only view with acute consternation the continuing tendencies to accommodate drug use amongst New age ranks.

Some have argued that their initial acquaintance with ASC's came through experimenting with drugs, and therefore why whould they cease their acquaintance via this source of experience? This argument sounds very shallow to those who are concerned with ASC's in their more extensive form. For those who are not fixated upon ASC's, drug use is clearly not conducive to clear-thinking in ecological matters and related concerns, but will instead merely maintain existing manifestations of incompetence.

A viable alternative lifestyle (or lifestyles) will rectify the behavioural shortcomings that are clearly evident in current society. Such a viable lifestyle does not mean "let go," which is the interpretation given to it by too many gurus, psychedelics, and psychotherapists. Rather, it means more psychological discipline in order to correct the abnormalities of mass media suggestion, self-interest, mental lethargy, banal entertainments fit for halfwits, and the fatal readiness to accept the first facile set of emphases leading to utopia. Naive minds are subject to exploitation sects at every turn; a continual objective should be to discipline the mind and to ensure one's careful evaluation of diverse alternatives. Of course, people who merely turn up at party-time as fodder for the gratification of "a good time was had by all" are unlikely to find a viable alternative prior to intellectual and intuitive expiry.

A viable alternative lifestyle presupposes a viable alternative thinking style. Owing to current confusion as to priorities, some may find that it takes time to select new lifestyle. It is better to effect the proper change in mind before adopting any spectacular behavioural tangent – just in case you regret it. Sanely programmed behaviour is often surprisingly non-exhibitionist.

## 10. **Meditation**

This subject has been much exploited during the past eighteen years or so in Western countries. A multitude of books have appeared on the subject, quite often for the wrong reasons, one fears. Owing to my adverse remarks on TM ("Transcendental Meditation") in *Psychology in Science*, some tend to assume that I dislike meditation. The truth is that I have been in the habit of practising meditation myself for a full twenty years now. I have never consulted a meditation teacher. I always meditate on my own, never in company. I do not sit cross-legged, but in a chair. If anyone asks me what great secrets there are for success in this subject, I am bound to state I would rather talk about the weather. Much better than great secrets are a few grains of intuitive commonsense. It might be helpful to state the following points:

a) The accusation levelled by the critics that meditation arrests the rate of literacy is sheer nonsense. They may be discussing people who are basically uncreative no matter what they do. My own strong interest in learning abilities commenced when I first began to meditate, and this interest has actually grown stronger with the years.

b) Some of the academic critics of "popular" meditation can themselves be described as being in a meditative condition during some of their more ruminative moments of study. This being so, they should not begrudge members of the public some similar relaxation during their leisure hours.

c) Some people seem temperamentally unsuited to meditation, particularly those who talk a great deal. If they are unable to stop talking, they may well find that some other activity has the same approximate benefits for them. In fact, they may be much better off with golf or knitting than some forms of cult meditation, which invoke abnormal mental patterns and can create undesirable fixations. I maintain that nobody really needs the extravagance of a "meditation master."

d) I firmly believe that meditation can be of medical benefit, but doubt very much if it can be really effective when undertaken solely with this purpose in mind.

e) The exotic vogues in meditation do not interest me seriously, only for amusement should I ever chance to read about them. I find some books in this idiom hilarious, and was particularly amused by the trend of "samadhi on cassette" which retails for less than £5, though I have not invested in it as a matter of principle.

f) I am quite happy to dispense with the term "meditation" if this seems desirable. If psychologists prefer, I am quite happy to call it positive thinking, though I hope that the contrast with negative thinking will be made clearly apparent.

## 11. **The Systems view of life**

This is an adaptation of cybernetics and systems research, and has recently become popular as a result of Fritjof Capra's *The Turning Point.* Capra is a physicist who views modern systems theory in a pertinent ecological context which stresses the differences between living organisms and machines. The systems view of living organisms is that they are basically self-organizing, a trait not imposed by the environment but established by the organism itself. The complex subject of brain function is of course included in this systems view, though it has frequently been neglected by holistic enthusiasts.

Despite the many interesting and worthwhile features of Capra's approach, including his admirably bold critique of nuclear armament, there is room for difference in the overall context of interpretation which he gives to the key denominator of the systems view. Capra approximately stresses the shift from the mechanistic worldview of Cartesian-Newtonian science to what may be tersely described as the holistic conception of reality in which the whole is more than the sum of the parts. For my own part, I am in basic agreement with this emphasis, but I do not agree with various extensions of this theme in the Capran format.

A significant distinction is made by Capra in referring separately to the holistic health movement, the human potential movement, the ecology movement, the feminist movement, and "a number of spiritual movements that re-emphasize the quest for meaning and the spiritual dimension of life." Capra appears to refer to the last-mentioned category as the New Age movements (in the plural), though other commentators have been much more generalizing. He goes on to observe that some individuals and organizations under the New Age banner have shown "clear signs of exploitation, fraud, sexism, and excessive economic expansion." It is not surprising that Capra prefers to refer to the future in terms of the "Solar age," a reference to the awaited usage of solar energy on a worldwide scale. He optimistically describes the abovementioned aberrations as transitory manifestations of the shift in value system, aberrations which should not prevent recognition of the genuine components in the contemporary changeover in values.[64]

I would like to add that the aberrations are not likely to cease so obligingly quickly if minorities do not become truly creative. This will not occur in the face of the highly random and fragmented education passing muster on the media as New Age. Capra expresses the hope that the diverse movements under discussion will recognize their communality of aim (i.e., as "creative minorities"). But the whole point is that such movements can only know their communality of aim if they have the same aim. The fact is that they do not have the same aim. Nor do they hold in common the same integrity, the same intensity, the same scope, or even the same interpretation of very basic concepts.

Capra cannot explain the anomalies manifest in the New Age repertories because his systems analysis of the two major modes of the mind (and the brain) is deficient. He does not specify the diffuse holistic subzones of thinking (and feeling), and nor the possibilities of advanced analytic thinking. Instead he presents the typical intuitive versus rational approach that will never do justice to the achievement of the whole becoming more than its parts. Despite his very brief mention of the integration of the two sides of the brain,[65] his predominant anti-rationality will amount to another lop-sided perspective unless due provision is made for a more comprehensive systems view. Capra aptly remarks that a reductionist approach is necessary to understand detailed neural mechanisms, and an holistic approach necessary to understand the integration of these mechanisms. But the inadequate application of both these approaches will result in a systems view that fades out at brain level in human psychobiology.

Those New Age and related movements which stress "let go" have no objective of furthering an era of better education, ecological sanity, the eradication of crime, to name but a few of the drastic requisites. Instead they flourish in anti-rational milieux of contentment in jettisoning all thoughts of today as well as tomorrow. As to the spiritual nature of some economic and other enterprises, it is arguably more advanced to be a conscientious materialist.

Such movements and enterprises flourish in an atmosphere of non-critique, where "all are one" and everybody is part of the same trend of intuition which is above irritating distractions of intellectual acumen. Hence anything goes, because nobody minds.

We learn from Capra that the psychoanalyst Stanislav Grof has written that psychedelic research (using LSD) is of a potential significance for psychiatry and psychology comparable to that of the microscope for medicine or the telescope for astronomy. Capra affirms that a person who takes LSD does not experience a toxic psychosis, as many psychiatrists believe, but rather journeys into the normally unconscious realms of the psyche.[66] Because of such misleading statements, I must unequivocally be considered a heretic within the Solar age version of systems theory and psycho-extension. I do not deny that LSD trippers may journey into unconscious realms, but I do urge that the toxic effects of such unnaturally induced transport will result in further imbalances within living organisms, imbalances which rapidly spread to other organisms in trends of ecological disaster. LSD may be appropriate in extreme cases of mental illness and dysfunction, but psycho-organisms wishing to discover their "unconscious" cannot be too strongly advised to remain sane while doing so.

There is such a thing as the wrong instrument in science and pseudoscience. A telescope would have been of little use in medicine; a microscope would not have encouraged astronomical expertise. Confusions in priorities are perhaps inevitable in the Jungian field when the collective unconscious is held to be an uncontaminated source of blessings. This is a convenient pretext for LSD enthusiasm, but is quite contrary to the implications extant from ancient Buddhist philosophers. These latter were not subscribers to Californian zen however, and their version of the "unconscious" is nowadays too analytical for simplified tastes wishing to take the easiest route to nirvana, or rather the nearest precipice. Simplistic error may spell the point of no return in systems disequilibrium.

Less objectionable is the Capran observation that the metaphor of the hologram has recently been applied to diverse phenomena in ways that are not always advanced with the necessary caution. Similarly, I would stress Capra's own lack of caution on the same page in listing as "high spiritual experiences": moments of perfect rhythm such as hitting a shot at tennis, skiing down a slope, a fulfilling sexual experience, contemplation of a great work of art, or deep meditation.[67] Most of these rhythms are of the extroverted variety, and may count only as social experiences, of significance in some situations maybe. But if such extroverted experiences are confused with advanced spiritual experiences, when is the Solar age going to reach its maturity? Not for a very long time maybe. One fears that the systems view of life has become mystical according to a fashion only, which is the common fate of meditation nowadays. Sport and aesthetics should be distinguished from the experience of cosmic profundities, in case an even greater spiritual dysfunction occurs in the interaction of mind and body.

Certain of Capra's emphases converge with his advocacy of Reichian and neo-Reichian therapy. He approves the "orgasm reflex" which is one component of this vogue.[68] Many psychiatrists and medics regard this form of therapy with suspicion, and I am certainly not the only nonprofessional to regard NeoReichian Gestalt as a blind alley.

If some people regard various forms of bodywork as a release for tension, then that may be justifiable for them. However, if the bodywork is considered to have more cosmic significances, one can logically and intuitively contest the claims of sensate mysticism. The answer to all systems necessity is not orgasm (however transcendently interpreted). The orgasm reflex is only a favoured answer for those with a truncated and mechanical systems view of life in which the body replaces the mind (and soul) as the vehicle of intelligence. A materialist alternative it is, and doubtless appropriate in that context along with Freudian stigmatization of all things mystical as mere infantile impulses. If there is to be a new age in the more meaningful senses of the phrase, then minds will have to be educated more than they are at present, in order to achieve the feat of an extension of consciousness in which mind (and soul) amounts to more than the bodily components.

### 12. **Panglobal attitude**

This denotes the incentive to cut across all boundaries of colour, creed, and nationality. In relation to ecology and economy, there is often much sympathy expressed for the Third World. The "lunatic fringe" who attach to new age concepts seldom have more than a nominal commitment to such incentive, and are nearly always oriented to ESP and alternative medicine, which are the most lucrative and well-advertised areas of interest.

In terms of practical research, few are informationally conversant in any detail with overseas developments and other ideological traditions. Though the panglobal incentive is acknowledged in theory, in practice many New age enthusiasts are (however inadvertently) centred in the "Western tradition," and very often in the twentieth century version of this. The Eastern traditions are usually represented only in amorphous variants that are often difficult for knowledgeable Easterners to accept as genuine. The prevalent hazy approach is not conducive to matters of clarity; this matter is now of potential importance in intercultural communications, owing to the increasingly educated sectors in Third World countries and Islamic countries.

The Islamic thinker Seyyed Hossein Nasr (who is well known for his interests in the sufi heritage) wrote in his book *The Encounter of Man and Nature* that the practices of decadent "occult sciences" are much more dangerous than materialism.[69] I accordingly employed this perspective in the excursus to *Psychology in Science*, in which scientific materialism and the relativism of a near literal "anything goes" situation in pseudoscience are viewed in due proportion. It may well be that some diffuse holistic deficiencies of mentation are even worse than rabid analytic penchants.

It is evident from the current political situation that a deep unity between the Western countries, the Islamic countries, and Israel, will not occur at materialistic level. It will have to be in the realm of metaphysical thought and discovery that this unity is precipitated. A new age of unity is going to require give and take in several directions. There may initially have to be an attitude of compromise. There are other metaphysical problems involved in Far Eastern juxtapositions that will have to be met by all parties concerned.

Various ideologies, both religious and materialist, tend to resist the flexible requirements of a potential panglobal unity. Vague gestures in this direction are of little use, and possess the inevitable status of rhetoric. This problem is one of those addressed by the research strategy of anthropography. The remaining chapters of this book are intended as guidelines towards necessary enlargements of view in respect of panhuman dimensions.

It is sometimes considered that the theme of a "perennial philosophy" is illustrative of a panhuman attitude. In certain respects it may be, but it is also evident that there are serious shortcomings attaching to this well known concept, which in general has achieved a very loose and glib usage. It would be unwise to base a projected panglobal unity upon inaccuracies; panglobal considerations do not relieve the exponent or researcher from the necessity for accuracy or realistic considerations. Quite to the contrary in fact. It is the lack of accuracy in obscurantist dogmas that serves to screen out and block panglobal wellbeing.

There are rather numerous factors requiring clarification in relation to the theme of a "perennial philosophy." In many popular treatments of evolution, there is no attention given to essential features of historical fact, but instead a reliance upon "exciting" fantasy, a cheap substitute for accuracy and depth. The incorporation of meaning should not entail distortion, but very often the reverse is true in current formats. Similarly, the subject of metaphysics is rarely given a sufficiently philosophical consideration, but instead a sensational context that would excite no deep interest in serious students. In respect of Asiatic contributions, the Western enthusiasts in this direction are too often reflectors of neo-Reichian thought, and hence fail to do justice to even elementary facets of contrasting trends and philosophies.

*CONCLUSION:* The ideals of the potentially productive new age are not in general implemented. The trends involved in Neo-Reichian Gestalt are particular causes of deterioration in ideals and concepts. Current "New Age" organizations like Esalen and the Findhorn Foundation constitute a cul-de-sac for progressive thinkers, and neglect spiritual and other priorities, instead promoting psychotherapies which do not clarify or further educational requirements. The narcissism of the "New Age" movement(s) is rightly notorious amongst sociologists and others. Perhaps it is most accurate to state that "New Age" elites (and lunatic fringe) mislead a majority who have not developed their critical faculties. Neo-Reichian and related psychotherapies masquerade under the auspices of mysticism and convenienty advocate non-criticism of flaws in the projected "counterculture," save those flaws evident in the activities of some Eastern gurus. The "New Age" movement is predominantly a Western phenomenon, and in some quarters is increasingly disdainful of much older and more intrinsic Eastern perspectives. Conversely, confusion has sometimes occurred between "New Age" eclectic trends and older (Eastern) traditions which had an entirely different orientation. Anthropography proposes that both partisans and critics of a new age should re-examine the various concepts and ideals involved.

# CHAPTER SIX

# A CLARIFICATION OF METAPHYSICS

The subject of metaphysics is variously ridiculed and glorified. It is an extremely confusing word in common usage, and attempts are rarely made to define what it represents – or what it should represent. From my own observation, the word can nowadays be taken to mean virtually anything; it can even be said that in the current climate of meaning, the subject of metaphysics is not only a vexed question but a hopeless one. Yet if the attendant meanings are uprated from devaluation, the situation is not at all hopeless for those who are not confused by hopeless distractions of meaninglessness.

The word metaphysics is derived from the Greek *metaphusika*, strongly associated with the Aristotelian corpus, though the derivative has long since lost its specifically Greek connotations. The *Oxford English Dictionary* defines the word metaphysics as denoting the philosophy of mind, or the philosophy of being and knowing. Yet it is often used as a term of castigation implying empty theorizing.

Some scientists employ the word metaphysical to denote only the unproven or theoretical aspects of data, without there necessarily being the slightest incorporeal element in such data. In other channels of expression, the metaphysical embraces all kinds of philosophical, mystical, occult, and religious matters, and very frequently without any bridle. More than any other factor, this loose usage of "metaphysics" has given the critics of such matters provocation to use the word as a term of abuse.

My intention in this chapter is to point out the original philosophical signification of the term in question, and to trace some important continuations of this perspective. I am therefore concerned here to separate the more classical meaning from the popular. This will not of course prevent loose usage, but it is as well to remind more people of what metaphysics did once signify. Further, the philosophy of mind in modern parlance may be overdue for a metaphysical clarification.

Owing to the assimilation of the Aristotelian corpus by medieval Christian theologians of Latin-speaking Europe, metaphysics acquired a Roman Catholic flavour in the Western world. But the use of the Aristotelian corpus by Christian schoolmen differed radically from its usage amongst philosophers in the Islamic world. These latter included Muslims, Jews, Nestorian Christians, and others of less certain religious affiliation. There were many different temperaments and thinking styles represented amongst these Eastern philosophers and scientists; not all of them reached the same conclusions, and not all of them started off from the same working assumptions. Suffice it to say here that there was a very substantial difference in outlook between Thomas Aquinas and Al-Farabi (d.950). The latter philosopher originated from Central Asia and was a tenth century expert in the Aristotelian, Neoplatonic, and other heritages. A leading modern Western scholar of philosophy has described Farabi as living the life of a sufi,[70] which is logically explicable on the basis of his contemplative lifestyle. Farabi was the first philosopher in the Islamic milieu to comprehensively classify the sciences in their transit from ancient Greek models. He did this in his Arabic treatise *Ihsa al-Ulum* (*Classification of the Sciences*), and amongst the sciences he listed was metaphysics. Farabi's recycled metaphysics is of more than passing interest, since the *Ihsa* gained a Latin translation in the twelfth century, and became one of the textbooks amongst the Christian scholars of Europe.

Farabi's sponsorship of metaphysics was not undertaken in a theological context, but from a remarkably impartial philosophical viewpoint. His method sidestepped conventional Islam, as a result of which some theologians criticized him in later centuries. But neither was Farabi an irreligious man. This distinctive cast of mind distinguished several of the famous and less famous philosophic entities of his era.

Farabi's attitude in metaphysics might here be summarized as: extending the scope of investigations into the nature of existence, in avenues of thought that may include psychical and theological aspects, but according to standards of a discriminative rigour which will not confuse pure being with popular contaminations. Hence a metaphysicist may believe in God, but not necessarily according to any set of conventional beliefs. The metaphysical philosopher may find that there are certain validities of approach in a subject like astrology, for example, but these validities are only likely to be discerned by other philosophers of similar acumen.

The Christian theologians of Latin Europe studied a considerable number of treatises which were translated from Arabic, though only a part of the extensive Arabo-Persian philosophical heritage became known to them. They were principally concerned with recovering Aristotle, whom they interpreted in a very different manner to that of Arabic-speaking philosophers. Aquinas and other scholars employed their research to buttress the religion of the Papacy, and not to further philosophy in the ancient manner. The result was a crippled Aristotelianism that limped into the Renaissance era as a professorial subject that was to cause Galileo and Kepler both amusement and sorrow. Deficiencies there were in Aristotelian logic long before Aquinas found it, but there were ways of improving upon it that were demonstrated by men like Farabi, but which were not cultivated by most of the Latin savants.

From the beginning, the Latin theologians were concerned to combat heretical tendencies in philosophy. Siger of Brabant was one of the heretics, adhering so closely to the outlook of the formidable Arab Aristotelian Ibn Rushd (alias Averroes) that it became dangerous to be considered an Averroist. But perhaps the most original of the Latins was Roger Bacon (d.*c.* 1292), who became a friar in the Franciscan order. He was one of those who studied Farabi in some depth from the material available in his day, and in his *Opus Tertium* he recommended the study of the *Ihsa*, which had since become known by the title *De Scientis*. Bacon drew heavily from the Arabic heritage, and was extremely unorthodox in his approach to philosophy and metaphysics by comparison with his Latin-speaking compatriots. He liked "occult" subjects just as many Muslim philosophers did, and one of his major inspirations has been pinpointed as an Arabic "pseudoAristotelian" treatise of the esoteric type which, in the Islamic world, frequently accompanied logical works in the more purist tradition of Peripatetic philosophy. This treatise was entitled in its Latin version *Secretum Secretorum* (*The Secret of Secrets*), and refers to a "universal science" which Bacon evidently attempted to emulate. An unusually industrious polymath, his own treatises exhibit a notable empirical streak that was lacking amongst his Christian contemporaries. Bacon was much more doctrinaire in theology than Farabi, but his piety was individualistic, since his pen erupted into polemic against the ignorance of established interests. Friar Bacon was some two and a half centuries ahead of Luther in certain respects, and dared to call leading contemporaries like Aquinas mere "ignorant boys" in the study of philosophy. Attempts were made to cordon his influence, and an obscure confinement was part of his lot.[71]

In an age that has forgotten the distinctions between Aristotelians, it is more than ever incumbent to grasp the differences between metaphysics as a science and metaphysics as a diversion.

It is ironic that modern writers on the occult deem all Aristotelians as misguided rationalists. This attitude is commensurate with an almost complete lack of knowledge of source materials. In other words, the modern occultists are imbeciles in their own subject. That is probably what Roger Bacon would have said in thirteenth century Aristotelian Latin, could he have known the fate of philosophy in later times.

One unorthodox subject which Friar Bacon would not favour was magic, towards which he expressed acute disapproval. This aversion he shared in common with the Muslim and Jewish philosophers; it was widely recognized amongst these thinkers that esoteric subjects could lead to wisdom but that superstitious magicians were fools and to be avoided accordingly.

By the sixteenth century, Europe was not so much a focus for philosophy but for magic. This latter was certainly not the only subject in the Renaissance spectrum, but it was a very popular one in the wake of widespread reaction against clericalism and professorial Aristotelianism. It was not all the Renaissance enthusiasts who possessed the creativity of Leonardo Da Vinci. Popular metaphysics was about as discerning as the arid Italian professors who disputed Galileo's discoveries with the very tangible telescope.

The fascination for magic became attached with due losses to the subject of Qabbalah, which was appropriated from the Jewish heritage by European Christians who in general lacked the scholarly talents of Jews. Renaissance Qabbalism of Christian strains might have merited an accusation from Friar Bacon of being the biggest clodhopping fiasco in centuries, or something to that effect. Further, the European enthusiasm for the Hermetic texts might have been a more fruitful episode if the magical obsessions had not intruded. The Hermetic tradition had fared much better amongst the Arabs and Persians several centuries before Ficino,[72] but European savants did not know anything of this missing chunk of medieval history for rather a long time.

Friar Bacon's famous namesake inaugurated the inductive method of experimental science. Sir Francis Bacon was not quite so modern as is often assumed, since he was familiar with "occult" subjects like alchemy which influenced his thinking to at least some extent.[73] Yet on the whole, Francis Bacon's approach was committed to experimental matters, and his attempted advancement of natural philosophy was influential to a degree that was arguably not beneficial in its consequences. He gave priority to the authority of observation and experiment, seeking in this way to offset the errors of academic speculation and the wilder occult ideas popularly in vogue. Baconian inductionism pursued the accumulation of increasingly reliable and precise facts which could be classified into appropriate axioms of knowledge. This methodology was almost painfully literal in its procedures; Sir Francis even favoured the inclusion of illiterate assistants in experiments in order to safeguard the objectivity of the experiment from any prior deliberation as to its result. Yet empiricism has very largely been stereotyped ever since by the basic assumptions of an objectivity which ignores a larger truth that only the enlightened are ever likely to demonstrate.

The matter of objective empiricism is rather similar to that of the deductive reasoning used in academic philosophy. The *a priori* logic was a subject of complaint for Roger Bacon, who had ample opportunity to observe the shortcomings of the logical theology that dominated his time. Friar Bacon firmly grasped that argument was not of the value of experience, but the implications of his phrase *scientia experimentalis* are much deeper than the inductionist sequel. This phrase has aptly been translated as the "science of experience." Friar Bacon meant that no theory is dynamic unless it is experientially tested; he not only believed in testability in the realm of natural science, but also (and more importantly) in the psychological realm where advanced experiences can be achieved by the attuned mind.

Roger Bacon's experiential calculus was neither inductive nor deductive according to conventional classifications. He was at odds with both Aquinas and his Elizabethan-Jacobean namesake. More crucially perhaps, the current amalgamations of reasoning aptitudes reflected in inductive-deductive models likewise miss out the key factors in the development of human knowledge. If the science of human development largely remains a subject of fantasy for cranks, it is because scientists and theoretical philosophers are content with that much less than is possible for the human mind.

While the inductionist Francis Bacon criticized the alchemical tradition for concealing procedures under a symbolism that evaded general understanding, the greatest empirical scientist of the seventeenth century actively maintained a secretive career of participation in alchemical matters. There have been various speculations made concerning Newton's more secretive interests, the more extreme of these speculations neglecting to take sufficient account of the archival evidence. Newton has even been called "the last of the magicians," which was perhaps an unfortunate turn of phrase indicative of the common tendency to associate obscure interests with magic. It can confidently be asserted that Isaac Newton was not a magician in the accepted sense of the word, though his discovery of gravitation often sounds magical to those for whom apple trees are customarily insignificant. He definitely was an austere Arian heretic and a believer in a secret tradition of knowledge going back to Pythagoras, though his use of mathematics was much less Pythagorean than that of Roger Bacon, who likewise studied alchemy and is one of the alchemical writers cited by Newton. There exists another difference here in that Roger Bacon drew upon the Arabic tradition of alchemy, whereas Newton's research was almost exclusively oriented to the later European versions.

According to his latest and most definitive biographer, Newton understood the content of alchemy to consist of "chemical processes, not mystical experience expressed in the idiom of chemical processes." If this assertion is correct, then Newton differed from many other alchemists, though by no means all of them, since a proportion of them were fundamentally desirous of making literal gold. It has been emphasized that Newton's studies in alchemy were accompanied by laboratory experimentation; recent interpretation has sought to correlate his extant experimental notes with the profusion of alchemical manuscripts acquired by Newton. Yet it is difficult to concede that finer points were totally lost upon Newton if he really investigated the extensive literature of pre-seventeenth century alchemy "as it has never been probed before or since," to cite the verdict of one recent researcher. At any rate, some in the history of pre-seventeenth century alchemy would have considered Newton an ignoramus if his motivations were entirely in the direction of transmuting metals. This would tend to place him in the category of a more erudite version of Edward Kelly, the Elizabethan prankster who lured the mathematician Dr. John Dee into the more undiscerning mists of alchemy and other pastimes of bathos.

It was about 1669 that Newton began a copious study of alchemy. He entered the very secretive and largely anonymous milieu of English alchemists, from which channels he evidently acquired much material. It is known that he composed an alchemical pseudonym, namely Jeova Sanctus unus, which was an anagram of Isaacus Neuutonus. Professor Westfall considers it possible that further research may reveal that Newton wrote pseudonymous treatises which he circulated amongst his alchemical acquaintances.

After nearly thirty years of evident devotion to practical alchemy, a "disillusionment" with the subject has been inferred for the period following Newton's move to London in the early 1690's. Though he continued to acquire more alchemical books, "he devoted no further significant time to alchemy" in experimental terms. By that date of course, he was famous for his *Principia*, a scientific treatise in which, amongst other things, he attacked Cartesian natural philosophy. This reaction to Descartes dated back to the late 1660's, when he rejected Cartesian concepts in his essay *On the Gravity and Equilibrium of Fluids*. This essay reflects the late (and Christianized) version of Neoplatonism exposited by Henry More (d. 1687), who had criticized the limitations of mechanical science. The influence of the Cambridge Platonists on Newton is definite, and some scholars have questioned the need to attribute any importance to alchemy in influencing his thought. But his notes on alchemy far outnumber those on the Cambridge Platonists (the ratio is about a hundred to one).[74]

The fact is that although Newton repudiated the mechanical philosophy of Descartes, he did not reject the new mechanical philosophy in its wider sense. It was the contemporary vogue in science, and Newton effectively pushed it into mathematical solidity. In so doing, he endorsed the Cartesian elimination of "occult" concepts from natural philosophy, and however unintentionally, sealed the rift between metaphysics and physics. Theological considerations may have justified this course in Newton's mind, since he believed that he had left room for the Christian God in his theories.

Now more than ever before, the operations of nature could be explained solely by recourse to the mechanical necessity inherent in particles of matter. Alchemy still offered a worldview in which nature was not a machine, which was possibly the real reason why Newton adhered to it. But the influence of the mechanical philosophy was absolute in experimental terms, and the completed *Princi-*

*pia* of 1687 set the pattern for modern mechanistic science. If Newton had been a less mechanical scientist, he might hve produced a sequel to the *Principia* which would have offset the triumph of mechanism. Twentieth century physics invalidates Newtonian science, but the mechanism has become a habit in too many quarters.

Ironically enough, it was metaphysics which spurred Newton to outmechanize Descartes, an unfortunate consequence of his mathematical industry, which was foreign to the Cambridge Platonists and the alchemists alike. Alchemy transited into modern chemistry, while the *Principia* became translated into a technology that has grown to lethal proportions. The dealchemicalized gold proved deadly.

The mechanical philosophy of Rene Descartes was a close partner in time to Francis Bacon's inductionism. Though the two approaches are distinct, there is an overall similarity in the rejection of factors not readily amenable to immediate logical verification via mathematical or experimental procedures. Whether or not Descartes was in fundamental dissent from Jesuit thinking, he was effectively in alliance with Francis Bacon's gesture of dispensing with the ancient view that man is *microcosmus*. In this view, the human being comprises a (potential) model of the greater world or macrocosm. In his *The Advancement of Learning* (1605), Bacon criticized this form of thought in its Paracelsan and alchemical guise. The philosophy of the microcosm-macrocosm was not of course indigenous to Renaissance Europe, and undoubtedly underwent some strange adventures amongst Bacon's contemporaries. It is still very easy to plagiarize this rather simple-sounding theme, though eccentricities of exponents do not necessarily reflect upon the usefulness of the principle itself as a working concept. The problem for many enthusiasts of principles in a simple form is that they would not very easily recognize the same principle in a more complex format entailing greater accuracy.

Though the logic of Descartes is often considered to have been the dividing line between medieval and modern, Aristotelian metaphysics was arguably as misrepresented in medieval and Renaissance Europe as the microcosm philosophy of Hermetic associations. The "neoplatonism" of Henry More was much more academic than that of Al-Farabi, in addition to the theological gloss that was lacking in the tenth century exponent of Plato and Aristotle. Nowadays Aristotle is largely a figure for disdain outside classicist circles, and the popular idea of the logician in error could do with a little more investigation than is customary. Scientific materialism is gratified by popular ideas, since the Aristotelian metaphysics have been eschewed in favour of the Aristotelian physical sciences. But the priorities were not always in this direction, and nor in the direction of an appropriation by a theology contrasting with the original.

Those books in the Aristotelian corpus that were early classified under the heading of Metaphysics deal with the "First Philosophy," which clearly correlated with the "wisdom" that was the objective of the Greek philosophers. Aristotle and his pupils clearly felt that this First Philosophy was the supreme science amongst the many sciences they studied. To them, metaphysics was a science that was more ultimate and more accurate than any of the other sciences in the curriculum.

We cannot be certain that we have the exact words of Aristotle in the extant corpus, since the treatises are mainly compilations of earlier notes and treatises, edited by followers of the Aristotelian tradition. Some scholars think that the *Metaphysics* was edited by Eudemus, as implied by classical authors. Be that as it may, the statements in these books reflect the attitude of the early Aristotelian school, however much is missing from the compilations.

What is classified as the fourth book of the *Metaphysics* begins with a definition of the primary science as "a science which studies Being *qua* Being, and the properties inherent in it in virtue of its own nature." In contrast, the other sciences all focus upon some particular portion of Being, which is hence divided up.[75] For the early Aristotelians therefore, polymathy not only included metaphysics, but metaphysics could stand aloof from polymathy.

The same book stresses that there is a more ultimate type of thinker than the natural philosopher, since nature is only a genus of Being. This more advanced specimen is "the universal thinker who studies the primary reality." Natural philosophy is here credited as a kind of wisdom, but not the primary wisdom. The text goes on to say that lack of training in logic causes some to discuss more ultimate questions prematurely, and that understanding is necessary to further such investigation.[76] It is natural philosophers who are being called to task here, since their tendency to materialist interpretation can obscure fundamentals. The physicists and others were liable to lose sight of ultimates in attempting to formulate ultimates from inadequate data and perceptions.

Largely neglected today are the implications of ancient distinctions between motivations. The abovementioned text states that the function of the philosopher is to discover the truth concerning the "peculiar modifications" of Being *qua* Being. But appearances can be misleading for the tyro. This is because "dialecticians and sophists" adopt the same appearance as the philosopher. Dialecticians discuss all subjects as a matter of course in their verbal career. Sophistry is more difficult to discern, "but philosophy differs from sophistry in the nature of its capability." Dialectic is a mere verbal exercise in subjects that philosophy attempts to understand, while "sophistry seems to be philosophy, but is not."[77] It was not the fault of Aristotle if the history of philosophy as now known includes a high proportion of sophists, albeit undeclared and often unrecognized.

The arguments of sophists are often ingenious, but a capacity for argument is not the key to wisdom. A fallacious argument can deflect from all hope of wisdom.

The same Aristotelian text of the *Metaphysics* refers with criticism to the theory of Protagoras, who appears to have defended a version of relativism in which all opinions are equally true.[78] This argument seems to have arisen in reaction to the dogmatism of those who insisted that persons not in agreement with them were wrong. Such a method of argument, if pressed to its logical conclusion, will merely facilitate a myriad of dogmatic opinions that will obscure the underlying truth of an ultimate reality. Protagorean relativism is still championed today, and hence is not an irrelevant matter of yesteryear.[79]

Many opinions have been expressed about Aristotle's "theology," which was an important part of the *Metaphysics*, but which followed a radically different rationale to the later Roman Catholic theology upon which it was grafted. Aristotelian texts are not systematic in the way that later commentators liked to think, and even today the definition of words like "soul (*psuche*)" is a matter for disagreement. Greek metaphysics was not theology in the popular sense, which Muslims like Al-Farabi and Jews like Moses Maimonides well understood.

It is well known that the Aristotelian attempt to give a logical and "mechanical" explananation of the universe is not satisfactory from the viewpoint of modern science. But then all the modern versions of explanation have similarly been found unsatisfactory by various parties. The comparative lack of detail in the Aristotelian version is arguably preferable to the laborious mechanism of Descartes or the mathematical half-truths of Newton. The *Metaphysics* reproves the Pythagoreans and Platonists for employing metaphorical language in the description of cosmic processes, but is ultimately driven to resort to this same expedient in describing causation. Modern cosmology still finds metaphor useful. Verbalism is often inexact for cosmic proportions. No verbalist can really be said to have disproved the Aristotelian contention that the ultimate cause, or Prime Mover, of the universal process is eternal, immutable, and immaterial, i.e., Mind or God. Yet the Aristotelian Absolute is not the creator of the universe, a contention which led to argument in debating history, which may here be regarded in general as being speculative when it is not dogmatic.

One dictionary definition of metaphysics is perhaps too dialectical in regarding it as a "branch of speculative enquiry," though apt enough in affirming its content as the first principles of things and concepts like being, substance, essence, time, space, cause, identity, and so forth.[80] That may at the most represent an approximate verbal idea of the rudiments of the First Philosophy.

Two thousand years after Aristotle, the First Philosophy was much in relegation in the axioms of David Hume, the theorist of Georgian England. In a famous passage in his

*Enquiry Concerning Human Understanding*, Hume refers to taking in hand "any volume of divinity or school of metaphysics," and finding the contents inadequate if lacking in quantitative reasoning or experimental reasoning. His prescription for such lack of content was: "Commit it then to the flames, for it can contain nothing but sophistry and illusion."[81]

Fortunately enough, Hume was not in charge of national or world libraries, and hence we are still in a position to compare Hume's contribution with many of those that would not otherwise have survived. The scepticism of this British thinker is not without its wit and subtlety, but one might well advise that his books be preserved from any calamity in order to attest their content as ingenious dialectics that are not demonstrative of wisdom.

One can sympathize with Hume's antipathy for doctrinaire theology, and even use many of his conclusions as a basis for new and more complete propositions. But the penchant for naturalism is no quantitative guarantee of accuracy, or even empirical probability.

What Hume did has for some confused reason been strangely admired. Insofar as the empiricist tradition was concerned, he split natural philosophy decisively from metaphysics, identifying the latter subject more or less exclusively with theology and ignorant of its extensions in experience. For Hume, every branch of science was to be anchored in experience, but an experience conducive only to natural science is only likely to be definitive for natural scientists and natural philosophers. Some might counter that Hume was also a psychologist, but his psychologistic reflections were markedly behaviourist in tone.

Hume has been credited with a philosophy of mind, a subject which is, properly speaking, an integral facet of metaphysics. But his presentation of this was inconclusive enough to warrant almost diametrically opposed interpretations. A recent analysis has concluded that Hume was a mind-body dualist admitting some degree of mind-body interaction, which seems preposterous to some readers. Others regard Hume as a behaviourist, while yet others see him as a radical subjectivist who reduced matter to mind. A further interpretation views him as a consistent sceptic with no constructive perspective on mind and matter at all. Whatever the truth in these various deductions, it is very easy to agree with the dualist interpretation that "much that is most characteristic of Hume's philosophy of mind must be abandoned."[82]

The philosophy of mind is currently in acute disarray. In general, materialist interpretations are committed to decrying anything that can conceivably sound even remotely similar to the Cartesian division between mind and body. Humanistic psychology panders to this bias by accepting the conflation of mind and body in a spirit of fashionable hedonism that is careful to dwell upon interpersonal relationships between bodies. Enjoyment is the order of the day; clear and intensive thinking hurts too much, since the mind is then too separate from the body to concur with all the current fancies as to what constitutes a real world and a mature human being.

To put it pithily, the philosophy of mind requires an intelligent assertion of the independence of mind from body in a non-Cartesian spirit. It is not mathematics or conventional theology that will arrive at the necessary interactionist explanation for what is both a commonsense and intuitive phenomenon. Descartes not only severed minds from bodies without allowing for an interactionist fulcrum in between, but denied animals any soul in his assertion of a totally mechanical universe of automatons. In short, his philosophy of doubt was an apt sequel to a philosophy of dogmatism, and was inversely proportional to progress.

An academic philosopher who tried hard to remedy the sterility in nineteenth century philosophy did not go far enough by the standards of current requirements. In Henri Bergson we have many of the best characteristics of academic philosophy. His book *Matter and Memory* first appeared in French at the very end of the nineteenth century, and was strongly in favour of a mentalist explanation of the mind-body problem.[83] But it was an inchoate mentalism, despite the fact that this French professor essentially concluded that the mind is a more expansive entity than the brain, and that the activity of the brain amounts to no more than an infinitesimal fraction of the mind's activity.

By comparison with many medieval professors of Europe, Bergson can be considered an enlightened Aristotelian in stressing the intuitive factor rather than formal logic. He interpreted the metaphysical teaching of Aristotle in terms of an intellectual discipline that pierces "by a strong effort of mental vision the material envelope of things," and which discloses "the unity that links being to being," from inert matter to man and hence to "the divine thought that thinks all things."[84] This merely sounds poetical to some scientists, but it should be remembered that Bergson may have made an understatement in his questioning reflection as to what would have happened if modern science had begun by considering mind – in other words, if Kepler, Galileo, and Newton had been psychologists. He suggested that progress during the interim would have meant a psychological advance comparable to the advance over Aristotelian physics achieved by the modern equivalent.

Yet Bergson would not go so far as to subordinate science to metaphysics. Instead he affirmed that they were complementary, his method being "to consolidate each by means of the other without sacrificing anything in either."[85] Yet this is now increasingly difficult, since consolidation of natural science tends to sacrifice practically everything else – even in terms of its own acknowledged extensions of empirical data which are accepted by some scientists and ignored by others.

It seems that even the mature Einstein considered "science" as the most objective factor known to human beings, though in his case metaphysics was a strongly underlying consideration. If Einstein had started life as a psychologist and not been influenced by logical positivism, he might have surged ahead of Bergson in the philosophical sense, and more directly negotiated quantum events. Until metaphysics has been reinstated in an advanced form, with a due priority over the physical sciences, it will be necessary to warn against "metaphysical extremes"[86] which consist of flotsam varying from pyramidmania and ethnocentric dialectic to "anything goes."

Bergson concluded his essay on metaphysics with the observation that the eclipse of the subject during the latter half of the nineteenth century was caused by the difficulty encountered by philosophers in securing a foothold in empirical science, which had become much too specialized. He deduced that "metaphysical intuition . . . . can only be obtained through material knowledge," meaning that a basis of empirical data was necessary as a guideline for intuition. He added that such intuition was not the mere summary or synthesis of material knowledge; metaphysics is therefore not a generalization of facts, but can be defined as "integral experience."[87]

Bergson himself did establish a foothold in empirical science, but one can urge that his definition of "metaphysical intuition" was at variance with the Aristotelian original, in that the First Philosophy is not susceptible to natural philosophy. This does not mean that metaphysicists have a unique monopoly of knowledge, because many metaphysicists are in actuality dialecticians and sophists. Nowhere is this disparity perhaps more evident in nineteenth century philosophy than in Hegelian dialectic.

A professorial logician, Hegel (d. 1831) expressed a glamourization of the German Enlightenment at the expense of, and in ignorance of, many other philosophical traditions in non-European locales. His triad of thesis-antithesis-synthesis loses substance in its historical application. He saw the dangers of the Kantian philosophy being assimilated to orthodox theology, but his own version of Spirit was phenomenologically inset into a cumbersome ethnocentric logic that effectively eschewed intuition.

It is understandable that Hegel became for Bertrand Russell the epitome of the impractical speculative philosopher, though in ethnocentricities the two were remarkably similar. Russell was one of the arch-opponents of metaphysics, of which Hegel was supposed to be the incarnation. This supposition should be corrected: what had happened was that Hegel's dialectic had become famous amongst dialecticians, proving extremely influential in university departments of philosophy, and also in marxist theory. Russell complained that Hegel had elevated the speculative philosopher – "sitting in his study considering abstract ideas" – above the statesman, the historian, and the scientist, in respect of a knowledge of the real world. The critic triumphantly seized upon the instance of the hapless Hegel publishing his proof that there must be exactly seven planets, proof made available only a week before the eighth planet was scientifically discovered.[88]

This kind of exposure of the theoretician is, of course, perenially necessary, but the assumption that the error is identical to the nature of metaphysics is woefully illogical. Bertrand Russell himself made certain looming errors which it is unnecessary to attribute to metaphysical assertion. But even in respect of his own vocation, Russell was apt to make nonsense of the very status of assertion, however empirical. He defined philosophy as "an unusually ingenious attempt to think fallaciously." Bearing in mind that Russell was recognized as the leading academic philosopher of his time when these words appeared in print, it is no encouragement to take any of his statements seriously. On the same page he refers to the Hegelian F.H. Bradley in the strain of: "When he was serious he was sophistical, and a typical philosopher; when he jested, he had insight."[89] One hopes that Russell was joking on such pages, since otherwise the logical conclusion is that he too was a sophist.

On the very next page of the essay in question, Russell asserts: "The more profound the philosopher, the more intricate and subtle must his fallacies be."[90] Are we to take it that Russell was yielding all claims to profundity, since as a typical philosopher (according to his own language), his only field of expertise was comic strip?

Bertrand Russell's approach has been dubbed logical atomism, reflecting his belief in a logic based on natural science and mathematics. He made empirical science the sole gauge of philosophy, and to all intents and purposes, his philosophic role was identical to that of the man of science. For him metaphysics was a term of abuse, and anything intuitive amounted to a heresy from the positivist canon of atomism and sceptical commonsense. At the end of his life he realized that science had made a wrong move with the atomic bomb, but it seems that he never did seriously confront the fact that the emerging new physics had made atomism one more scientific illusion of the past.

One of the views for which Russell expressed a pronounced aversion was Bergson's emphasis upon intuition. Bergson's philosophy was characterized by his sceptical contemporary as "merely traditional mysticism expressed in slightly novel language." More specifically, Russell defined traditional mysticism as "contemplative, convinced of the unreality of time, and essentially a lazy man's philosophy." The critic did concede that Bergson's "great and remarkable innovation" was to have partnered mysticism with a belief in the reality of time and progress, but this too was dismissed as romantic and irrational.[91] Russell's own realism is not convincing in relation to new scientific perspectives in which his logical atomism amounts to novelism. Ironically, if he had been more intuitive, he might have been considered more progressive by the new physics.

Definitions of traditional mysticism are frequently attended by a myopia that could easily be corrected by a due investigation of the historical facts. For instance, Bergson was by no means the first "mystic" to accommodate the validity of time and the necessity of progress; lazy research is frequently a prop for biased views. Russell's sense of progress was every bit as speculative as Hegel's planets.

Rather than classifying Bergson as an irrational mystic, a more scientific approach can legitimately point to one important deficiency in the Bergsonian philosophy of mind, one which does not invalidate his philosophy as a whole. Bergson stressed that intuition transcends intellect, though he did not neglect to emphasize that it is by means of the intellect that intuition develops evolution-wise beyond the constraints of mere instinct. The distinction between intuition and instinct is not made in Russellian and Koestlerian vogues, but Bergson himself did not distinguish between substantially different wavelengths of "intellect." If this whole matter is transposed into terms of the analytic/holistic modes of mentation, then my own emphasis is that an advanced form of controlled "linear" consciousness is the crucial means of adjusting advanced intuitive (non-linear) consciousness to the sphere of time and cultural progress.

These advanced wavelengths in the analytic mode are geared to the intuitive faculties, and are not in conflict with the latter (as occurs in less advanced wavelengths). The integration of these two complementary foci constitutes a degree (or rather degrees) of discernment well above the average, and is liable to be much more rare than is sometimes facilely envisaged. The advanced "linear" complement is liable to require a specific development of its own at advanced levels, and it is arguable that many mystical types are incomplete in this respect, which is one explanation for some tangible errors.

From this perspective, Bertrand Russell was more incomplete in discriminative faculties than Bergson, even though the former assumed that he already possessed such attainments in full by virtue of his dedication to science. Attainment is not necessarily coexistent with the mere fact of dedication, a drawback that is undoubtedly an ingredient of the situation of numerous professed mystics. By comparison with developed discernment, many mystics and logicians are likely to be at a junior stage which might even be called lazy if stronger efforts are not forthcoming.

It is a proposition here that Bertrand Russell was not so much a philosopher as a competent mathematician, early renowned for his collaboration at Cambridge in *Principia Mathematica*, considered a milestone in the history of mathematics. Russell was annoyed with Kant and Hegel because they awarded a low status to mathematics, though this should not lead to the assumption that Kant and Hegel were surpassing philosophers. Russell complained that ever since the time of Zeno the Eleatic, idealist philosophers have attempted to discredit mathematics by producing contradictions designed to reveal that mathematicians had not arrived at metaphysical truth. Modern academic philosophy still aspires to *a priori* knowledge, and mathematics is sometimes considered to contain *a priori* knowledge of a high degree of certainty. Kant denied that arithmetic follows from (deductive) logic, but the nineteenth century academic philosopher Gottlieb Frege demonstrated to the contrary. Russell accused idealist philosophers of having responded to Frege by not reading the authors concerned.[92]

The crux of the issue is really that Kant and other moderns conceived of certain knowledge as being the product of a process of (*a priori*) reasoning; other faculties were foreign to them. Arithmetic is another form of logic, and capable of some very different usages. There was probably a great difference between Pythagoras and Bertrand Russell.

The truth is that many contemporary scientists cannot understand mathematics in an *a priori* context. A recent theory in mathematical format has proposed a "virtually *a priori*" explanation of the universe, envisaged as a precedent for a mathematical metaphysics. It is so complex that many physicists are unable to decode it, and as a result it is in danger of reaping an oblivion amongst natural scientists comparable to the reputed fate of Frege's demonstration amongst some philosophers.[93]

New and formative quantum-relativistic models in physics now sound pronouncedly metaphysical even to physicists who concede their powerful cogency and importance, and are now potentially crucial in the history of science. It is unscientific to call something metaphysical because one is averse to its implications. This habit has undesirable pseudo-empirical overtones, perhaps even comparable to misrepresenting a certain truth associated with the Greek thinker Protagoras. The physicist David Bohm has remarked upon the Protagorean statement: "Man is the measure of all things," which he interprets in the sense of measure being a reality that is *not* external to man. Yet some who habitually looked at everything externally imposed their perspective upon what Protagoras said. Hence they came to the erroneous conclusion that measure was a relative phenomenon, something subject to the caprice or taste of each individual. In contrast, for Bohm measure is a form of insight and mental harmony that can only arise when someone makes truth and factuality priorities instead of their own whims and desires.[94]

This perspective might here be called essential realism, in extension of the physicalist notion of realism prevalent today that stresses only a limited factuality. Whether or not one gives Protagoras the benefit of the doubt in the enunciation of his famous principle (i.e., he may have misconstrued it from a more knowledgeable source), subsequent Protagorean relativism made measure equivalent to whim, displacing an ultimate standard of insight.

It should be well known that a shoddy handling of quantum theory can acquire relativist overtones, leading to a virtual "anything goes" position. By contrast, emerging quantum-relativist models in physics can supply missing pieces of the universal puzzle at sub-atomic and other levels. Bohm remarks that "anything goes, or nothing goes" is an apt description of the situation applying in a black hole, where time and space as we know it vanishes. But as the same physicist states, current quantum mechanics is a "very truncated, limited, abstracted set of formulae which gives certain limited results having to do with only one moment of an experiment." Quantum mechanics requires an extension in order to accommodate time and the actuality of the universe. The physicist Eugene Wigner has proposed that it is the consciousness of the observer that gives actuality to everything, but Bohm is not satisfied with this solution to the quantum regress. As an alternative to the incapacity of quantum mechanics to explain process, i.e., the influence of the past on the present, Bohm has devised the formulation of the implicate order and also the concepts of "injection" and "projection" of successive moments in time which relate to "cosmic memory."[95]

The necessary feat of explanation in physics is now comparable to explaining the fundaments of a sequential "left brain" process at cosmic level in extrapolation from the present-centredness of a "right brain" focus in sub-atomic terms. If there is much that sounds metaphysical, it is only that smaller minds inevitably have to stretch their capacities in order to assess a cosmic counterpart.

Recovery of an ultimate standard of insight will have to manoeuvre past the Scylla and Charybdis of relativism and scientific materialism. The discovery of a greater factuality than conventional science wishes to acknowledge is likely to mean a greater sense of responsibility in those deemed the official leaders of the human community. The recovery of a greater order in science is not without its paradoxes for those committed to the sloganism of "against the moralists."

As the Nobel prize-winning chemist Ilya Prigogine aptly endorses: "We can no longer accept the old *a priori* distinction between scientific and ethical values."[96] Even this sounds conveniently metaphysical for those wishing to jettison responsibility.

A recent and noteworthy spokesman of metaphysical theory relating to the brain is the neuroscientist John Eccles. His ethical stresses are above average in scientific ranks, and his theory of dualist-interactionism deserves close attention. Boldly proposing a self-conscious mind in interaction with the brain, Eccles firmly parts company with the various materialist theories of mind-brain identity.[97] In the strongly defined metaphysical sense, only pronouncedly mentalist strategies can seriously hope to rival the Ecclesian expertise in brain data, and there are to date very few of these alternative strategies explicitly formulated (e.g., the anthropographic strategy). As an appendage to natural theology, the Ecclesian theory is much closer to Cartesian dualism than alternative strategies, a feature reflected in the evolutionary data incorporated by Eccles. What is perhaps more surprising is that such a pronouncedly theologico-metaphysical viewpoint has been an influence second to none upon current and continuing ideas of the superiority of the "major" (left) hemisphere over the "minor" (right) hemisphere of the brain.

It can be urged here that a philosophy of mind which almost completely devalues the holistic mentation mode (equivalent to the "minor" hemisphere in reductionist terms) is committing an error of limited factuality comparable to a physicist ignoring the discoveries in quantum mechanics that have created the new physics. Because of this omission, it is unlikely that in practice such a philosophy could achieve major stimulation of analytic mode potentials, however much verbalism was resorted to. In actuality, this error amounts to a metaphysical version of Bertrand Russell, though much more cerebrally scientific than sceptical commonsense.

Dualist-interactionism can be said to have greatly improved upon the Cartesian philosophy by creating a theoretical bridge between mind and body via a predominantly one-hemisphere cerebral orientation. But dualist-interactionism does not greatly improve upon the Cartesian division between human souls and the rest of nature. Animals are effectively left as automatons, and there is no overall inter-species key to unlock the mechanistic impasse of Monod and other scientific materialists. It is an anthropocentric universe that is outlined, heavily dependent upon left hemisphere talents of verbalism for salvation.

In contrast to the Ecclesian schema, I maintain that the philosophy of mind admits of a much more extensive cerebral orientation, and the inclusion of an inter-species key which releases thought from both Cartesian and Monodic constraints of conditioning. The key might still be thrown away in some quarters even if it were empirically demonstrated as probabilistic truth, but since we live in a century when this not infrequently occurs in respect of important problems and solutions, the question of a clarified metaphysics constituting the reality is less startling to sober thinking.

## CHAPTER SEVEN

# THE PHILOSOPHY OF EVOLUTION AND HUMAN DEVELOPMENT

Evolution is a subject that still means many different things to different parties. I have no intention of proferring a potted version in the thriller style beloved by some contemporaries. Truth is often stranger than fiction.

A philosophy of evolution is not necessarily any the less viable than conventional scientific theories of evolution. Darwinian and neo-Darwinian ideas are now widely questioned even in conventional ranks, and new cosmological perspectives relating to the "Big Bang" and related phenomena are by no means standardized. As two empirical cosmologists recently affirmed: "Our theories of how the universe unfolded are never proved true. They serve only as guides to their successors."[98]

The question is: can a philosophy of evolution get closer to the truth than a scientific theory? Some would reply in the negative if there is no scientific data in accompaniment. But unless one attributes a high degree of comprehensiveness to such data, mere extrapolation from such data amounts to one more unproven theory which is superceded by another one. Even probabilistic accuracy enters limbo. Is there really no hope of certainty?

If a philosophy, as distinct from an empirically testable theory, can penetrate the evolutionary mists, then who is going to be able to verify its achievement? This is a very pertinent question applying to both partisans and critics of philosophies.

A minimal definition of the endeavour can be asserted here: a philosophy of evolution suffers if presented in an "exciting" novelistic manner. The novelistic idiom may belong to one type of creative imagination, but imagination very often does not possess any element of either "intuitive" certainty or probabilistic truth. This does not mean that more discursive philosophies of evolution do not frequently amount to the novelistic. But in general modern appetites cannot distinguish between the "spiritual evolution" of ancient philosophical classics and the garbage of commercial science fiction.

A viable philosophy of evolution will acknowledge empirical perspectives according to a scale of observation and experience that seeks definite knowledge and not novelism, that seeks to transcend shallow probabilities, and which takes into account a range of polymathic data that is generally excluded from specialist empirical disciplines and novelism alike.

The question "what do we mean by evolution?" may have to become "what do I mean by evolution?" If specialist disciplines persist in zero-rating evolutionary potentials, and if novelism delights in distorting priorities of experience, then it is up to the philosopher to call into question the anomalies and to attempt to rectify them. The answer is not to be dogmatic, but there is the necessity to emphasize basic priorities in the ongoing potential of the subject as an experiential reservoir for humans liable to die of thirst.

One of these basic priorities is that the quality of human life experience is more important than the zero-rating afforded by the Darwinian conclusion of "survival of the fittest." Far too many people are still confused by genetic theory, which is anachronistically insisted upon by Darwinist types as an explanation for both human and animal thinking and behaviour. Current sociobiology perpetuates this error, but the shortcomings here are readily apparent even to extreme materialist thinkers. No invocation of any metaphysical factor is required to correct elementary flaws in the conventional evolutionary corpus of theory and myth.

The fact remains that the quality of human life experience is disfigured and crippled by Darwinian concepts, which have not improved upon orthodox theology for the most part. If many people are currently content to regress to the animal level, there is no need for surprise in view of the mental conditioning which they accept so unthinkingly.

A cogent disavowal of overall Darwinist conceptions of evolution has recently been expressed by the astronomer Fred Hoyle. In the foreword to *The Intelligent Universe*, he aptly describes Darwinism as a nihilistic philosophy which was accepted by "so-called educated opinion" after publication of Darwin's *Origin of Species*. Hoyle concludes that this nihilism committed humankind to "a course of automatic self-destruction." Hoyle is amongst a minority of scientists who have expressed such a view; if the minority became a majority, we would be liable to see great changes for the better in global conditions, even if such changes occur too late in the ecological and related crises.

Hoyle is now one of those scientists who emphasize a new-found (to science) order *and* purpose in the universe, by contrast with the conventional scientific materialist notions of chance and physical necessity. Yet there are different ways of interpreting purpose at this cosmic level. Hoyle complains that in contemporary Western religions, it is affirmed that "God" created the universe, and that "God" can intervene in the universe, though the universe cannot interfere with God. This leads to what Hoyle calls an unanswerable question: why should the universe exist at all? He also duly cites the recent admission of a distinguished modern theologian: "What we cannot understand is that God, who has no need of the world, should have reason to create (it) . . . ."

The logical objection to creationism is offset in Hoyle's commentary by the proposition that "God" exists "only by virtue of the support received from the universe."[99] This argument is not in contradiction to a cosmic intelligence, which is here viewed as an immanent factor. This perspective is much more logical than conventional theology, though it need not be considered at all theological. The scientific explanation of "God" is still a very open-ended matter.

One problem with modern scientific attitudes is that they tend sometimes to conclude that questions about the meaning of the universe could not formerly have been answered in a scientific, or even a sensible, manner. Science inevitably hedges against religious faith in a larger-scale intelligence than ourselves, but more unjustifiably ignores "mystical" subsets and dissenting groups. These latter are not all to be facilely classified as pseudoscientific. Meaning is not the prerogative of empirical science, however enlightened this latter enterprise becomes.

A standard attitude even amongst progressive scientists is that only by the accumulation of a multitude of facts via observation and experiment, "and by then making reasoned deductions from the facts, can one ever know."[100] This ignores any intuitive knowledge, which is not equivalent to faith any more than is scientific knowledge. Further, intuitive knowledge itself is apt to build upon experiential facts. The problem with mystical knowledge is that differing ranges of observation are not specified in the reports and rumours of experiences, which means that one man's purported illumination can be another man's preparatory tuition.

The factor of intuition did gain a place in Bergson's theory of creative evolution, though this factor was resented by the advocates of commonsense. Bertrand Russell described Bergson's famous *L'Evolution Creatrice* (1907) as "merely a poetical picture appealing to the fancy." Russell's major accusation was that the book in question contained no argument, and therefore there was nothing in it to facilitate a conclusion as to whether the philosophy it exposits is true or false.[101] If Bergson was a poet, then Russell might be classified as a rhetorician, but neither attribution of merit proves whether the attendant philosophies were true or false. Nor does the lack of argument in any thesis necessarily prove it is unworthy of being a claimant at least to partial truth – which is a booty not always falling to empirical stylization, which is often proved to be something less than partial in the posthumous light of day.

The scepticism meted out to Bergson is strangely similar to that befalling Teilhard De Chardin, the more significant perhaps because Bergson (a professor of philosophy) was not a theologian and did not couch his work in theological terms. Does this mean that scientific sceptics are not merely opponents of theology on valid historical grounds, but also opponents of anything savouring of the metaphysical on less valid grounds of sheer conditioning to a scientific belief system?

De Chardin, unlike Bergson, was a Jesuit father. His major work *The Phenomenon of Man* could not be published until his death owing to its prohibition by his religious superiors. In the preface, the author states that "it must be read not as a work on metaphysics, still less as a sort of theological essay, but purely and simply as a scientific treatise."[102] It may be this definition which has drawn such a scorching response from critics in scientific ranks. It is apparently a scientific crime to be utopian in respect of the future possibilities of humankind, though ironically enough in this respect, De Chardin's concept of a progressive momentum in history (and prehistory) may be too linear to realistically accommodate cyclical reversions to more alpha grades of density.

While some forms of utopianism are not to be dismissed so readily by those members of the human species capable of scientifically creating a comparative utopia by contrast with technological nightmares, an inevitable criticism of De Chardin's treatise is that it ends with a statement of the Christian faith as comprising the envisaged utopia or Omega Point. Furthermore, this statement is exclusivist in its approach to "ancient religions," which are said to be "narrowly bound to untenable myths, or steeped in a pessimistic and passive mysticism." These ancient religions are out of step with science, affirms De Chardin, but Christianity is interpreted as forging ahead from the scientific shock that is "rapidly causing its rivals to disappear."[103] It is difficult for some commentators to be as charitable as they otherwise might be if such exclusivism did not rear its head in a scientific treatise.

Another valid criticism of the same treatise is its vague attribution of consciousness to the higher animals. De Chardin does not adopt the Cartesian perspective of the animal as mere automaton, but neither does he definitively repudiate it.[104] In this sense therefore, he is convergent with the views of many Darwinists, who have not been particularly venturesome on this point.

Since orthodox science and orthodox religion seem to converge strongly in repudiation of "ancient religions," I will take this opportunity of contributing a philosophical defence of the more intrinsic ancient perspectives. I can offer no apologies for this defence, since in my view, the ancient (and less ancient) heretics were closer to the truth than their detractors. The matter is one of clarifying the meaning of evolution, and distinguishing between contractions and expansions in both scientific and mystical concepts. I may add that such clarification in concepts has been surprisingly neglected by numerous "mystical" partisans, including the latter day "Platonist" metaphysicists of academic philosophy.

One of the ancient perspectives which Teilhard De Chardin was evidently attempting to expel from rivalry with his favoured doctrine is that known by the awkward term metempsychosis, denoting a subject which has frequently been (very) poorly researched. The Christian Platonist Henry More was evidently a (largely clandestine) subscriber to this heretical view, to judge from the verse invoking Plotinus in his *Philosophical Poems* (1647), a verse which refers to "the pre-existing soul" which "enters bodies here below." This matter was not well clarified however, and More's contemporary Ralph Cudworth, another of the Cambridge Platonists, dismissed the Platonic teachings of pre-existence and transmigration of the soul as "offensive absurdities."[105] The full force of Christian dogma was not always in abeyance amongst Christian Platonists, but Darwinian biases are closely approximate in respect of transmigration. Though the subject is taboo in the canons of both materialist science and orthodox theology, a rationalist of Voltaire's critical stature could observe that ideas of metempsychosis are "neither absurd nor useless."[106] It remains to determine the nature and extent of the perspectives in this direction that are commonly neglected by doctrinaire interests and popular misrepresentation. While Western views in favour of transmigration have frequently been expressed inadequately and ambiguously, it is often assumed that all Eastern views on the subject are somehow regressive. One could wish that a more competent research was prevalent, since as usual, the truth is contrary to misrepresentation.

It is relevant here to compare Teilhard De Chardin's viewpoint with that of an Eastern mystical philosopher whose book was published the same year as the original *Le Phenomene Humain* (1955). This Eastern contribution also follows an evolutionist framework, and does not contradict

Darwinian biological evolution in respect of the basic conception of the human species following on in an interlinked chain from subhuman species. But in most other respects, the content is very different from both the Darwinian and Teilhardist interpretations of the evolutionary phenomenon. I am referring to a much neglected book dictated in English [107] by the late Meher Baba (d. 1969), an Irani Zoroastrian by birth, who lived much of his life observing strict silence. The synchronous publication tends to invite a comparison, particularly since both the Jesuit anthropologist and the Persian mystic were highly original in their own milieux of expression, and because their respective books are likely to be much copied by other writers having an easily available precedent.

There are three particularly notable features about the Iranian contribution. Firstly, it is unusually systematic and technical, and differs from many other metaphysical works in its lack of emotive expression. It nowhere claims to be a scientific treatise, but it is not primarily a theological treatise either. Secondly, it offers a unique exposition and correlation of Arabic and Persian terminology used in sufi literature and Sanskrit terminology employed in Vedantic tradition. Thirdly, it is thoroughly panpsychist in its interpretative details. Panpsychism is the term applied in Western philosophy to concepts of the universe in which all animate and "organic" inanimate matter is invested with an "inside" or soul-like essence. These concepts are conventionally deemed preposterous, and in fact amount to heresy in Darwinian and neo-Darwinian perspective.

According to Meher Baba's evolutionism, all matter ultimately consists of evolving entities who myriadally inhabit all the species and even mineral and atomic existence. These entities evolve over astronomical lengths of time, since they develop in consciousness potential from the stage of gaseous matter to human beings. Consciousness is firmly attributed to the lower species, including plants and insects, though of a very rudimentary nature. The evolutionary pattern is stated to be one of successive sojourns of an individual entity in the various species, i.e., mineral, vegetable, reptile, fish, bird, animal, and human, in proportional ascendancy from the less evolved to the more evolved species. The pattern is regular and methodical, and does *not* involve any retrograde passage between species-forms as is frequently found in more well known doctrines of transmigration. The explanation of the causal factors operative in this evolutionism is also unusually detailed, and specifies a uniquely intricate version of the *sanskara* (impression) concept which is found in Sanskrit texts but not there treated in any detailed evolutionist sense. These *sanskaras* or impressions are accumulated during evolutionary experience and shape the emergent consciousness that is increasingly adaptable to the momentum involved in the transit from one species-form to another. The mind-stuff is composed of these impressions, which are not only acquired through experience in a physical form, but are also expended in a mathematically proportional process of inputs and outputs.

The ingenuity of this interpretation, upon close inspection, is as logically feasible as other evolutionist doctrines if concession is made to the possibility of its primary components. It is both methodical and comprehensive of eventualities, contrasts, and variations. As an Eastern theory of evolution, it is singularly dynamic in its causal sequences, and does not involve any repudiation of the basic Darwinian premise of a development through lower forms to higher ones. But is it even approximately correct? It is not fair to lump it with other theories of transmigration owing to its absence of anomalous retrogressions. It is very remote from any anthropocentric Cartesian doctrine, and firmly outlines purpose in a full-scale evolution that is sorely missing from Western expositions. How then are the more unbiased investigators to assess it? Perhaps the only immediate answer can be that it is most scientific to investigate all coherent theories before disregarding any of them.

It is a fact that both scientific cosmologists and theologians nowadays focus upon the "creation" of the universe in causal explanations. What is the Persian panpsychist able to say on this larger-than-life subject? There was no widely known "Big Bang" theory in the middle of this century, and he is original enough without being incompatible with the latest stellar deliberations. His metaphysic specifies the first inanimate form in creation, but in a non-creationist context from the theological point of view. This is because he maintains that the pre-creation situation was that of an Absolute that cannot be described as either conscious or unconscious. Instead he defines it as the "original unbounded absolute vacuum state of God," which more than a few physicists and astronomers could now agree with by analogy at least. Consciousness does not exist in this vacuum state; for consciousness to occur and develop required the process which we now call the universe. This perspective contradicts the conventional theological assumption that the universe was created by a conscious agency which is not itself involved in the universal process. Rather, the mystical evolutionist argument of Meher Baba has it that the absolute vacuum state *is* complete in itself *but* requires to achieve consciousness of itself via the process of evolution. This leads to a complex microcosm-macrocosm thesis which is altogether omitted in conventional religion.

According to the same panpsychist, humans do not require to evolve a more advanced physical form. The objective is the refinement and expansion of consciousness within the human life-span. This is contrary to space fiction and much standardized evolutionary theory. The increasing discoveries of the great age of *homo* – now in terms of millions of years – would tend to bear out this contention of an endpoint in the human form. But the endpoint in consciousness is much more complex than the uniform occurrence of entities possessing a human body. Like other mystics, Meher Baba refers to a higher evolution of consciousness, which is variously exposited with appreciable differences in range of detail. He affirms a reincarnation sequence (in accordance with the balance of impressions) and acknowledges an after-death state, but there is no great importance attached to the latter, since it is held that the ultimate conscious expansion can only occur in relation to a human life-span. The contention is that this ultimate expansion in the individual achieves conscious identity with the original vacuum state of the Absolute. Unlike many other twentieth century mystical accounts, an unusual emphasis is placed upon the dangers of partial advancement in the "higher evolution" of consciousness, an emphasis which is refreshingly realistic and difficult to find nowadays. The Persian panpsychist affirms that a malfunctioning entity at a critical level of partial advancement can, in extreme instances, negate its own laboriously acquired human individuality and, by a process of psychic disintegration, revert to a rudimentary level of infrahuman evolution (i.e. mineral); the causal process here is very atypical, and something quite apart from the normal course of evolution where no retrogression occurs. This kind of exception is not illogical if one believes in reincarnation, but such parapsychology is unlikely to prove popular on the commercial media, since vested interests in miraculous powers are unlikely to desire a sane estimate of what disintegration could occur if such faculties were misused.

All this does of course sound fictitious to those critical of microcosm-macrocosm philosophies, despite its ingenious recasting, replete with details that are very difficult to find elsewhere. However, it is remarkable as a coherent explanation for so many tangible (and intangible) events. It is perhaps worth noting that conventional theology has more difficulties in explaining several different types of event, and that conventional evolutionary theory is nowhere near as consistent as was believed by the early Darwinians.

Inconsistencies abound in the views of some Western believers in reincarnation who attribute the phenomenon only to humans. The reluctance to accept the transmigration of souls from one species to another amounts to a form of "Cartesian" belief which in some respects is even more unconvincing than orthodox theology. Unless there is a logical interconnecting principle between humans and the many other species and forms of existence, the subject of reincarnation is at a distinct disadvantage in relation to materialism and Cartesian philosophy alike. Such points are widely neglected however.

The reputation of panpsychism in modern Western philosophy is very much that of an aberration, though it is customarily dismissed to such an extent that very little in the way of compelling argument is ever brought against it.

Added to this, there are different versions of panpsychism, not all of them very clear, and tending to cause confusion as to what it is that is so much beneath contempt. Elements of panpsychism can be found in various of the Greek philosophers, but not always clearly expressed, and often in alliance with the metaphor that was characteristic of their times. But paganism has long been considered old-fashioned in the march to progress, as Henry More and others found. One of the eighteenth century opponents of panpsychism was Immanuel Kant, the German professor whose stress on Christian morality elevated European Reason to the apex of human consciousness and disparaged intuition even in Plato. To the pious Kant, even the Stoics had morally erred in proclaiming "virtue" as being fully attainable in the present life of the wise sage. Kant's devaluation of wisdom is no logical encouragement to believe that all mysticism is a myth.

Yet panpsychism is not nearly so foreign to modern Western philosophy as some would like to believe. A century before Kant, the Jewish philosopher Baruch Spinoza stated in his *Ethics*: "All things are animate in various degrees." There is much in Spinoza's philosophy that is obscure, and the panpsychist components were perhaps quite deliberately rounded off (or made angular) by their incorporation into a Cartesian style format – though his whole tendency of interpretation was different to that of Descartes. It is not impossible that this heretical Jew had some knowledge of the Qabbalah tradition as it was known to his own race. The Jewish Qabbalah was a diversified phenomenon, to be distinguished in much of its repertory from the derivative Christian Qabbalism, and included variants of a panpsychist perspective. The Hebrew term for transmigration was *gilgul*, and the usage of this word and its significations met with the disapproval of the orthodox rabbis. During the thirteenth century, Jewish Qabbalists regarded transmigration as an esoteric teaching which could only be alluded to in their writings, and never systematically essayed. But in the fourteenth century it became more openly exposited, and was said to occur in all forms of existence, including plants and minerals. The Qabbalists of

Safed subsequently accepted this teaching, and were the cause of it becoming a widespread popular belief amongst Jews. However, there were many permutations of the *gilgul* teaching, with much metaphor and superstition in train. Such a teaching is very easily distorted by persons only superficially acquainted with it.

The relevant Hebrew words for this Jewish form of panpsychism were translations of the Arabic term *tanasukh*,[108] well known to philosophers and sufi types. A late Jewish representative of the Arabic repertory was Sarmad, a contemporary of Spinoza who was active in Iran and India. Educated in an Islamic environment by leading philosophers like the liberal Iranian sufi Mir Findiriski, he ended his days at the Mughal court where his unconventional lifestyle and outspokenness aroused official stigmatization of him as a heretic. He was executed in 1660–1. Reared in the Arabic tradition of philosophy, but also steeped in the Jewish tradition, an extant contemporary report reveals him as an exponent of *tanasukh* (*gilgul*) in a typically abstruse and metaphorical format as favoured by sophisticated Asiatic thinkers.[109]

It is apparent that many Muslim philosophers in the Aristotelian tradition discredited transmigration or else ignored it in their writings. This probably reflects, in part at least, the customary Aristotelian caution against the confused neo-Pythagorean version of transmigration that was in vogue amongst some ancient Greek circles. But perhaps a stronger influence was the orthodox Islamic disapproval of the subject. For instance, one of Sarmad's teachers, Mulla Sadra Shirazi, endorsed the anti-transmigrationist arguments of the Aristotelian Ibn Sina (Avicenna), an eleventh century thinker of a complex and strangely dual output, who assimilated the Greek tradition of philosophy to Islam. Yet the disapproval of *tanasukh* on the part of Islamic orthodoxy did not prevent all Muslim philosophers from expressing more approving judgments. One of the exceptions was Qutubuddin Shirazi,[110] a thirteenth century Aristotelian of Iran who was also intimate with sufi perspectives. Qutubuddin Shirazi is an important figure in the largely neglected history of medieval science. He was one of the team of astronomers who worked at the Maragha observatory in North-West Iran, and he evolved a planetary theory of Copernican overtones that was later reworked in its passage from the Iranian milieu.[111] Though one of the forerunners of Copernicus, he is still virtually unknown to the history of science as taught in the West, and his part in the history of philosophy remains to be maximally determined.

The extremely diverse medieval tradition of Sufism is not nearly so distinct in all of its facets from the Aristotelian tradition as is conventionally assumed. Yet major sufi exponents like Jalaluddin Rumi (d. 1273) did not require the role of a philosopher as it is understood in the West. Rumi was definitely not a theologian in the orthodox sense, and it is evident that his habit of intricate poetic expression was one means of employing unorthodox themes. It was in poetic form that he expressed in his *Mathnavi* an evolutionary formula that has been variously interpreted:

> "I died as mineral and became a plant,
> I died as plant and rose to animal,
> I died as animal and I was man."[112]

In this and other similar passages, Rumi alludes to something that he did not define in terms amenable to current classifications. The Cambridge scholar R.A. Nicholson concluded that Rumi was referring to the Aristotelian theory of the triple nature of the soul, and in this respect suggests a parallel in Milton's *Paradise Lost*.[113] Yet it may be relevant here that the British poet, like Rumi, was actually more of a Platonist than an Aristotelian. The tripartite Aristotelian division was vegetative-animal-rational, to which was sometimes added the angelic in later formats. The fourfold scheme is compatible in part with the complete verse of the *Mathnavi* quoted above, which could refer to a human developmental theme such as was exposited by sufis in diverse formulae. Yet, by the very fact of more inclusive terminology, it is not totally convincing that Rumi did not mean to imply a more long-term evolutionary sequence, and a major compendium of reincarnationist thought has accordingly included the verse in question.[114]

The associations of a (non-Darwinian) biological evolution

are not easily to be rejected. A primary factor in respect of this consideration is the evidence left by the redoubtable eleventh century Muslim polymath and scientist Al-Biruni. In more than one of his outstanding treatises, he briefly outlined what is clearly discernible as an inter-species evolutionary theory, though the Darwinist world has made light of this by deducing that it is not sufficiently complex to merit comparison with the natural selection theory of Charles Darwin. This superiority in detail is, however, unconvincing in its attempt to ignore the looming factor that the inter-species sequence was scientifically intuited and conceived long before the Darwinists were bred to inchoate developments. Biruni was evidently aware that humans had evolved through the lower species and then through to primates and the anthropoid stages. Further, and undeniably powerful proof of his acumen, is afforded by his important conclusion that animal life exists at a very low level of cellular organization in sponges and corals. European naturalists did not equal (let alone surpass) this zoological acumen in plant-animal transitions until the era of the French researchers Cuvier and Lamarck over seven centuries later.[115]

It can here be suggested that the daunting research of Al-Biruni was aided by his acquaintance with panpsychist data of the *tanasukh* philosophy. It would have been that much easier for him to have grasped organic details during his empirical investigations after assimilating *tanasukh* emphases, however cautious he may have been with regard to the differing versions of transmigration.

Since it is only very recently that the full extent of Biruni's vast knowledge of the sciences has become apparent to scholars (with resultant difficulties in catching up with the revisions), one should be careful not to ignore related philosophical details that extend to mystical sectors.

Owing to the associations of those doctrines of transmigration which incorporate retrograde incarnation, e.g. humans reincarnating as animals, the whole subject has understandably received criticism and even outright rejection from many commentators. But there is quality material available which tends to prove that discerning panpsychists did not hold any such view, which represents a popular superstition extrapolated from a core teaching that utilized metaphor. Aziz ibn Muhammad Nasafi was a Persian sufi writer of the thirteenth century, and exhibits a sophisticated approach to *tanasukh* that is worthy of consideration. He reports the subject in a manner which attests his partisanship, with emphases that are likely to surprise readers accustomed to the more "orthodox" sufi literature. Nasafi's various treatises enable a reconstruction of largely forgotten sufi teachings, which are distinct from more popular versions of transmigration. In his *Tanzil ul-Arwah* (Souls Brought Down) he states that ascending transmigration (*naskh*) signifies that an entity casts off one form and assumes a new and higher form. In this way, the "part-soul" first arises in the form of the elements, then assumes the plant form, then assumes the animal form, then assumes human form, and finally assumes the likeness of "angels." In contrast to this, descending transmigration (*maskh*) signifies that an entity assumes a lower form which corresponds to its character after failure in the human form. But despite the disadvantages of a corrupt text, it is possible to read Nasafi as emphasizing that the soul can transit from a "higher" man to a "lower" man. This gives a radically different accent to the conventional literal interpretation of a frequent retrogression of the human entity into subhuman forms. Confirmation of this sophisticated interpretation is to be found in Nasafi's statement that: "Although man is human in outward form, in his moral and spiritual composition he is sometimes an ant or a mouse, sometimes a wolf or a panther, or even a demon and a Satan, and other things also." Nasafi makes it quite clear that a man can assume the qualities of inferior creatures in his present human existence. It is therefore apparent that *maskh* is symbolic of lost potential, though interpreted literally in popular traditions. Whereas *naskh* was a firm evolutionary view which it is unnecessary for the most part to decode into symbolic components, an evolutionary view which had the extraordinary advantage of directly anticipating the Darwinist biological evolution, though from a very different interpretive standpoint.

Emphasizing the cosmic nature of the *tanasukh* evolutionary perspective, Nasafi writes: "All the species of the material world are journeying to reach their goal and end. The destination of them all is the human species, which is the perfection of the whole." He adds the warning that humans can go against the cosmic objective, and create a violent movement in antagonism to this objective. One could currently deduce that Darwinism has aided this violent reverse through its lack of dimension in the balance of psyche.

Nasafi also clarified the topic of the "angels" stipulated in the *naskh* sequence. In his *Kashf al-Haqaiq* (Unveiling of Realities), he affirms that each man in whom intelligence (or wisdom) is the controlling factor is an angel, or even superior to an angel, while yet in human form. In contrast, each man who is dominated by nature is "a Satan or a beast or even worse than the beasts."[116]

Nasafi shows every sign of having been one of the more enlightened sufi types, in contrast to the "orthodox" vogues which were popular and often much narrower in outlook. A common idea is that "Muslim sufis" did not believe in anything panpsychist, but this is a sweeping generalization based upon inadequate scholarship and conventional preferences. It is more accurate to assert that, since transmigrationist views amounted to a heresy in the eyes of the zealous legalists and theologians of Islam, those sympathetic to such views were very often wary of expressing their deepest thoughts other than in the form of poetry and adroit references incidental to other exegeses.

One of the most famous names in the heritage of sufi philosophy is that of Muhiyuddin ibn al-Arabi (d. 1240), born in Spain but later domiciled in Syria. He is scholastically considered to be more "philosophical" than most of the other names of sufi mystical association. Professor Nicholson duly commented that Ibn al-Arabi "always writes with a fixed philosophical purpose, which may be defined as the logical development of a single all-embracing concept, and much of his thought expresses itself in a dialectic bristling with technicalities." Nicholson also described Arabi's pantheistic philosophy in terms of a system which "perhaps, all things considered, is the most imposing monument of mystical speculation the world has ever seen."[117] While this judgment was admirably liberal, the choice of description is misleading, since Arabi stressed experiential concepts as distinct from the speculative and dogmatic. His logic was in acute contrast to that of the medieval schoolmen of Europe; there appears to be a deliberate lack of order in the presentation of Arabi's system, and he is not easy to read in translation. His "dialectic" is not of the later European variety, and the technicalities of his style employ much metaphor that make it abundantly clear that he was not a literalist. This mystical philosopher faced severe disapproval from the orthodox, and various attempts were made to discredit him and to murder him. It is not surprising to find that the ingenious technicalities of his presentation include a suitably cautious reference to transmigration in the context of remarking upon the differences of opinion amongst Muslim literati concerning the event of "Resurrection." He reports the view of some that this event will occur via reincarnation, and is careful to add that these spokesmen quote Quranic passages and authenticated sayings of the Prophet in support of their contention.[118] This passage is no proof that Arabi believed in transmigration, but he would not have put himself to the potentially dire trouble of proving any intimation of his on a subject that had no chance of tolerance. Some proofs are not possible of premature acceptance, as even Galileo found. Modern Darwinian scientists and dogmatists of respectable non-fanatic auspices will not even credit the fact tht a complex evolutionary sequence was known to medieval sufis and polymaths; how then are even deeper matters possible of a civilized scientific investigation?

Though Ibn al-Arabi is too mystical for the tastes of scientific materialism, a much more scientifically proportioned sample of the evolutionary theme is to be found in Abu Bakr Muhammad ibn Zakariya al-Razi, known to the Latin-speaking scholars of Europe as Rhazes. He notably furthered medical practice at Baghdad prior to his decease in the early tenth century. He is less well known for his distinctive philosophy, though this has frequently been stated to be of a Platonist idiom – a typical simplification in matters of potted reports of more expansive wisdom. While his empirical achievements substantially outstripped those of many Aristotelians, his most essential philosophy is less clear than it might have been owing to manuscript losses, though an ancient Iranian colouring of Zurvanite overtones is clearly discernible. It is evident enough that he believed in a very sensitive version of transmigration, and his emphasis upon the necessity of saving animals from pain does not fare well in the current empirical climate of laboratory mutilation. Razi was extremely bold in his disclaimer of ethnocentric penchants surfacing in religion, and is known to have been on close terms with Chinese visitors to his native Iran. One wonders what this redoubtable empirical panpsychist would have made of the ethnocentric Koestlerian argument directed (in part at least) against the transmigrationist beliefs of Hindus and Buddhists.

Koestler has urged that "if consciousness is an emergent quality, the ugly paradox of the solon (immortal soul) – implicit in all Eastern and Platonic philosophy – ceases to exist." He deduces that we nowhere find completely self-contained wholes or solons, but only holons, meaning "double-faced entities which display the characteristics both of independent units and of inter-dependent parts." He gleefully seizes upon the fact that a flatworm, if cut into six slices, will regenerate a complete individual from each slice within a matter of weeks. One of Koestler's major targets, it is only fair to mention, is the conventional transmigration theory (rife in India and Tibet) of humans reversing into animal forms.

The Koestlerian confusions over the question of individuality unfortunately (for the Koestlerian argument) result in the embryonic kidney being taken as an equivalent to crushed and re-formed sponges possessing individuality.[119] Both Al-Razi and Al-Biruni are likely to have been amused at this holonic conflation. They might have empirically pointed out that popular modern science is a fitting successor to ancient popular superstition. Razi at least might have added, with a philosophic acerbity, that anyone with sufficient leisure and sadistic tendencies who wants to cut up worms into pieces and then watch them rejuvenate, should at least ascertain which species are the more emergent and which are those possessing more individuality, if the ugly paradoxes invented by modern puzzle-makers are ever to become of immortal significance. Failing this, one could suggest that vivisectionists undergo the same operations they inflict, just in case their kidneys have a higher survival value than their emergent consciousness.

An implicated associate of Razi was the unorthodox sufi exponent Al-Hallaj (d. 922), who aroused the antipathy of canonists and courtiers owing to his repudiations of prevalent elitist convenience and ignorance. Much of his literary output perished in the condemnation attendant upon his execution at Baghdad, but it is quite evident that much of his teaching did not follow an orthodox pattern. One verse attributed to him includes the assertion: "For a hundred thousand years I have lived and worked and tried in every sort of body."[120] Though some conservatives might deem this of poetic relevance only, the verbal heritage of Hallaj was deemed pointed enough by his detractors for it to be kept under official prohibition for over three centuries until the Mongol conquests, by which time only fragments survived.

The liberal Persian work known as the *Dabistan-i-Mazahib*, written in the mid-seventeenth century, reports the sufi exponent Muhammad Nurbakhsh as distinguishing between *tanasukh* and *buruz*, that is, between the evolutionary process of transmigration and the reincarnation of a completed human soul "for the sake of perfecting mankind."[121] Nurbakhsh was another of pronouncedly unorthodox tendencies, a fifteenth century Iranian in whose wake came the Nurbakhshi order of dervishes. The distinction he made has been far more common in Mahayana Buddhist lore; in Tibet it was a popular and official convention for "incarnate lamas" to be attributed a very high spiritual status. The eyewitness reports of the sympathetic (and critical) traveller Madame Alexandra David-Neel, who herself gained a rank in the lamaist system of Tibet, afford reliable evidence that such claims and attributions were abused by some lamas, who were anything but exemplary of a completed evolution. In fact, the useful documentation of David-Neel[122] reveals that the desire for occult powers and spiritual status was almost as widespread in old Tibet as it is in the contemporary West. This does not of course mean that the subject of a spiritual evolution is devoid of serious meaning, but it does mean that the relevance and application qualitatively varies to a pronounced degree.

It ought to be more well known how an experiential tradition can lose content in terms of human removes from the original exemplars, or from those exemplars most expert in its essential features.

Though the nineteenth century philosopher Arthur Schopenhauer has been called a panpsychist in Western annals,[123] there are pronounced differences between Schopenhauer's writings and his Eastern sources of inspiration. He is more accurately to be classified as a neo-Kantian phenomenologist. Schopenhauer was from the start an admirer of Kant, though he revised the emphases of his predecessor. His major incentive in this was provided by the ancient Indian texts known as the Upanishads, texts which he did not read in the Sanskrit but in the very laborious translation of Anquetil Duperron that became available to European literati in the early years of the nineteenth century. Buddhist texts also had some influence upon him, and his "pessimistic" philosophy[124] equates more with the so-called nihilism of the Theravada school of Buddhism than with Vedantic characteristics. Reincarnation was purely allegorical in his view, and he implies his belief in the eventual nothingness of the soul. The Buddhist *nirvana* and the Vedantic reabsorption in *Brahman* were considered by Schopenhauer to be "myths and meaningless words" in terms of ultimate significations, though he was fond of using the term *nirvana* in a negative context. He was one of the first to point out the resemblance of the Vedantic *maya* (illusion) to Kant's phenomenon, but this is arguably a superficial comparison. Certainly, Schopenhauer's concept of the will was not equivalent to the *atman* of the Upanishads, though the latter was an inspiration for the former. Schopenhauer's concept of the ascetic denial of the will and his realistic assessment of suffering have advantages over Hegelian dialectic, which Schopenhauer abhorred. He wanted to improve upon Kant's denial of the possibility of being acquainted with realities beyond phenomena, to reveal a way in which metaphysics could be applied to consciousness and not left in a speculative limbo. But despite his clearer terminology, and despite the statuette of Buddha which accompanied the bust of Kant upon his writing desk, Schopenhauer only found the beginning of the way by the more enlightened Eastern panpsychist standards – which is not to deny his merits in attempting to de-ethnocentricize his horizons in a milieu that subsequently considered him an alien to Western society because he based his ideas on Oriental philosophy.

This neo-Kantian understandably reacted to the professorial claim of Schleiermacher that philosophy should be founded upon religious faith. He was also ahead of a subsequent view in academe that was diametrically opposed to that of Schleiermacher: namely, the view of Moritz Schlick and other logical positivists who maintained that philosophy should be founded upon natural science. By comparison, Schopenhauer was very reasonable in affirming that natural science only touches the surface of existence, though perhaps less reasonable in certain respects than some of the contemporary Romantics, with whom he also disagreed. In respect of Oriental precedents, he was very much behind the times in being completely ignorant of the philosophical and experiential extensions of the Duperron version of the Upanishads that he studied so assiduously and cherished so highly. In his set of essays entitled *Parerga and Paralipomena* (1851), he wrote: "In the whole world there is no study, except that of the originals, so beneficial and so elevating as that of the *Oupnekhat* (Upanishads). It has been the solace of my life, it will be the solace of my death." Anquetil Duperron's *Oupnekhat* was not translated from the Sanskrit, but from the Persian version of the Upanishads prepared in the 1650's by the Mughal prince Dara Shikoh. Shikoh was a liberal aristocrat of strong sufi affiliations, and by the time he consulted the Hindu pundits on the Sanskrit heritage, had as his mentor the heretical Jewish philosopher Sarmad. Both Sarmad and Shikoh were on the best of terms with Hindus, and the prince was evidently well disposed towards panpsychist views. He produced his own distinctive treatise on the confluence of Sufi and Vedantic tradition, a measure for which he received the disapproval of orthodox Muslims. Like his teacher Sarmad, he could talk in a non-dogmatic manner with members of several different religions, to the extent that he could easily be mistaken for an adherent of this or that religion.[125] But such philosophy and its extensions were blotted out in Western annals, in which the seventeenth century represented only the mechanical philosophy of Descartes, the "panpsychist" monadology of Leibniz, the inductionism of Francis Bacon, the dogmatism of Hobbes, the empiricism of Locke, and whatever Spinoza was supposed to have said in his metaphysical paragraphs.

Various Romantics and Rationalists have been associated with concepts of metempsychosis that adhered to the German Enlightenment, partly through interest in Sanskrit classics. Johann Gottfried von Herder (d. 1803) is sometimes implicated, but it has been affirmed that he abandoned the idea of metempsychosis by 1774. His *Conversations about Metempsychosis* (1782) have been interpreted as a refutation of J.G. Schlosser's then recent dialogue *About Metempsychosis*, which had defended the subject, one which Lessing had "merely suggested" as a possible explanation for human ethical progress in his much discussed *Education of the Human Race*.[126] Herder has been contrasted with Kant, whom he strongly criticized, in a context amounting to "relativist" versus "moralist," variety versus uniformity, local versus universal standards.[127] But did either of these thinkers understand the nature of the soul and its development? It is arguable that Kant knew very little about universals in the evolutionary sense, and Herder's locality of mind may have prematurely jettisoned concepts of greater value for human development. That Romantics and Rationalists dabbled in concepts of transmigration, and even abandoned such concepts, is no proof that such concepts have no value or relevance. How many Empiricists would definitively know their antecedents or future states by the mere repudiation of apparently fantastic concepts?

One could be far more realistic than Schopenhauer in inferring that the stark quality of a long-term evolutionary transformation of human ignorance is the most apt fate for the myriadal expressions of egoism, myopia of thought, and general constriction of horizons. One is under no logical constraint to believe that humans and animals have only one life-span simply because so many people find it unbearable to think otherwise.

Just as Schopenhauer was out of attunement with Mughal era philosophical understanding of the Upanishads, other forms of neo-Kantian "panpsychism" lack the dimensions of the more intrinsic Eastern versions. The philosopher of science, Sir Karl Popper, has recently remarked on the panpsychism of the nineteenth century mathematician William Kingdon Clifford and other neo-Kantians. But Popper conflates this modern Western panpsychism with Spinoza, the earliest Presocratics, and with materialism. He concludes that it is in error, like materialism, because it is too predictable or deterministic in its conceptions.[128] This strangely parallels the "intuitive" verdict of Bergson that neither mechanical causality nor teleology can give a sufficient interpretation of the evolutionary process.[129] Bergson's modified teleology, or vitalism, was here confronting the cumbersome teleology of Leibniz, and was perhaps in need of an increased intuitive momentum in order to grasp an even deeper evolutionary spectrum of events and potentials. Bergsonian vitalism, as with more conventional metaphysics, did not arrive at the discernment of some pre-moderns.

Intrinsic Eastern panpsychism is not deterministic in the way that materialist and other mechanistic theories are; it is both purposive in a refined teleological sense and emergent in consciousness extensions.[130] It has advantages in explanation over both the vitalist and organicist approaches in modern biology, approaches which are other alternatives to the Darwinian paradigm. The vitalist approach has not been capable of experimental proof, while organicists emphasize testability in the competition with neo-Darwinian mechanists.[131] Panpsychism is not testable in laboratories. Laboratory testing amounts to pinball wisdom when it comes to matters in advance of the probabilistic, matters which are of a greater scope than piecemeal statistics.

The mathematical philosopher Leibniz, despite his recognition of the animal soul, was unduly deterministic in his teleology as a result of his adaptation to Christian theology. The Aristotelianism of Ibn Sina (Avicenna) was subject to an equivalent adaptation to Islamic theology, though he also developed a pointedly mystical (and metaphorical) philosophy of a different order. The intrinsic panpsychism greatly supercedes the metaphysics of the extant Aristotelian corpus, which should not be taken as definitive for all views at the Lyceum. The intrinsic panpsychism is also much in advance of the largely oblique and metaphorical references that can be found in the Dialogues of Plato.

According to Sir Karl Popper, panpsychism is irrefutable in that it is not testable (in the laboratory), and even if conscious states are attributed to all atoms, the problem of explaining the states of consciousness of higher animals remains as difficult as it was previously. This is anachronistic reasoning, since some problems are created by experimental science and its philosophy. For instance, Popper affirms that little can be gained by linking mental states to physics rather than to biology.[132] But it is not really scientific to split physics and biology in the customary specialist manner. Intrinsic Eastern panpsychism unites the emergent conscious properties in both fields of smaller and greater organisms (i.e. physics and biology), and is the only coherent evolutionary format to do so in terms of a progressive phenomenon. Other formats are effectively Cartesian.

A well known and influential Popperian definition of a scientific theory is that the criterion of its scientific status is its falsifiability, its refutability, or its testability. But falsification of a theory or truth is not always definitive in the slightest, particularly if it is irrefutable, and so the mere absence of mundane testability should not in itself be considered proof of something unscientific, but only as indication of a problem for mundane tactics. Such tactics exemplified the logical positivist approach of the academic philosopher Moritz Schlick and his colleagues of the Vienna Circle, and persist in official science and in variants like Popperian philosophy. It is maintained here that such tactics have helped only to saddle twentieth century thought with a static evolution. Popper is not antimetaphysical in the dogmatic Humean sense avowed by Sir Alfred Ayer,[133] and in his autobiography has helpfully expressed the conclusion that Darwinism itself is a metaphysical research programme. Logically enough therefore, the Humes ought to have that much more scientific difficulty in burning heretical books.

Popperian conflation of panpsychism with materialism is metaphysically rendered nonsense by a consideration of the fact that metaphysical Darwinism and neo-Kantan panpsychism omit (at least) three basic factors in the intrinsic panpsychist evolutionary worldview:

1. The clarified non-Cartesian perspective of an evolution from the physicist's material of atoms up to and including the higher animals, an evolution that is alive, progressive in species-traits, and increasingly complex in its emergent dynamic of consciousness. This consciousness is correspondingly infinitesimal and instinctive in the lower species, but not eradicable by virtue of preference for the theological convention of animals = automata = no souls. In this respect, materialist thinkers have sometimes proffered an excuse for their own dismissal of subhuman rights and potentials, since theological materialists have relegated the larger proportion of living matter to the status of dead matter. Both Bertrand Russell and Herbert Marcuse referred to the incident when the Society for the Prevention of Cruelty to Animals requested the Pope for his support of their project. He refused it, giving the reason that humans owe no duty to lower animals, and more pointedly, that it is not sinful to ill-treat animals, since animals have no souls. It is not difficult to improve upon this diabolical perspective. The Hegelian materialist Marcuse rectified the theological deficit by asserting that materialism is not tainted by such ideological abuse of the soul, and has a more "universal and realistic concept of salvation" – admitting the reality of Hell only upon earth, a Hell created by man, a Hell which includes the ill-treatment of animals on the part of a human

society "whose rationality is still the irrational."[134] The enlightened materialism of Marcuse is far more humane than its theological counterpart, but still ignores the most realistic and universal evolutionary implications of salvation.

The animal soul requires more recognition, however subhuman in status it is deemed to be, a recognition furthermore that does not commit the error of mistaking transmigrationist metaphor for evolutionary and de-evolutionary fact. Higher in the scale than the animal soul is the human equivalent, though one frequently assuming bestial characteristics (and hence transmigrationist metaphor). These bestial characteristics have been diversely manifest amongst theologians, priests, materialists, shamans, pseudomystics, scientific vivisectionists, and sundry sordid occultists. Sublimation of such undesirable characteristics requires a more competent form of education than is currently prevalent, but the more "romantic" ideas on education are unlikely to do more than instil a sense of poetry into the disjointed scheme of values that is frequently the prerogative of the "neo-Kantian" attempt at evolutionary theory. Phenomenology requires to become startlingly objective in order to avoid relativist errors that are even worse than effete moralism.

2. The clarified concept of an after-death state which is not viewed as being of the same importance as human existence via reincarnation. Philosophically, it is possible to argue for this two-fold concept as the most logical solution to the complexities of an emergent human consciousness that differs so widely amongst the human species in both quantitative and qualitative frequencies. Yet since both conventional theology and materialism customarily ignore logical solutions, I will limit myself here to more empirical considerations that have recently been charted with a remarkably high degree of probabilistic accuracy. I say accuracy owing to the experiential dimensions of certainty and behavioural change that have been attendant upon cases of what is now known as the "near-death" experience. If persons reported as being clinically dead subsequently transpire to have been intensely alive in consciousness, then this factor merits at

least some investigation on the part of those supposedly intensely alive. It would be extremely dogmatic to affirm that the "near-death" experience is a myth, and of mythical implications for a post-mortem condition.

For some years now there have been many reports available of the experiences of people who have been clinically dead for a brief period. In 1979, a science correspondent of *The Observer* had cause to write that doctors who were prepared to give attention to these experiences – particularly those with a "transcendent" aspect – reported a consistent and profound change in the attitude of the subjects to death. The majority of these patients emerged from their clinical suspension with an "absolute certainty" that their eventual physical death would amount to entry into the mode of further existence that they had already experienced. These experiences were "almost always accompanied by a joy and certainty scarcely comparable to anything in ordinary life." But a consistent feature of attitude in the subjects was their new determination to "complete their unfinished business in ordinary life to the very best of their ability." These near-death experiences did not lead to unworldliness, but rather to an increased sense of personal and social responsibility. The tendency to unworldly or extreme behaviour seems more common among those who talk of extradimensional experiences without having had them.[135]

The urge to "put things right" in one's life pattern is one corollary of an experiential encounter with the implications of cause-effect, which in the mere talkers amounts only to a free and easy version of karma. If there is any truth in the much abused karma concept ("as a man sows, so shall he reap") then it is as well to view it in a more intelligent fashion than some enthusiasts and critics have done. For instance, it is a facile argument to stress that it is an overwhelmingly deterministic concept, because the actual implications are that a good harvest is very different from a bad one and equally possible. It may not be at all deterministic to escape the bad harvest, but a result of emergent efforts to clarify the consciousness. In other words, the priests of the Hindu caste system were unduly deterministic in stressing, for convenient elitist reasons, that it was a bad harvest every year for the outcastes, no matter what efforts were made to transcend the status quo. It would seem that some have freewill to be as tyrannical as they wish, though they are totally inept at interpreting any subtlety or complexity, which is doubtless proof enough of their evolutionary immaturity.

Despite the findings of systematic research, much controversy exists in official circles over the interpretation of the near-death experience. Many medical and scientific authorities regard these experiences as "mental deviations engendered by emotional and psychological stress, due to the close proximity of death," writes one psychiatrist. Some researchers into near-death experiences have suggested a possible neurological basis for these in conformity with the holographic theory of the neurosurgeon Karl Pribram, who has concluded that the brain functions holographically, i.e., the brain mathematically constructs physical reality by interpreting extradimensional frequencies. Since primary reality is composed of frequencies only, this "frequency domain" transcends the time-space boundaries of ordinary consciousness. Pribram has expressed the view that holographic theory is much closer to mystical and Eastern philosophy than conventional science, and that "some of the mystical experiences people have described for millenia begin to make some scientific sense." From this theory, near-death researchers have logically extrapolated that consciousness can still function holographically without a brain.[136] Though feasible to some, critics tend to object that near-death experiences occur via the brain, since the subject is still alive. In fact, whatever one believes about an after-death state, one has to concede that the brain is very much an ever-present factor during the physical life-span.

In this context, it is relevant to counteract certain unjustifiable misuses of holographic theory, which tends to be employed for some extreme tangents of view that are neither scientific nor intrinsically mystical. I am referring to the promotion of ESP. According to some interpretations, one would be led to think that all brain talk is merely reductionist and that ESP enthusiasts effectively have no brains. The analytic/holistic modes of mentation oriented to the brain hemispheres are ignored in favour of a hypothetical transcendence of space-time. This is about as realistic as equating space with intuition. It can be pointed out that unless one achieves the highest state of transcendence and maintains this on a permanent basis – which might be equivalent to a discarnate entity by comparison with normal standards – one will necessarily remain in the situation of having to cope with brain patterns.

Near-death experiencers who have resumed personal and social responsibilities are strongly cultivating the "left brain" (left hemisphere) mode that is often dreaded and derided by holistic enthusiasts who are averse to discipline. An essential aspect of social health and salvation is customarily missed out by ESP enthusiasts, who accordingly cancel out some essential frequencies which ensure a greater range in consciousness. Psychedelic recourse is no answer, but only an invitation to disordered frequencies which are deemed mystical only by partisans of a faulty hologram which constructs a third-rate reality that is another form of illusion.

3. The phase of human development that is more important than the after-death state in Eastern panpsychism is sometimes referred to in Western lore as the "spiritual path," a concept prone to very numerous interpretations. Interests in this field have been customarily scapegoated as heretical in Christian theology, which has never been particularly partial to evolutionary concepts. On the other hand, Darwinism offers a gloomy view of evolutionary end-products, and in its "survival of the fittest" speculations, totally ignores the importance of character development. This places mechanistic evolutionary schemes at a considerable disadvantage to those systems which do stress a character development of an intricate complexity and purposive situation in the universe. Such an intricate complexity is apparent in intrinsic Eastern panpsychism.

The Darwinist horizons which lead to a mercenary intensification in military and economic ranges inevitably corrode educational values, since there is no objective of a finer character development insisted upon in Darwinian extrapolations from natural selection. In the Darwinian (and neo-Darwinian) scheme of life, it is merely sufficient to preserve personal interests and to be successful at one's job or profession, hoping to die as happily and as financially rich as possible. This outlook is often an amiable partner of conventional theology, which similarly relegates to death any hope of radical transformation in the psyche.

Very similar in effect to these constrained and habitual approaches is the current "countercultural" equation of a collective unconscious with all things good and pure, so that drugs and other forms of self-abandonment can be conveniently and facilely linked with the activation of "unconscious" prerogatives. The result is often a living death from overdose, which is increasingly saddening now that children under teenage are increasingly turning to artificial stimulants in the increasingly permissive society.

It is still not sufficiently understood in general what the implications are in the current situation of permissive conditioning factors that have been let loose in Western society in the wake of the sex prophets. A recent report states thsat the National Federation of Parents for Drug-free Youth has managed to persuade thirty-four states in the U.S.A. to pass laws prohibiting the sale or manufacture of drug-using equipment. But this still leaves sixteen other states in which decisions are not yet forthcoming in support of this cause. This campaign against drug use only came into existence four years ago when the founder Joyce Nalepka took her sons to a pop music concert and saw with horror that children barely in their teens were taking "almost every kind of drug imaginable."[137] This permissive trend commonly involves addiction to alcohol at around eleven years of age, followed by a progressive swing to marijuana-smoking combined with alcohol. In a large number of cases, addiction to cocaine or heroin occurs in the age group of the mid-teens – which is arguably too young to die. Yet attempts to stem this tide of casualties meet with accusations of patriarchal morality from the partisans of the "uncontaminated unconscious" vogues, to whom all discipline is equivalent to repression. These accusations are particularly questionable in view of the fact that it is mainly women who are most concerned about the fate of their children, and that *it is very often males who are at the centre of drug-pushing and related activities.* Even anxious mothers are considered to be overbearing representatives of the patriarchal society, and even more so it seems when they are not susceptible to the commune overtures of free love from those males who have strong interests in this field of "creative" expression.

In view of such social matters, it is less surprising to find that not a few of the adherents of "spiritual path" concepts are actually following the mandates of humanistic psychology and its ideals of hedonism. Creativity is often a catch-phrase here; interpersonal processes lead nowhere if personal and social responsibility is avoided. The recruits for new therapies are told that these will heal all stresses, but in practice the recruits frequently get difficult relationships and dissatisfaction, and often are no more fulfilled than craving for the next session of excitement and sensation. Many of them are terrified to be alone, perhaps because this is alien to the success of the practitioners.

One can legitimately conclude that the truth is never what it seems in the sales of "spiritual" goods. Unfortunately, too many of the applicants for the spiritual path go where they are most reassured in their bad habits.

The person acquiring a deep layer of mind will tend to find it difficult to transmit more than a fraction of his knowledge. Knowledge of anything hard won is rarely in demand nowadays. By current standards of the permissive society, it is logical enough that people ask for irrelevant toys instead of useful instruments. If there is any truth in the Western guru concept, then not a few Western gurus are fakes by virtue of the booming industry in toys and playtime therapies.

Despite the aversion of humanistic psychology to traditional norms, the "Christian saint" ideal tends to dominate this field in respect of the new convention that it is wrong to criticize (except to criticize the scientific Establishment, a habit liberally indulged in at the cost of other necessities). But even the ethical man may commit an unethical error if he refuses to intervene in cases of teenage murder and nightmares of psychedelic hypnosis.

Ironically enough, the man (or woman) who follows traditional emphases (Eastern or Western) of frugal living and thorough application to the task of reorientation, is the odd one out amongst the liberated trendies and the "esoteric" jet set. Space fiction evolution and commercial ESP vie with television and cassettes in the rat-race of Sunday afternoon alternatives to sheer boredom. Some of the pop-gurus are representative of modern materialist culture at its worst. Alan Watts died of alcohol poison after a career in free love that causes even nihilists to conclude that he was not fundamentally trying. Yet he is still remembered by some as a zen-cum-taoist hero. Each to their own, as long as it is advertised for what it really is. I dare say that Watts would have been kicked out headlong from any self-respecting zen monastery in early medieval China.

Apart from nihilistic renditions, another popular projection of the "spiritual path" concept is that of a constant preoccupation with paranormal powers. Some people evidently find it very difficult to accept that traditional accounts warn of extra-sensory powers as distractions, and even as dangers. However, there is far more money to be made in pop-parapsychology than in more reflective labours. Some years ago a well advertised Indian yogi disappointed his more well-read followers by emphasizing his ESP feats. Those Western enthusiasts for whom Patanjali is merely old-fashioned found it far more exciting to believe that times had changed for the better. Otherwise, it would have been too boring perhaps, which is very often the case with a fashionable plateful of desultory red herrings.

An argument for determinism could be constructed from the predictable behaviour of so many fashion-seekers and narcissistic celebrities. But the predictable scope for exceptions to the rule tends to belie the constraints of mechanism in all extensions of evolution and deevolution. Materialistic versions of a spiritualized evolution are not evidenced in some traditional interpretive and behavioural channels. Intrinsic Eastern panpsychism describes variations of states and stages in an evolutionary context that serves to explain why instances of intrinsic achievement are so radically emergent from ignorance. There is anything but determinism involved here, since the individual has the opportunity to maximally develop potential or to maximally ruin that potential. A mathematical argument could be constructed to prove that a non-uniform arc of cause-effect ratios contains latitude potential for both extreme deviational frequencies and harmonious continuum-frequencies in an individual consciousness. But this would lack conscious proof for those limited to the lower extremities of the arc of ratio. Perhaps it is that every Galileo must first establish the testimony of his own eyes before gaining proof that the local know-alls do not understand telescopic vision or the universe.

As for the current argument that any finer concept of evolution is unrealistic – and hence to be relegated to the status of a vague idealism – this is logically offset by the intrinsic panpsychist contention that only those applying a sufficient ongoing dedication to matters of consciousness clarification will ever evolve in realistic terms that outstrip lazy and indifferent attitudes. Those who carp at the possibilities may keep their jobs and their sense of composure at all costs, but may suffer unknown losses in entity. Yet much more serious losses may accrue to the parasitic elements amongst the spiritually elite, whose stunted and reversed potential in the arc of cause-effect ratio is traditionally said to cause a disintegration of their entity at a critical juncture. If there is anything equivalent to higher mathematical laws of order, then one would expect the balance-sheet to be calculated with due exactitude. That there is a tough aspect to the universe need not be denied even by the more squeamish. Predatory tendencies exist in profusion amongst the subhuman and human species, and there are innumerable grim deaths in nature that often result from mere seasonal changes. Surprisingly enough, this kind of realism is totally lacking in many current versions of spiritual evolution. It may be that the truth is being unduly concealed for one reason or another, through ignorance maybe, or even through subterfuge. The remedy for a static human evolution is not simple-minded part-truth, but a more comprehensively emergent education in purposive priorities inherent in cause-effect chains of an evolving universe of consciousness.

# CHAPTER EIGHT

# A CROSS-CULTURAL PHILOSOPHY

In the current world situation, it is surely pardonable to conclude that neither science nor religion is a sufficient unifying factor of concensus or truth. Countries the world over do respect technology more than any form of religious belief, but the ideals of technology are a dubious substitute for a viable intercultural philosophy that specializes in human nature and its potential.

The respective partisan attitudes of different culture blocs are not particularly amenable to an intercultural philosophy that might usefully instruct, advise, or guide. In the West, scientific materialism is in general considered the universal standard of truth, though in Latin countries the Roman Catholic church is attributed the same capacity. On a global level, scientific materialism, marxism, and various religions compete for supremacy. Any non-technological and non-dogmatic intercultural philosophy must rest content with stylizing its bases, leaving ideologies to affirm their prerogative in channels of political expression.

Though Al-Farabi and some other medieval philosophers are sometimes described in terms of a political philosophy, this tends to be misleading in view of current attitudes to politics. Al-Farabi's purpose was not to dogmatize, but to throw light upon what an ideal society could be if the requisite conditions were established. Various subtle concepts are not readily assimilable by forceful political penchants.

Since all attempts to outline an ideal society are currently dismissed as utopian, I will not venture upon forbidden territory, but will instead focus upon various developments and interpretations that have a bearing upon cross-cultural interests and latitude, using the example of past events generally neglected.

The definition of philosophy and mysticism is perhaps a guide to what constitutes inflexible scientific and religious orthodoxies. But it is apparent that localized versions are frequently preferred in such definitions by persons who would not consider themselves orthodox. Many of the more scientifically minded investigators are understandably offput by Western preferences for academic philosophy on the one hand, and for Christian mysticism on the other. But there are other extremes possible amongst Westerners, though much less ethnocentric. The physicist Fritjof Capra is one of those who cannot be accused of an ethnocentric stance, and indeed his latitude for the Far East is in many respects praiseworthy, though prone to a neo-Reichian perspective. In Capra's view, the new physics is itself a form of mystical truth. He defines Eastern mysticism as meaning Taoism, Hinduism, and Buddhism. Surprisingly to some, he excludes the mysticism of the Middle and Near East from this definition, instead classifying this with Western philosophy, which he considers to possess mystical elements to a limited extent. This relegation is made on the grounds that mysticism played only a "marginal role" in the West, contrary to its role in the East (i.e. the Far East). But objections can be raised against this classification; one is not at all certain that the accent on geographical situation is correct in terms of the qualitative implications. Indeed, it can be urged that the Capran dividing-line is inappropriate in both a philosophical and a mystical context. Capra's solitary reference to sufi subjects specifies only Muhiyuddin ibn al-Arabi,[138] one of the most well known names in the philosophico-mystical galaxy historically verifiable in the heritage of Islamic milieux.

For my own part, I am quite content to consider Ibn al-Arabi as part of the Western philosophical heritage of mysical dimensions, which is not inappropriate in view of the fact that he lived his early years in Spain. Indeed, this extension may actually be helpful in dissolving the barriers of separativeness that have habitually arisen between local formats of philosophy and mysticism. But I think it also true to say that Ibn al-Arabi and his confreres were very much a part of the Eastern heritage as well, particularly in view of the extensive array of source materials that are discernible in his voluminous writings and which strongly implicate some vintage pre-Islamic traditions.[139]

It is difficult to inform both conventional and modern perspectives that the tradition now known to some scholars as "high Sufism" is one of the major links with the ancient civilizations of the Near and Middle East, which in turn were part of the much older archaic chain of cultures that appears to have spanned both East and West in terms of basic religio-cultural characteristics. From the mystical point of view, some of the apparent geographical differences in this sequence may even be illusory.

What is perhaps best referred to historically as "popular Sufism" is something very different in manifestation and emphasis to its sophisticated namesake. Yet variations in quality were also very marked in the traditions of Hinduism, Buddhism, and Taoism, to mention only the more well known of the Far Eastern mystical heritages. These internal qualitative differences are far more important for assessment than the geographical demarcators between ethnic and doctrinal units. Yet these qualitative variations are commonly glossed or ignored by the partisans of specific traditions, and also by scholars of comparative religion.

There is perhaps no study more vitiated by sectarian bias than mysticism, particularly when it is closely associated with salient religious denominators. One is led to conclude that even erudite scholarly pursuits are sometimes refined variants of sectarian conditioning. In studies of Sufism, for instance, the subject has not infrequently been coloured by the views of scholars with a Christian background who interpret sympathetically but according to their own canons of religiosity. Much the same can be said of some Muslim scholars.

One of the finest orientalist scholars of this century was Louis Massignon (d. 1962), who not only demonstrated a high standard of scholarship in a difficult field, but also achieved a notable and rare distinction as an active worker in the social cause of the underdog Muslims in the face of French colonialism. He was one of those who took part in public demonstrations during the 1950's against the French war in Algeria. Massignon was inspired in part by the example of Mahatma Gandhi (d. 1948), and at the end of his life it seems that he broke his conditioning patterns far more than most literati. Yet his *magnum opus* on the sufi mystic Hallaj dates to a much earlier period of his life. By the very fact of its detail, this book discloses elements for an alternative interpretation to the one Massignon early constructed to account for the facts. This major work was originally a doctoral thesis, and reflects the author's Roman Catholic background, carrying strong "martyr" overtones that are more in accord with the Christian rather than the sufi tradition. Suffice it to say here that it is possible to conclude (as I have done elsewhere) that Massignon unwittingly cast Hallaj in an idiom of popular Sufism, contrary to the strong indications that the Arabo-Iranian mystic was actually an exponent of "high Sufism."[140] However, Massignon did effectively rescue Hallaj from earlier, and much more serious, defacements of the record.

Serious distortions of the historical record are evident in the attitude of some Westerners to the patriarchal organization of Islamic society; it is sometimes imagined that orthodox strictures were typical of sufi attitudes. Ironically, this stigma actually obscures the role of women in sufi activity from at least the eighth century A.D. The historical reality is that large numbers of women found an outlet for their energies in forms of sufi activity and affiliation, though with varying degrees of prominence. Such outlet was denied them in orthodox religion. Upon close inspection of data, a surprising number of known male sufi exponents show influence from female sources. The specialist scholar Annemarie Schimmel observes that there are many references in the traditional biographies to saintly/ascetic mothers who influenced their more well known sufi sons.[141] The Islamic emphasis against monasticism ensured a strong female role in sufi activity via family involvement, but there were also some very independent female ascetics. The most well known of these latter is Rabia, the eighth century Arab woman who lived as an ascetic in the marshlands of Basra (in modern Iraq), and who appears to have influenced contemporary males of sufi fame.

In later sufi circles, the Iranian mystic Fariduddin Attar decisively helped to perpetuate memory of Rabia in his eulogistic account of her incorporated in an influential twelfth century compendium of sufi biographies. Attar represented the sufi trend that evaded orthodox formalism by a variety of literary devices, including allusive poetry, and also by other means of teaching.

While it was customary in orthodox Islam to downgrade the social importance of women, the liberal (and genuine) sufi exponents like Jalaluddin Rumi made a detour around such blockages by giving tuition to a substantial number of female disciples. Further, it was not unknown for males in sufi ranks to have a female teacher. Ibn al-Arabi had at least two of these, namely Shams of Marchena and Fatima bint Waliyya. This Fatima was a twelfth century sufi tutor of Cordova, and hence an early "European" mystic, whose long life synchronized with the beginning of the female tradition in Roman Catholic mysticism.

There have been differences of view on the low status accorded to women in Islam. The notion that women in Islam have no soul cannot, affirms Schimmel, be found in the *Quran* or the traditions (*hadith*) of Muhammad.[142] Yet it is undeniable that subsequent events in Islamic history did effect a markedly subordinate female status.

It was the specialist scholar Margaret Smith who concluded that the position of women in Islamic countries deteriorated during the third century after the death of Muhammad.[143] This is attributable to the increasing codification of Quranic tradition by the canonists of the emerging legalism, who inflexibly applied their interpretations of early Arabian conditions to non-Arab milieux which had been absorbed by conquests unknown in Muhammad's day. These legalists were not known for their intuitive abilities, and their pedantry was in direct opposition to sufi penchants which claimed a different heritage from Muhammad. Much sufi history is a record of friction with dogmatists, though there were also many dogmatists who became popular as sufis, usually as a result of their conviction that they had achieved the merits of this fabled category.

The word sufi has for long been a blanket term, very glibly used by some partisans, and often asserted by dogmatists to mean Muslims only. The historical facts, together with philosophical acuity, do not bend easily to such popular conventions of insular thinking. Like practically all other mystical classifications, the word *sufi* is devalued. I use it here for convenience so that people will know what approximate trend I am referring to. But suffice it to say that the detractors of "patriarchal" Sufism are in a highly ambiguous and historically contradicted position as regards a substantially female-participant tradition. Ironically, their attitude is similar to that of the dogmatists who could not discriminate between quality of experience and quantity of professed exponents.

The subordinate status of women in Islamic society was paralleled by other Eastern conventions in the Confucian society of China and the brahmanical milieu of India. Both Buddhism and Jainism changed this status quo in some areas; Buddhist Tibet was probably the most lenient sector for official recognition of female rights, but even here males still took the senior roles in both the monastic and "unreformed" organizations comprising Lamaism.

It is not generally understood that Islamized Turkish culture maintained a significant undercurrent of archaic lifestyles via the Bektashi communities of dervishes. Constituting one of the many dervish orders of popular Sufism, they were unusual for the equality of the sexes which they fostered in their membership. Their admission of women to their meetings on an equal basis with men provoked condemnatory criticism from the divines of Turkey, who were eager to castigate such parity as immoral. Such features of Bektashi organization have been traced to older Turkish roots in the shamanistic culture of the Central Asian Turks. This is a significant and complex matter, and one that links sufi manifestations to the archaic phenomenon of shamanism, which is more commonly associated with Mongolian-Siberian locales. Shamanism is currently an enthusiast subject, and is rarely given accurate treatment. Some writers do not take into sufficient account just how varied a phenomenon it was, and that extant forms of it in the ethnographic record are derivative, and admixed with degenerate elements. Known shamanistic forms of expression have sometimes amounted to mere ventriloquism and a very superstitious fetishism. On the positive side, women in the Mongoloid tradition could hold positions equivalent to those of male shamans.[144]

A specimen of Turko-Iranian blood (approximately) was the sufi matriarch known as Hazrat Babajan (d. 1931), who hailed from a Pathan community in the Afghan zone, and who lived in British-occupied Poona at the end of her long life in India. This extraordinary entity was a complete enigma to the British Raj, who had to tolerate her presence on the edge of the cantonment precincts owing to her many devoted followers, who included Muslims, Hindus, and Zoroastrians. I have elsewhere described her lifestyle, which was a robustly outdoor one spent underneath a tree at Poona. Though born a Muslim, she exhibited no trace of any doctrinaire or sectarian penchant. She came from an aristocratic family, but had totally severed herself from this background in her long years of wanderings as a mendicant beggar. According to a strong report from declared eyewitnesses, she had once been buried alive by orthodox Muslims in the Punjab, her crime having been mystical utterances which were deemed to be heretical by male custodians of the religious law. How she escaped from this dire predicament is not on record, but it is reliably reported that she objected to being referred to as a woman. She affirmed her masculinity in a sense that has a deeper meaning than is common. She would refer to all her visitors, male or female, as children, and conceivably she knew enough about life to fully justify these nuances.[145]

It is possible to consider Hazrat Babajan as a successor to a tradition that is remotely prehistoric in origins. At the same time, her very unconventionality demonstrates how difficult it would be in truth to accept the simplistic generalizations and misleading conclusions that have so often been made with regard to the subject of "shamanism." So few people yet understand the Turkic train of occurrences that it is perhaps premature to align Babajan, even indirectly, with any kind of shamanism at all.

Both the Turkic and Iranian heritages are strangely unknown to popular media in Western literature by comparison with other Eastern traditions. Iran is currently the focus for a powerful modernist versus traditionalist debate, and one cannot help but feel that the traditionalist stress is weakened by the totalitarian oppression carried out by the Iranian theological elite. But if modernists bolster the influence of Western materialism, there is no certainty that an equal hazard would not arise. An enlightened modernism appears to be required, one that will not forget the worth of those who are now often considered traditionalists in retrospect, but who were often considered heretics in their day.

A sixteenth century Iranian who fled to India from a then prevalent milieu of persecution in his native land was a Zoroastrian ascetic known as Azar Kaivan (d. 1618). He was on good terms with liberal Muslims but did not officially change his religion. However, he was nothing of an orthodox Zoroastrian (despite the mistaken nineteenth century assumption that he was a high priest), but was instead the exponent of an esoteric tradition that has remained obscure. Yet this was not so much esoteric religion, but esoteric philosophy. Kaivan and his disciples were "Zoroastrian ishraqis," that is to say, distinctive heirs to the *ishraqi* (illuminist) tradition primarily associated with the Iranian sufi philosopher Shaikh Sohravardi Maqtul (d. 1191). The latter met a premature death as a heretic, murdered by orthodox bigots who were resentful of mystical and philosophical genius. Azar Kaivan avoided such a fate by keeping himself at arm's length from contact with the eminent, and by enjoining secrecy upon his ishraqi circle.

This practical application of esoteric measures was a very logical recourse for any philosopher with an eye to self-preservation and the safety of his pupils. Indeed, one can say that it was a recourse resulting from the most empirical encounters with ignorance.

The neo-ishraqi philosophy of Kaivan's circle incorporated Greek philosophy (and Arabic Hermeticism) after the example of Maqtul, and also accommodated a more atypical acquaintance with Sanskrit philosophy. This was not only mediated through Persian translations, but via direct contact with Hindu sages. His Iranian disciples included multilinguists of liberal views which render them a subject for very favourable comparison with the contemporary Renaissance thinkers of Europe; the range of the Kaivanis (as I have chosen to call them for convenience) was actually greater than that of the latter, since they not only had access to "Western" sources of textual tradition, but also to diverse Eastern sources. Experiential extensions are a finer point more difficult of comparison here.

In terms of evolutionary thinking, the Kaivanis[146] were transmigrationists, i.e. panpsychists. Peripheral students have assumed that this was a consequence of the influence exerted by the liberal milieu of the Mughal emperor Akbar, during whose reign Azar Kaivan emigrated to North India. But a more accurate conclusion is that the Zoroastrian ishraqis were drawing upon a much older and pre-Mughal *tanasukh* tradition maintained by exponents of "high Sufism" like Aziz Nasafi and the ishraqi scientist Qutubuddin Shirazi. Azar Kaivan did not himself require the Akbarian syncretism of Hindu-Muslim ideas inaugurated by Akbar, though he must have found this expansiveness a very congenial climate after the grim horrors possible in imperially dogmatic Safavid Iran.

The expansive attitude of Kaivanis towards other religions is very notable. Their policy was one of conciliation with all on as many points as possible, though in relation to matters of dogmatism and superstition, they evidently resorted to sophisticated measures of indicating errors by adroit means causing only minimal offence, if that.

The late Henry Corbin was the leading Western scholar of the manuscripts relating to the ishraqi tradition. He gave only slight attention to the Kaivani branch of this tradition however, and many of his readers are unaware of the ishraqi extensions. There are several differences between Corbin's approach and my own which relate to cross-cultural features, and which it is perhaps unavoidable to emphasize here. Despite his admirably industrious labours, Corbin unfortunately adopted an anti-historicism which is not advantageous for the study of this kind of material. Much of the symbolism and abstract ingredients of ishraqi treatises are obviously not in need of a historical approach, but other factors definitely do merit historicist evaluations. Corbin tended to omit completely the "Aristotelian" ingredients of this tradition. He also ignored implications of certain key metaphysical themes (e.g. panpsychism). In terms of a pluralism of traditions, Corbin limited his range of application rather surprisingly, though his disposition here was actually much in advance of average specialist penchants of study. The institutional curriculum that he officially inaugurated at the end of his life extended to Islam, Judaism,and Christianity, but did not encompass Asiatic traditions east of Iran. Also, he tended to express a shia bias against the sunni heritage in Islam. It is my contention that his phenomenology actually abscured much of the essential ishraqi tradition and its methodology. Despite these necessary criticisms, it can be said to his great credit that he recognized the value and importance of a submerged tradition that very few other Westerners were even aware of beyond casual references.[147]

The belief that a return to the essence of things invalidates the reconstruction of historical fact is potentially disastrous for essential history and essential philosophy. Corbin outgrew the phenomenology of Heidegger and sidestepped the existentialism of Sartre, but he perpetuated his own form of Husserlian phenomenology. A phenomenological humanism on European lines is ill-suited to a polymathic range in alignment with essential philosophy on Eastern lines.[148]

The Kaivani-ishraqi groups of Mughal India included Zoroastrians, Muslims, Hindus, Jews, and one (at least) Christian of European blood. There was no requirement involved of changing religion, and this non-concern with doctrinaire preferences has made it more difficult for some scholars to appreciate the ramifications of Kaivani activity. An esoteric philosophy will inevitably regard religious externals as being of peripheral importance. These ishraqis are legitimately to be accounted as sufi participants, but not in the limited popular context of the sufi = Muslim persuasion. As for the groups concerned, the question of such classification was irrelevant, since the formal mystic is experientially dead, rather like the sophistic philosopher.

It is also a matter of historical fact that Jews had earlier been closely involved in sufi thinking and roles. What are scholastically referred to as "Jewish sufis" existed in late medieval Egypt in the form of a complex philosophical and pietist trend which lasted for some generations. They did not become Muslims, but they were not orthodox Jews; they studied and preserved much sufi literature from the Islamic milieu.[149] Amongst the influences upon this trend was the Jewish philosopher Moses Maimonides (d. 1204), who himself is (at least indirectly) implicated in the emerging annals of "high Sufism." Such psychological affiliation was more than usually possible for the more discerning Aristotelians.

One distinctive Aristotelian was the Jewish sufi Sarmad (d. 1660–1), affiliated to Kaivani activity in both Iran and India. Some might prefer to call him a Qabbalist in the (authentic) esoteric tradition going back to Ibn Gabirol, the Jewish philosopher of Islamic Spain, an attribution which is logically in keeping – providing that this tradition is clearly distinguished from the dummy versions of Qabbalah which grew worse with the passing of centuries. Sarmad was the antithesis of dogmatism, and was hated at the Mughal court. He seems to have been much more of a firebrand than Azar Kaivan, and did not so obligingly restrain his nonconformist expressiveness. Though he was an expert in Arabic philosophical literature, he scandalized the dogmatists of the court by adopting the lifestyle of a *qalandar*, i.e., a nonconformist sufi type often indistinguishable from Hindu ascetics when found in India.

The enemies of Sarmad dispensed with him by executing him as a heretic. The liberal trend in Indian politics reversed with the ensuing reign of Aurangzeb, and the Kaivani phenomenon disappears from the record at this critical juncture. Yet there are indications that its spirit did not die out.

Much information on the Kaivanis can be found in the Persian treatise known as the *Dabistan*, written and compiled during the mid-seventeenth century while Sarmad was still alive. This treatise has not in general been adequately evaluated by scholars, mainly owing to the unfamiliarity of its contents, a feature particularly marked in the lengthy section on Persian sects. The *Dabistan* is a distinctive manual on comparative religion and philosophy, and is remarkable both for its range in cross-cultural reporting and for its unbiased approach. There have been scholarly uncertainties as to its authorship, but weighty conclusions favour a Zoroastrian pen. More specifically it can be added here, the penmanship is clearly deducible as Kaivani. I shall refer to the author as Mobad Shah, which is one of the names of authorship appearing in surviving manuscripts.

It is difficult to assess some of the more demanding ishraqi works without a sufficient knowledge of their purpose. They do not comprise standard mystical fare, which is not always a particular sign of achievement owing to the lack of originality too frequently evident. It was partly owing to this factor that a man like Abu'l Qasim Findiriski (d. 1640) maintained a role as an Aristotelian philosopher at major cities in Iran. Surrounded by despots, fanatics, and pedants, he did not unduly emphasize to the heedless matters for which they were entirely unprepared. Yet this Iranian savant lived a dual life; he is known to have travelled in India in a more pointed role of sufi dimensions, associating with the circle of Azar Kaivan and being in personal contact with Hindu yogi types. This Aristotelian Kaivani would be an enigma by contemporary philosophical standards, but perhaps he would prove contemporaneously adaptable if he could somehow be contacted in thought across the centuries. If asked his identity he would doubtless answer politely in flawless Persian that he was an Aristotelian – though he might mutter under his breath that he had seen so many unfledged "sufis" in popular dervishism that even in more liberal India the mystical tag was a victim of dogmatism and sheer whim.

While Findiriski was writing polymathic and scientific treatises, the author of the *Dabistan* produced a wide-ranging work on religions and sects which eclipsed the parochial dimensions of many contemporary sufi-style compendiums of biography and hagiography. The distinctive opening lines of the chapter on the sufis states that they, "like other philosophers, always were, and are, scattered among all nations of the world."[150] Even more atypically, Sanskrit equivalents are given for the word sufi, e.g. *jnani*. The nineteenth century British scholar Anthony Troyer early grasped that this definition cut through all boundaries of nationality and local religion. But other scholars have merely deemed this latitude a confusion in reporting, owing to their commitment to insular orthodox associations.

Those analysts who have sought to find confusion in the *Dabistan* where it does not actually exist are in the unenviable position of being several centuries behind tangibly attested historical developments which are not dependent upon the caprice of modern hindsight.

The *Dabistan* has met with animosity in some scholarly quarters owing to its exceptional liberalism. Apparent idiosyncracies of style are found in passages which demand a more than average affinity with the perspectives of the intrinsic sufi philosophy. The real idiosyncracies are evident enough in the narrow outlook of some specialists.

One dogmatist who became radically liberal as a result of an encounter with a Kaivani teacher in North India was a Portuguese Christian referred to as Antun (Antoine) Bashuyah in the *Dabistan*. He was a wealthy man, probably affiliated to the Jesuits, and evidently of evangelical zealousness. He not only renounced his riches, but adopted the lifestyle of a nonconformist *qalandar* after the pattern of Sarmad and other sufi types. This ex-dogmatist also practised the *ahimsa* (non-violence) principles of the Kaivani circle to which he belonged, the leader of which was a Zoroastrian by birth. In his new milieu, he learnt how *not* to impose his new views upon others. This does not mean to say that he did not become a "secret Christian" in the more Hallajian sense, but such secrecy is not compatible with the exoteric fare of stentorian evangelism.

One of the orthodox Muslim accusations against Hallaj appears to have been that he was a "secret Christian," owing to references he made in an apocalyptic vein to Jesus. But there was not the slightest Christian orthodoxy in such terminology, any more than Hallaj can be considered typically Islamic. Hallaj can well be called a "secret Zoroastrian" in view of other atypical extensions of his terminology.

The *Dabistan* includes a lengthy chapter on Hinduism, and demonstrates a wide knowledge of different sects and teachings of the Hindus. This chapter covers brahmanical orthodoxy, the Vedanta philosophy, the Sankhya philosophy, the Yogis, the Shaktas, the Vaishnavas, and others. The author demonstrates clear affinities with some Yogic practices, and makes it evident that the Kaivanis had their own form of what is now commonly known as kundalini yoga, complete with its own Persian terminology that paralleled the Sanskrit. But unlike some vulgar modern manuals, he does not attempt to describe attendant methods in any detail. In sophisticated circles that subscribe to the basic concepts involved, it has been considered a proof of total incompetence to teach "kundalini activation" in a systematized form; it is said that there are elements of grave danger (sufficient to cause illness) in "forcing" development, not least because unhealthy obsessions can arise that render victims an easy prey to exploiters. Gurus who make a fetish of kundalini yoga are amongst those most likely to be fakes; despite current advertising, the public is seriously uneducated on such points. The *Dabistan* author and his confreres would doubtless have been vastly amused at twentieth century vogues in this subject, which confuse tantric sexuality with the "unblocking" of the kundalini power. Quite to the contrary here, the more traditional and demanding cross-cultural yoga maintained that the desired cosmic power was effectively blocked by preoccupation with sexuality. However, many moderns in both the East and West are averse to demanding emphases, and hence substitute preferred amusements instead. This is the common fate nowadays of other traditional teachings also.

Demonstrating its declared aim of impartial reporting, the *Dabistan* describes certain notorious shakta (tantric) practices without rebuke. Sexual rites of the commune and human sacrifice do not commend themselves to every so-called aspirant. The documentation is now valuable, and would merely have been twisted beyond factual recognition in certain other avenues of reporting. But the *Dabistan* author was evidently aware that it is necessary to indicate whether or not the annalist approves of views described, since otherwise objective reporting can amount to an unenviable exercise. This he does without making undue intrusions upon his subject matter. His method was to point to inconsistencies between ideals and lesser ideals, and between ideals and behaviour.

In a very different category to debased tantric lifestyles was the example of Chatur Vapah (d. 1637), a Hindu yogi whom the *Dabistan* author knew personally, and who was partly responsible for the latter's education in his tender years. Chatur Vapah was originally a brahmin of Gujerat, but renounced the world in the manner of a *sannyasin* (renunciate). He was one of the numerous Hindus who participated in Kaivani activity during the early seventeenth century, and was active in the Agra locale of North India. He was a famous ascetic name in the area, and even Muslims deferred to him. The *Dabistan* describes Chatur Vapah as a *jnani* (wise man), nowadays a term of increasingly reduced significance. Amongst his companions were dervishes who said that he had such powers as that of walking on water. Such attributions were and are common in yogic and dervish lore, but there is no indication that Chatur Vapah regarded such powers as being of any consequence. Often the only reason why orthodox Muslims gave any credit to such infidel entities was on account of the occult powers for which they were reputed. It is unlikely that the author of the *Dabistan* would have wished to reduce this tolerance, and it is not really surprising to find him occasionally indulging in hagiography with regard to Zoroastrian and Hindu saints. His use of this stock ingredient of reporting is superior to that found in some contemporary compendia written in Persian, which were zealous of attributing powers only to Muslim saints.

The intercultural dimensions implicated in the philosophy of Chatur Vapah antedated and paralleled those of Mahatma Gandhi, who affirmed, "I am a Christian, and a Hindu, and a Muslim, and a Jew." Bigoted Hindus even accused Gandhi of being a secret Christian; the situation is in this respect reminiscent of the Hallajian precedent. Gandhi admired the Sermon on the Mount, but did not hesitate to express his view that "much of what passes as Christianity is a negation of the Sermon on the Mount." He here stipulated that the errors were due to "Christianity as it is understood in the West." Though Gandhi remained a staunch Hindu, he asserted that "all faiths . . . are imperfect, and liable to error; reverence for other faiths need not blind us to their faults." He was averse to all proselytizing, whether the conversion drive was made by Hindus, Christians, or Muslims. By 1932 he had broken his own earlier conservative conditioning that tended to defend the caste system, a conditioning that had persisted despite his inveterate attack on the stigma of untouchability.[151] One could wish that more conservative traditionalists would become radical and humane iconoclasts of the non-materialist kind.

Prior to Gandhi's volte-face on caste restrictions, Hindu intellectuals could legitimately minimize his non-Westernized contribution. In a wider context, the question of the viability of traditional Indian philosophy was posed by Sir Sarvepalli Radhakrishnan, the distinguished professor of philosophy at Oxford and Calcutta. He commented at the end of a well known book that the problem facing Indian philosophy is whether it is to be reduced to a cult, with no application to present facts, or whether it is to become "a great formative element in human progress, by relating the immensely increased knowledge of modern science to the ancient ideals of India's philosophers."[152] Perhaps the key to this problem is whether modern science is conceived in the image of a Swami Vivekananda or a Bertrand Russell; unlike Vivekananda, Russell represented scientific materialism, which too frequently has no other application to present facts other than in technology. The cult of technology is now more stifling than many religious cults, and frequently obscures the merit of philosophies that are too easily equated with cults by those wishing to ignore all alternatives.

One of the Indian religio-philosophical traditions exhibiting a consideration for subhuman life that is apt to puzzle comparatively insensitive Westerners (whether scientific or religious) is that of the Jainas. The *Dabistan* includes a section on the Jainas, who constitute one of the oldest surviving religions in India. Certain similarities with the Buddhists led the *Dabistan* author Mobad Shah to conflate Jainas with the Buddha; this was an error probably made easier by the fact that Buddhists had then ceased to exist in India. Mobad Shah says that he had met many Jainas, and evidently admired their extreme adherence to *ahimsa* principles (which were also a feature of Kaivani activity, though not to such a pronounced extent). He relates a graphic incident in which a Muslim dervish sat outside the shop of a Jaina merchant of Gujerat, in Western India. The dervish picked an insect off his robe and was about to kill it in the automatic manner that is customarily reserved for flies and similar forms of life. An agitated merchant emerged from the shop and offered the dervish money in order to stop the fatal action. This reflects the Jaina aversion to killing any form of life, even insects like mosquitoes, since all species are considered to possess souls. It was a wily dervish who profited from this exchange by striking a bargain of a hundred rupees in order to save the contested insect. One might conclude that the dervish was much less spiritually principled than the merchant, who possessed such conscience for his ideals.

Though Indian Buddhists no longer existed at that time, Mobad Shah was industrious enough to contact a Tibetan Buddhist, who was doubtless engaged on a pilgrimage to Indian sites associated with the Buddha's life. This Tibetan was apparently a lama, but the report is brief, running to only four pages in the English translation of the *Dabistan*.[153] The reason for this brevity is supplied (with refreshing honesty) by Mobad Shah in the detail that his talk with his informer occurred via an interpreter, and that complexities could not be satisfactorily relayed through the intermediary. There is no trace of bias in the report, and Mobad Shah accurately describes the lifestyle of lamas as ascetic, and adds respectfully that they had no equals in magic. This refers to the extraordinary reputation for shaman-type abilities that the lamas possessed in Tibet and adjoining areas.

According to Christmas Humphreys, founder of the Buddhist Society in London, Lamaism has represented "a mixture of the best and worst of Buddhism." He affirms that nowhere save in Tibet have there been so many men who have become masters of themselves, but that nowhere else save in Tibet has there been "so much sorcery and 'black' magic, such degradation of the mind to selfish, evil ends."[154] This memorable statement was made by a knowledgeable and sympathetic Buddhist, but seems to have been rarely dwelt upon by Western enthusiasts of magic, who are often undiscerning in their choice between "black" and "white." Yet it is well known to Tibetan lamas that there were continual lapses in Buddhist practice in medieval Tibet (and later times), lapses which necessitated reforms. Westerners in general do not possess the same knowledge of occult matters that Tibetans do, and have very often ignored basic emphases which are available in English and other European languages. It is evident to some what kind of magic it was that Aleister Crowley represented, though attempts to explain this are met with evasion by enthusiasts of the sadistic.

The attempt to teach some people priorities in values is rather like hoping that political violence will subside. Some Western social thinkers who have believed that increased secular education was justifiable under the military Chinese takeover of Tibet are in an unenviable position now that the Gang of Four policy has been exposed by the Chinese people. The violent gospel of Western Marxism did much more than send thousands of monks to concentration camps and force Tibetan women to mate with Chinese soldiers. The attempt in the new form of education, inaugurated in the 1960's, to erode all sense of Tibetan individuality and replace it with Chinese patriotism, is very questionable.[155] The argument that the Tibetans were too indoctrinated by religion is rather easily countered by the argument that the substitute was that much more coercive in its indoctrination programme.

Another religion to find that greater numbers were formidable was Sikhism, also given space in the *Dabistan*. Mobad Shah knew some of the Sikh leaders of his day in the Punjab, and claims a close acquaintance with the seventh Guru Har Rai (d. 1661). It is also apparent that he was personally acquainted with Hargobind, the sixth Sikh Guru who was in office during 1606–1644. He gives an account of the life of Guru Nanak (1469–1539), who was by then a legendized entity, but nonetheless important in the Indian tradition of dissent. Though an opponent of orthodox Hinduism, Nanak retained transmigration in his worldview, one of the features which distinguishes his extant teaching from the Islamic elements with which he is sometimes associated. Early Sikh activity had a strong pacifist colouring, but this was substantially modified later as a consequence of friction with Mughal interests. The fifth Guru Arjun died a grim death in 1606 after supporting a rebellion against the Mughal emperor Jehangir. There was a subsequent hostility between Sikhs and Muslims, but Mobad Shah avoided this deadlock. His evident friendship with Sikhs even gave him the opportunity to politely report unseemly popular habits amongst Sikhs which had formerly been in vogue prior to reforms.[156]

The *Dabistan* is an outstanding work in a tradition of liberalism textually rare in either East or West prior to the twentieth century. Most of its criticism is implicit, toned down to cause the least offence. The audience for which it was designed were probably liberal Parsi Zoroastrians, liberal Muslims, and the more literate Hindus who frequently learnt Persian at that era. Its format is unusual. For instance, it includes a treatment of both Sunni and Shia Islam, but gives a completely separate chapter to the sufis, hence emphasizing the non-doctrinaire category of the latter. There is a distinctive chapter on the philosophers, relating to both the Platonic and Aristotelian traditions, that clearly allows for similar differences from religion.

In the introductory pages, the *Dabistan* author clearly states some of his intentions: to report something of the knowledge of ancient nations and the speech and behaviour of modern peoples, without hatred, envy, and castigation, and without siding with one against the other. An integral part of this statement of tolerance is the explicit consideration that the reports used derive from (a) those informants with the capacity to perceive what is concealed in tradition (b) those informants attached to external forms. With true oriental subtlety, he does not specify which reports are which. That would no doubt have spoiled the possibilities of perception on the part of readers.

The stated nature of this treatise is therefore clearly different from some current phenomenological exercises of reporting, which effectively adopt a relativistic stance. Though the *Dabistan* can be interpreted as advocating a liberal pluralism of ideas and institutions, which might seem reminiscent to some of John Stuart Mill, the nineteenth century British logical philosopher,[157] there are contrasting dimensions of liberalism in these instances. It might be salutary to reconstruct what would have been Mobad Shah's reaction to Mill's positivist emphasis in such works as *A System of Logic, ratiocinative and inductive* (1843). Mill was a fervent admirer of the positivist "philosophy" of Auguste Comte, a contemporary sociologist who repudiated all metaphysical avenues of discussion. Mill accordingly emphasized that the social and human sciences should be made as precise and empirical as the natural sciences. Mobad Shah might have pointed out that premature precision in natural science amounts to a negative philosophy if its scope is considered the rule for other faculties of perception and knowledge.

Some forms of liberalism are lop-sided in the attention given to secondary features at the expense of primary stimuli to expansiveness. The modern Western forms of liberalism, ranging from the eighteenth century *philosophes* to current phenomenological trends in the history of religions, are by no means exempt from legitimate accusations of missing the point of a finer range of discrimination and intuition.

# CHAPTER NINE

# THE PERENNIAL PHILOSOPHY AND PERENNIAL FOLLY

The history of philosophy runs to a rather narrow convention in many current treatments. In this chapter I will venture an unconventional variation that may lend a less stifling and less parochial quality to the subject.

Since many people associate philosophy with the modern Western thinkers since Descartes, other dimensions of the term are subject to undue compression. While many Western academic thinkers tend to exclude pre-modern and Eastern thinkers from the favoured canon, popular aspersions upon philosophy as a logical cul-de-sac are clearly conditioned by an ignorance of events and trends not generally well known. The replacement of these heavily conditioned perspectives by the popular "perennial philosophy" has not been attended by any impressive degree of accuracy or discrimination. I will therefore focus upon matters which are not commonly aired by either the insularists or the enthusiasts of diffuse holistica.

Ancient Iran fares very badly in most accounts of philosophy and religion. Sects like the Mazdakites of the Sassanian era customarily receive a few lines that might please the compilers of potted philosophies, but it is evident that complexities in Iranian "mystical" philosophy have rarely been plumbed by the variety of annalists who have touched upon this subject. One suspects that the same is true of other countries also, but I will begin here with a cluster of traditions that are quite obviously poorly represented in general.

A wide variation is evident in the ingredients comprising the longest chapter in the *Dabistan* – namely, that devoted to the Zoroastrian and related Iranian religions, sects, and philosophies. As we have seen, the *Dabistan* was an unorthodox Persian work of the seventeenth century, and an unusual entry for so late a date is the brief account of Mazdakite tradition as relayed by some contemporary Mazdakites personally known to Mobad Shah. These individuals are stated to have practised their tradition secretly among the Muslims of the Iranian milieu. The description fits the corrupt form of the Mazdakite tradition, though a censorious attitude is not resorted to. The Mazdakites date back to the pre-Islamic Sassanian era, and it has been difficult for scholars to ascertain exactly what their beliefs and attitudes were, though these are known to have differed radically from clerical Zoroastrianism, and deducibly included such themes as transmigration. Perhaps the main point to convey here is that derivative mysticism is frequently misleading where philosophical values are concerned. It is now apparent that there was more than one unorthodox Zoroastrian tradition during Sassanian times, but any continuation does not imply an identical form for the more intrinsic principles represented.

A prominent feature of Mobad Shah's presentation of Zoroastrianism in the *Dabistan* is that very little of it amounts to the conventional guise of that religion. Numerous sects are briefly described which are for the most part unknown in other sources; Mobad Shah says he had met a few persons representing these sects. They were probably very small minorities, and included some discernible peculiarities. But the tradition which gains more space than all the others put together is that of the Sipasis or Abadis, i.e. the Kaivanis. The author presents them in an impartial manner along with all the other traditions described in his book, but there are clear indications that he had himself been personally reared in this tradition. This is not obvious to casual scrutiny however, a fact worth remembering in relation to the more sophisticated Eastern rationales of mysticism and philosophy. This matter is additionally complicated for casual scrutiny owing to the close associations of the Kaivanis with the Iranized tradition of Greek philosophy and intercultural Sufism.

The European savant who "discovered" the *Dabistan* (from Muslim sources) was Sir William Jones (d. 1794), the British Sanskritist who was also fluent in Persian. Jones thought highly of the work, and described it as "the most amusing and instructive book I ever read in Persian." This was in 1787, in the maturity of his career as a scholar. But he did not perceive all the complexities of the contents, and though sympathetic to sufi ideas (for a British scholar), he was not as alert as he could have been to Zoroastrian intricacies. Jones believed the work to have been written by a Muslim, but this relates to the factor of the verses of one Muhsin Fani being quoted in the work – which cannot be taken any longer as proof of authorship. He thought that the last two chapters, on philosophy and Sufism respectively, must have been written by a different hand, since they did not deal with any conventional religious material. Jones also made far too much of the "historical" dynasties mentioned in the Sipasi section, a feat of literalist interpretation which could have been remedied by a greater knowledge of the Pahlavi style allegory employed by Kaivani writers. But such knowledge was very difficult to obtain (though it might have been suspected), and the Jonesian horizons of the British Constitution and Newtonian philosophy were not the best yardsticks for orientalia, despite his unusual catholicity. Ironically perhaps, despite the rather literalist favour shown by this savant to a previously unknown treatise of unorthodox Zoroastrian dimensions, he had earlier been responsible for a controversial repudiation of the newly discovered orthodox Zoroastrian heritage, which he had dismissed as nonsense, a repudiation extending to the Gathas of Zarathushtra in the form then known.

As a young man of only twenty-four, Sir William Jones had written a highly acidic (though anonymous) epistle to another of the leading orientalist scholars of Europe. Jones accused Anquetil Duperron of having introduced fallacies into historical research on Iran, and maintained that enlightened European scholarship had no need of Duperron's *Zend-Avesta*. Jones was here defending the scholarly tradition of Oxford, which Duperron had radically challenged in his new translation of Avestan and Pahlavi texts which he had acquired from a Zoroastrian priest at Surat. Duperron's *Zend-Avesta, Ouvrage de Zoroaster* (1771) came from the same hand that caused Dara Shikoh's version of the Upanishads to ignite the enthusiasm of Schopenhauer. The learned world was stunned by the Zoroastrian revelations, since the new French translation presented an entirely different tradition to that previously reconstructed by the Oxford scholar Thomas Hyde (d. 1703) a few generations earlier. Hyde had primarily worked from Greek, Latin, and Arabic authors, and was deficient in Zoroastrian texts. But more seriously perhaps, he was handicapped by his penchant for Christianizing interpretations. Hyde quite feasibly concluded that the Iranian prophet Zarathushtra (Greek: Zoroaster) had been misinterpreted by the Greeks and Sassanian sectarians, but his Judaeo-Christian version of Zarathushtra's actual teaching is too biblical for more recent experts.

Duperron's translation revealed a highly ritualistic religion which some found unacceptable as fact, including the young William Jones. The critics were substantially wrong, even though Duperron's translation later transpired to be inaccurate owing to his priestly source. But this did not change the ritualistic complexion of the phenomenon. The first volume of Duperron's work incorporated the ritual text known as the *Vendidad*, which has been aptly described as consisting "chiefly of minute directions about ceremonies of ritual purification and the art of combating demonic influences." It reads uninspiringly even in more recent translations.

Unlike Hyde, Anquetil Duperron (d. 1805) was a Roman Catholic, and his translations of Eastern scriptures did not convert him. In the later years of his life, he accomplished much theological and political pamphleteering, and expended much energy in the attempt to persuade the French government to recapture India by the means of an overland campaign through Turkey or Russia.[158] More edifying, though still limited in scope, were the subsequent developments in Iranist scholarship. Pieces of a textual jig-saw puzzle were accumulating, but some very simplified interpretation was in fashion. A predominantly Protestant Christian perspective for long prevailed, retaining the basic theory of Hyde, which was made compatible with Duperron's deduction of a "pure theism" as the essence of Zarathushtra's teaching. The official Western interpretation of Zoroastrian history and religion was one of assuming that the Zoroastrians themselves had long ago lost an accurate knowledge of Zarathushtra's teaching. This was legitimate enough as an explanation for texts like the *Vendidad*,[159] but Gathic implications and later Persian texts were rather too conveniently left in limbo. Nobody should want only selected pieces of a jig-saw puzzle if it is the complete picture that is desired.

The Christian sense of confidence in knowing all about pure theism, on the basis of the Old Testament, tended to be strengthened when it was discovered during the nineteenth century that most of the *Zend-Avesta* could not be regarded as the words of Zarathushtra, but only the archaic "hymns" known as the Gathas. Yet the Zoroastrian priests had long been attributing the whole of the Avesta to their figurehead.

There have since been many sequels to the Jones versus Duperron confrontation amongst Iranist scholars, duels of interpretation occurring in the pages of learned journals and specialist commentaries. The subject of Zarathushtra is one of a continuing fascination, since there is a strong textual basis for the archaic entity, but a general context of uncertainty with regard to legendary elements. Flights of fancy have undeniably made their appearance, perhaps most marked of all in the pages of Nietzche's philosophical *Thus Spake Zarathustra*, which should of course read: Thus Spake Nietzche. Yet divergences in more scholarly interpretation provoke the conclusion that academic errors have not infrequently been substantial.[160]

The Western assumption that the Zoroastrian tradition was entirely divorced from its origin is rather too facile when it is realized that a work like the *Dabistan* has been customarily ignored by Iranist scholars as a late syncretic text of little or no relevance to earlier eras. In another camp, orthodox Parsi priests have denounced this liberal treatise as heretical. It can be conceded here that there is a general basis for the "Semitic prophet" paradigm favoured by Christian scholars in relation to Zarathushtra, in that a reforming precedent contrasted with the conservative priestly aftermath. But the philosophy of this paradigm is unenviably ahistorical in denying the relevance of the esoteric version of Zoroastrian tradition as palpably evidenced in surviving texts. This matter has been complicated by the vogue for Western Theosophy amongst the Parsis of India, a vogue which should not be confused with Kaivani lore, though this confusion has in fact occurred in both popular and academic circles.

This suggested connection should not be taken to mean any exact duplication of teaching or event – which was linguistically impossible – but can be conceived in terms of a sequel of Iranian componency that can serve as an ethnoarchaeological focus for possible approximations in orientation. The neceessity to see beneath miscastings is relevant to an investigation of both Zarathushtra and the much later Kaivani philosophers.

The *Dabistan* incorporates a version of ancient Zoroastrian religion that tallies in some respects with the "pseudo-history" of the late Pahlavi-style text known as the *Desatir*, which gained favour amongst the members of the Theosophical Society.[161] Allegorical considerations apart, a typical attitude of scholars has been that because the "pseudo-Pahlavi" format is not historical, the school of Azar Kaivan bears no relation to ancient events. But the point is that the valid historical data on the Kaivani school is also jettisoned, dismissed as a religious syncretism that is irrelevant to Zoroastrianism. It could be that history is being violated by this attitude. One contention of mine is that the figure of Azar Kaivan cannot be so conveniently separated from considerations of the archaic Zarathushtra.[162] Both were Iranian nonconformists. The possibility of a similarity in consciousness orientation is one of the factors bearing upon the question (for some) of what is perennial in experiential philosophy. Or to put it more pointedly, Azar Kaivan can be viewed as a continuation and extension in time of the Zarathushtran event, in comparison to which the priestly conventions of Zoroastrianism were anachronistic and pseudo.

My approach to these philosophical and historical matters is radically distinct from the recent interpretation which considers orthodox Zoroastrian tradition as the accurate successor to the Zarathushtran event.[163] If it is true that Zarathushtra lived *c.*1400–1200 B.C.,[164] or even earlier, then clearly it is a very ancient phenomenon that is under discussion, and likely to stretch the inelastic horizons of the traditional chronology which dates the author of the Gathas at *c.*600 B.C. While it can be considered a step in the right direction to grant honour to Zoroastrian abilities rather than to the preferences of Christianizing orientalists, to grant the laurels of expertise to ritualists (which the Kaivanis were not) is no real improvement upon the "Roman Catholic" interpretation of the Oxford scholar R.C. Zaehner, an interpretation which proved influential.[165]

What Leibniz chose to call the *philosophia perennis* is much more difficult to detect than it need be if subject to the imposition of paradigm by different religious orthodoxies. The ishraqi philosophy of Iran antedated Leibniz by several centuries in this concept, and furthermore extended its range to a universality of wisdom (*hiqmah*) in which ancient pre-Islamic civilizations were prominent participants.

A much more recent attempt to chart a perennial philosophy was the more well known version of Aldous Huxley. His much-read anthology *The Perennial Philosophy* substantially incorporates Christian ingredients, though he did extend coverage to several other mystical traditions. His sources in respect of the latter are perhaps revealing: Dean W.R. Inge, D.T. Suzuki, Alan Watts, Sir Sarvepalli Radhakrishnan, the Tibetological scholar W.Y. Evans-Wentz, Ananda K. Coomaraswamy, Rene Guenon, Shri Aurobindo Ghose, Chuang-tzu in the Giles translation, Al-Ghazzali's *Confessions*, E.H. Whinfield's translation of Rumi's *Mathnavi*, selections from Ansari and Attar, and R.A. Nicholson's early work *The Mystics of Islam* (1914). The list is not exhaustive, but was one that was more easily available to the liberal Christian reader earlier this century, and would largely earn the description of popular mysticism from current scholars in the history of religions, though specialists are likely to be more acidic in their appraisal. But it is a fact that even a specialist orientalist scholar like Nicholson expressed some very simplified interpretations of sufi mysticism and philosophy that are liable to make today's cognoscenti wince.

Simplicities apart, Huxley's anthology is so well known

that it justifies comment. Huxley was liberal, and the problem is not that he made unfair judgments of the non-Christian traditions, but that so little about them emerges from his pages. His introductory classification tends to reflect general ideas on mysticism: the "lower gate" of entry to the perennial philosophy is preferred by "strictly practical teachers like Buddha, who have no use for speculation." (Now granted that Buddha had no use for speculation, but why is he assigned to the lower gate ?) Whereas the "upper gate" is that of "the born philosophers and theologians." This is meant in respect of formulations of metaphysics, but the conflation seems pronounced. The "middle gate" is that preferred by Huxley, namely that applying to the exponents of "spiritual religion," i.e., the devout (*sic*) contemplatives of India, the Sufis of Islam, the Catholic mystics of the later middle Ages, and the more mystical representatives of the Protestant tradition.[166] The sociology of the *Dabistan* is not in evidence in Huxley's approach, but he does incorporate certain admirable cautions not found in more recent works. For instance, he makes it clear that "miracles" and powers were warned against as distractions by sufis and Hindu teachers; the Buddha also dismissed these sidetracks.[167] This caveat alone makes Huxley's book superior to much current fare, in which psychic powers are widely advertised as something greatly desirable.

One accusation that can legitimately be made against simplified versions of the *philosophia perennis* is that there is little or no indication of variations and differences in experiential intensity. It is all very well to speak (as Huxley did) in terms of the same meanings being perpetuated in relation to ultimates. But this can merely mean that anybody can testify to a popular perennial philosophy by invoking, e.g., the Vedantic clause of "*Aham Brahmasmi*" (I am Brahman). The greatest criminal could easily do that given sufficient incentive or cupidity. The actual experiences signified or deducible remain a virtual mystery by comparison with the ease and facility of exploitative claims relayed to an audience of uncritical consumers.

There is now more need than ever to qualify factors relating to an accurate and comprehensive perennial philosophy in view of the increasingly facile cash-in tactics in vogue.

According to Huxley, one of the "four fundamental doctrines" at the core of the perennial philosophy is: humans can realize the existence of the ultimate Reality by a direct intuition, which is superior to discursive reasoning.[168] On this issue unfortunately, there is a widespread tendency to assume that an inchoate intuition represents the ultimate realization; remarkably little distinction is made between the alpha and the omega of the experiential code, leading to a policy of narcissism in peripheral and distorted forms of the perennial philosophy. This is the more convenient for bandwagon gurus owing to the submergence of all necessity for discrimination – which is jettisoned along with discursive reasoning in the scramble for intuitive status. Yet *jnana* (wisdom) and its corollary of *viveka* (discrimination) is a traditional mainstay of fundamental yoga – which is not to be confused (as it often is) with the penchant for gymnastic exercises that is sometimes cultivated as a substitute. The Vedantic jnanis who appear in the *Dabistan* are not likely to have been impressed by Huxley's subsequent "intuitive" confrontation with mescalin and his advocacy of the drug experience, since in India this is a common resort of lacklustre holy men who become addicts of hemp and related substances.

The perennial philosophy very quickly becomes perennial folly in the minds and behaviour of those lacking in a basic sense of discrimination as to what leads where.

Huxley's belief that psychedelic drugs could guide the intuitive aspirant towards cosmic consciousness is not the only instance of aberration amongst apparently intelligent Western gurus who become mouthpieces for make-believe instead of the ultimate reality.

It is perhaps too much to hope that an experiential code for the perennial philosophy will ever become articulated for the benefit of those who decry all possible relevance of verbal explanation. Yet such repudiators are only too ready to listen to beguiling simplifications; perhaps the truth is that anything demanding is deemed irrelevant in the interests of entertainment. If there is any truth in reincarnation, then it is apparent that many people require a very long time to mature experientially. This realism is more logical to the critics of contrived wonders.

It seems that what is most needed in the history of the perennial philosophy is a knowledge of what really occurred. Yet history is nowadays increasingly zero-rated. People prefer science fiction and other forms of contemporary mythology consonant with samadhi on cassette. Even some scholars are extremely lax in the evaluation of known historical materials.

A celebrated scholar in the history of religions who adopts a strong phenomenological approach is Mircea Eliade. His books are frequently cited as authority by the less scholarly writers on "esoteric" subjects. His early familiarity with the Hindu tradition has given him a reputation as a Tantricist.[169] Not all partisans of Eastern thought agree with Eliade in his methodology. This is because he describes different traditions without demarcating the discrepancies or abnormalities evident in them (or between them); often he endorses the cruder elements discernible. Since this stance, apart from being an increasing issue in social science, tends to be associated with the *philosophia perennis et universalis* (to use a problematic phrase of Ananda K. Coomaraswamy), it merits attention here. Eliade's latitude is not at issue here; he has covered so many different traditions that his range can be said to eclipse the more pedestrian efforts of many others. But his methodology is a different matter altogether.

Eliade has distinguished his methodology from that of the structuralist anthropologist Claude Levi-Strauss, affirming his use of a different approach to the "materialistic reductionism" of the latter. But Eliade bends a great deal to structuralist antihistoricism. He finds in the indifference to history one reason for the popularity of Levi-Strauss, whose criticism of anthropological historicism he deems as being very timely. Eliade explains this antihistoricism as "a protest against the pessimism and nihilism of some recent historicists." According to Eliade, other (non-structuralist) anthropologists have expended too much time and energy in reconstructing the history of primitive cultures and too little time in understanding their meaning. To Eliade, it follows that "man can be understood without taking consciousness into consideration." He pleads for a hermeneutical effort, not a demystification, stressing that meaning and significance must be grasped.[170]

Despite his attempt to veer away from the extremes of phenomenology as a historian of religions, Eliade's methodology amounts to a phenomenological skirting of comparative evaluation of traditions and trends. Lack of adequate analysis makes it easier for dubious trends to be sanctioned by such a methodology. Eliade is quite right to feel that the historical documents have more content than the conventional historian will allow, but the factor of meaning has much more variation than Eliadic phenomenology allows. One first has to demystify errors of meaning before exposing more accurate meanings and more comprehensive contours. It is a step in the right direction to react (as Eliade does) to the pessimistic existentialism of Sartre, but in other respects too many steps backwards into a phenomenology partial to orgiastic religion allows small scope for depth in meaning. A macrohistory of intrinsic depth cannot by definition avoid taking the requisite steps to qualify the microfeatures which both enhance, and detract from, cosmic significances.

Eliade's pursuit of meaning very often neglects to distinguish between intrinsic meanings and aberrant meanings. It is comparatively rare in his writings to find a clear demarcation in this respect. One of the exceptions was his observation that the "process of desacralization of human existence has sometimes arrived at hybrid forms of black magic and sheer travesty of religion." He refers here to the "aberrant aspects of pseudomorphs" of the pseudo-occult and neospiritualistic. Further, various political movements and social utopianisms are seen to have a mythological structure and a type of religious fanaticism, e.g. marxism. According to Eliade, Marx continued one of the major eschatological myths of the Asiatico-Mediterranean world, namely the redeeming role of the Just, substituting the proletariat for the anointed messenger; marxist classless society and the consequently anticipated disappearance of historical tensions have their closest precedent in the myth of the Golden Age; Marx is construed as appropriating for his own purposes the Judaeo-Christian eschatological hope of an absolute end to history. Eliade adds that it is not only the "little (pseudo) religions" and political mystiques that exhibit "degenerated or camouflaged religious behaviour" – but also movements with an avowed secular or antireligious orientation, e.g., movements for complete sexual freedom.[171]

Though one can agree here that the profane frequently exhibits a variant of sacred associations, one could wish that the phenomenological history of religions dealt with major, occult, and archaic religions in the same way when these give evidence of penchants for camouflaged profanities.

The Eliadic tactic of finding a spiritual meaning in all things religiously ancient is at complete odds with both commonsense and mystical gauges of the *philosophia perennis*. The latter proves exacting in its more uncamouflaged contours. But when degenerate features are camouflaged, under whatsoever label of meaning, the content remains spurious, and can frequently be harmful.

An instance in which Eliadic phenomenology does not stress any qualitative demarcations is provided by an article that deals with a sufficient number of contrasting ancient traditions to necessitate acute distinctions. This article deals with the Phibionite gnostics, Indian Tantra, Manichaean asceticism, Zoroastrianism, Sufism, and "archaic level" tribalism.

The Phibionites were a so-called gnostic sect of Alexandria. Gnosis has achieved some strange interpretations in modern annals. According to Eliade, the possession of gnosis enabled the *pneumatikoi*, i.e. gnostics, to consider themselves beyond social rules and ethical interdictions. But it is arguably only phenomenological hindsight which deems the gnostics to have been free to practise asceticism or sexual libertinage, a situation which reminds Eliade of the Upanishadic rishis (a strangely unqualified reminiscence) and (more scholastically accurate) the Tantric yogis. One can agree, however, with the assertion that the most striking parallel to the Shaiva and Tantric sexual rites is that of the Phibionites, the main source for which is Epiphanius, the church father who (as a young man) attended their meetings in fourth century Alexandria. The agenda of these meetings included communal sex and an elaborate rite of eating semen. Eliade refers approvingly to this in terms of a sanctification, but such gloss is misleading for those still requiring to be educated. In the anthropographic view, there was nothing in the least bit mystical or spiritualizing in such habits, which comprised only a social venue for the local sensationalists, to put it as politely as possible. Yet according to Eliade, "the ultimate goal of the Phibionites' sexual rituals was . . . to accelerate the reintegration of the precosmogonic stage, that is, the 'end of the world,' and . . . to approach God through a progressive 'spermatization.'"

Some of those readers with abnormal dietary requirements might feel agog with anticipation at the scholarly proviso that we are still insufficiently (*sic*) informed about the Phibionite rituals and beliefs "to make an adequate comparison" with the Tantric *maithuna* procedures referred to by the medieval commentator Abhinavagupta, and the Shaiva ceremonial known as *kundagolaka*. Since I believe that neither of these lastmentioned diversions have anything to do with the *philosophia perennis*, I will not describe them here, but only report Eliade's remark that all these systems "seem to have in common the hope that the primordial spiritual unity can be reconstituted through erotic bliss and the consumption of semen and the menses." One would at the least expect a repudiation of these aberrant gourmet proclivities, but instead Eliade refers to them in the context of "relevant conceptions." There is no criticism, but instead tacit approval. Are some scholars to be taken seriously by the man in the street? Certainly not by educated members of the public.

To camouflage the profane as sacred amounts to the mockery of meaning and the acute devaluation of meaning. In such a milieu, crass idiocy will flourish, since there is no stipulation as to the validity of meaningful content.

Such a milieu was cultivated by a fringe element in Indian cultism from (at least) the time of the brahmanical revival in opposition to Buddhism.[172] Some Hindu Tantric sects favoured rites which included the ceremonial eating of genital secretions, though this feature was harmless by comparison with certain other practices on record. The sexual practices documented in later Tantric sects appear to have existed as early as the first/second centuries A.D., according to the Tibetological scholar Guiseppe Tucci. Yet there is also discernible a symbolic code in Tantric texts, more particularly the Buddhist Tantras (which have differences of format from the Hindu Tantras). The symbolism of "five luminous lights" appears in the Buddhist Tantras, Manichaean cosmology, and sufi treatises. In the Indian milieu, this symbolism underwent distortions. The actual usage of symbolism varied prodigiously between wise men, fools, and exploiters. It still does.

Eliade sounds (or rather reads) disappointed to find that the "seminal" value of light symbolism was ignored in the sufi tradition of Najmuddin Kubra (d. 1221). This Iranian teacher of Central Asia gives a systematic description of the perception of "coloured lights," part of an intricate system of associations relevant to specific sufi developmental processes. But there is no lurid aberration of format, and for this reason perhaps, it is still little known despite Henry Corbin's (incomplete) presentation of this symbolism. But instead of drawing conclusions that might advance Corbin's research, Eliade abruptly moves on to the more exotic theology of a tribe in Columbian Amazonia, said to exhibit an archaic level of culture.

After reading some modern expositions of Tantrism, the reader might well conclude that it was no wonder that for Manichaeans (or at least the early Manichaeans), the perfect life entailed an uninterrupted series of purifications. This involved a stringent concept of the separation of spirit (= light) from matter. Sexual intercourse was considered to prolong the captivity of light in the physical body. The "end of the world" meant the end of this (individual) captivity. Many moderns do not, of course, favour this emphasis, and humanistic psychology has become very vocal in its equation of the mind with the body, a trend favourable to neo-Reichian Gestalt, which finds it easier to preserve constraints in partisans once their mental autonomy is removed. Much modern psychotherapy is invalid for the simple reason that it is not dealing with the mind at all; that would be too difficult for the inexpert.

Manichaeanism and Sufism converge in the Iranian tradition, which Eliade touches upon in its more archaic extensions in the article under discussion. He aptly observes that when legends concerning Zarathushtra were written down, the biography of this prophet "was already almost completely mythologized." It was stated by the priestly annalists of the *Denkart* that Zarathushtra was born from *haoma*, a "divine liquid" analogous to the Vedic *soma*, concerning which there have been scholarly arguments. But there are grounds for thinking that the *haoma* associations were a priestly contrivance for the purpose of buttressing the ritualism of Zoroastrian orthodoxy. *Haoma* figured in ancient ritual and was conceived as being full of *khvarenah*, an important term in Iranian lore over which there have been further arguments. We may follow Eliade's affirmation that in the older Iranian conception, *khvarenah* was "a supernatural light possessed by every human." But Eliade insists upon describing *khvarenah* as a fluid (of spermatic associations), the cue for which is derived from late Pahlavi texts, and not the earlier Gathic and Avestan texts, which have a different symbolism altogether.[173] Hence Eliade's article leaves diligent readers with the onus to assert the necessity for distinction between ritualism and reform, the need for accurate meanings of terms and concepts, and the need for the imperative distinction between discriminative wisdom and the "left hand" perversity of cultist and related imbalance. The Eliadic advocacy of "left hand" Tantra has tended to unduly colour the spectrum of traditions that orgiastic tastes distort in order to provide sanction for aberrations. The neo-Reichian "tao of physics" has not improved upon such phenomenology by the haphazard mistake of equating the Brihadaranyaka Upanishad with the sensual preoccupations of left-hand (*vamachara*) Tantra.[174]

The text known as the *Denkart* is a Pahlavi work dating no earlier than the ninth century A.D. in its extant form. This is the primary source for the legend of Zarathushtra,[175] which must therefore be treated with acute caution in respect of history. The links of the orthodox tradition with archaic events are extremely questionable, to say the least. As the Swedish scholar Henrik Nyberg observed, the text of the *Denkart* is much corrupted; the Zoroastrian priests had always been primarily concerned with ritual and the recitation of myth. The compilers of the *Denkart* were probably not trained writers, and produced this text at a time (in the Islamic era) when "Book Pahlavi" was already a dead language, and one which they accordingly handled with difficulty. Nyberg concludes that the copyists "only half understood the contents," and that the modern editors were at an even greater disadvantage. The literary consequence of these linguistic vicissitudes is a "somewhat bewildering text, some of whose enigmas will perhaps remain unsolved forever."[176] It should be added that Nyberg was usually an incorrigible optimist in such matters of decipherment.

There are obvious difficulties in tracing the Zoroastrian tradition back some two millenia or so prior to the *Denkart*. Such difficulties can be freely conceded here without giving up the attempt, and similar attempts in other avenues. A dogmatic stance in such efforts is inadvisable, but what can be far more abruptly emphasized are at least three basic points which have a relevance to current ideas on the *philosophia perennis*:

1) Some erudite and less erudite scholars have unintentionally misled the public into a false sense of liberalism that in large part proves only perennial folly.

2) At the risk of being unpopular, honesty demands that several current trends purporting to represent mystical dimensions of the past should more accurately be described as hedonistic apologies for current laxity in thinking and behaviour.

3) The spirit of conservative scholarship can contribute to dishonesty when it rejects extended meaning out of hand. Recognition of extended meaning does not necessarily amount to a phenomenological approach.

A major influence upon the tradition of conservative scholarship has been (however indirectly) the sceptical philosophy of David Hume. His oft-cited *Natural History of Religion* is a treatise not without merit in the necessary criticism of vanities, though Hume's knowledge of history was largely of the classicist variety as cultivated by Georgian ethnocentricists secure in the hey-day of the British Empire. While one need not take too much notice of the amiable sceptic as he warbles about Stoic superstitions (he sounds almost like Kant on such points), it is easy to agree with him in such questions as: "Is it strange, when mistakes are so common, to find every one positive and dogmatical?"[177] One could underline in red his observation that religious zeal is no proof against hypocrisy. Recent discoveries can only confirm the Humean conclusion that "the most voluptuous and most abandoned of men" have aligned themselves with religious precepts. Typical of his own cast of thought, he affirms that happiness is not to be dreamed of, and that the best course of life is a moderate one which avoids the extremes of joy and melancholy, wit and madness, pleasures and disgust, hope and disappointment. This is not to be confused with the "middle way" of some mystical philosophies, since for Hume, this course resulted in "as far as possible, a mediocrity, and a kind of insensibility, in everything." This is the outcome of his philosophy in this historical rumination upon religion, and he may be said to have achieved his aim in terms of an indifferent profundity. He ends the treatise by saying that he makes his escape into "the calm, tho' obscure, regions of philosophy."[178]

While Hume is correct enough about much superficial religion and mysticism, it is arguable that he did not know very much about philosophy, but only about a form of mediocre commonsense that was insensible to a self in extension of a mere bundle of perceptions or impressions.

Hume's theory of the self has sometimes been confused with Buddhist perspectives; indeed, the physicist Ernst Mach entertained a similarly negative view of the self as did Hume, and considered that his own view had affinities with the Buddhist worldview. This kind of equation gained strength from prevalent Western interpretations of Buddhist texts, interpretations which were (in part at least) shared by Theravada Buddhists in the East. The Pali Canon of Theravada Buddhism was the focus for early Buddhist studies in Europe, since it was the oldest in the sequence of corpora. The nihilistic overtones were often exaggerated, particularly by Christian critics. A recent scholarly analysis has emerged with very different implications. The *anatta* (non-self) teaching appears in the earlier parts of the Pali Canon, namely the *Suttapitaka*, though the *Vinayapitaka* (on monastic rules) is also relevant. Perez-Remon observes that nowhere in these texts is the reality of the self (*atta*) absolutely and explicitly denied. The *anatta* doctrine taught in the Nikayas (of the *Suttapitaka*) has a relative value, not an absolute one as has been supposed. These texts, reputedly the words of the Buddha, do not state that the self has no reality at all, but that certain things which the untutored man identifies with are not the self. This is the logical reason given in the texts as to why one should become detached from extraneous things. The *anatta* doctrine therefore only denies selfhood to the things that constitute the non-self, showing these things to be empty of any ultimate value and to be repudiated accordingly.[179]

This perspective renders it unnecessary to adopt the controversial interpretation earlier proposed by Mrs C.A.F. Rhys Davids, who made extensive contributions to studies of early Buddhism. In her earlier works, she adopted a negativist interpretation of *anatta*, affirming that this argument was directed against the notion of a soul (and hence against the Brahmanical worldview). But in her later books she changed her view almost completely, concluding that *anatta* was a later accretion of monastic origin, obscuring the original teaching of Buddha, which closely approximated to the Upanishadic theme of *atman* (the self, in the sense of the intrinsic self).[180] Other scholars have not been in agreement,[181] but there are yet different ways of interpreting the "self" as the ego rather than as the *atman*. Another well known Western Buddhist affirms that Theravada Buddhists did narrow down the Buddha's teaching to a doctrine of "no soul" for which there is no scriptural authority; yet the Buddha was not teaching the *atman* doctrine, but emphasizing that the self (or ego) is subject to change (*anicca*) and suffering before it dies in Buddhahood to gain an incomparably greater consciousness.[182]

Like the more myopic Theravadins perhaps, the negativism of Mach and Hume narrowed down the potential of philosophy to pedestrian convenience.

The pedestrian mentality acquired more oracular auspices in the ancient Chinese tradition associated with the *Yi-Ching* (Book of Changes). This well known text has achieved a fame amongst Western enthusiasts that is probably greater than that of any other Chinese classic, including even the *Tao-te-Ching*. Seldom perhaps does any text so clearly reveal the vicissitudes of usage and interpretation by different mentalities. This manual became an official Confucian classic, but its exact relationship to Confucius (551–479 B.C.) is not so easily discoverable. It had formerly been used as an oracle during the Chou dynasty of the first millenium B.C., but early Confucian circles gave it a more philosophical complexion with the aid of new commentaries. Confucius himself mentions a *Book of Changes* dating from the Shang dynasty (second millenium B.C.), though it is problematic as to what this consisted of. But the sixty-four hexagram version of the Chou dynasty should be distinguished from the early Confucian usage of the same version. Subsequently, this version was reinstated as a divinatory manual during the Ch'in and Han dynasties (third century B.C. to third century A.D.), and the *yin-yang* lore associated with the *fang shih* ("magicians") gained prominence as a code of interpretation. The much standardized terms *yin* and *yang* do not appear in the oldest commentaries on the *Yi-Ching*, only in this later "magical" phase which some scholars have aligned with Taoistic influence. Afterwards the Confucian scholar Wang Pi was instrumental in replacing the *yin-yang* interpretation with "a philosophy of statecraft" (as Richard Wilhelm called it) that harked back to the earlier Confucian interpretations of a metaphysical and cosmological character. It seems to have acquired a very formal usage in later centuries prior to the Neo-Confucian innovations of the Sung era in which the *Yi-Ching* was viewed as the only Confucian classic capable of opposing the metaphysical views of the Buddhists, towards whom the orthodox Chinese were averse. The syncretism of the Han dynasty was even more in evidence during the Ch'ing dynasty (1644–1912), owing to the reaction of Confucian scholars to the attitudes of the Sung literati and the resultant preference for Han commentaries. Thus the divinatory usage of the *Yi-Ching* was not frowned upon in general, though the erudite Ch'ing scholars would doubtless have been more than a little puzzled by twentieth century Western consumption of the *Yi-Ching*. This compilation of diverse writings is frequently a coffee table adornment in the fortune-telling idiom; one has the distinct suspicion that the more abstract philosophy associated with it is too complicated for simplistic digestion.[183]

In brief, the *Yi-Ching* may well comprise a perennial document of sorts, but diverse vicissitudes of interpretation and audience have largely been wide of the mark in the much discussed return to the original philosophy of the sage Confucius.[184]

A major stimulant to current Western faddism in the *Yi-Ching* as oracle was the penchant for divination expressed by C.G. Jung. He sided with the tradition of Taoist priests who tended to specialize in fortune-telling via the *Yi-Ching*. Jung saw in this divination a "spiritual nourishment for the unconscious elements or forces."[185] Thus every throw of the dice (or rather coins and yarrow stalks) was somehow spiritually nourishing. Since Jung had elaborated a very inadequate version of the "unconscious" by comparison with the much more discerning prototype of the ancient Buddhist Yogacara school, one can suggest that he was similarly at odds with ancient Chinese wisdom as distinct from diffuse holistic accretion. The belief in total efficacy of a fetish grants an uncanny conscious power to the manipulators of the fetish.

Jung makes the comparatively diminutive qualification that the *Yi-Ching* insists upon self-knowledge, and that the method by which this is to be achieved "is open to every kind of misuse." But he confuses the mode of divination with this self-knowledge, and does not appear to have grasped the unconscious dimensions of his own statement that this method of divination had been put to superstitious use at all times. One may regard this as a fact, a status which one cannot grant to Jung's assertion that the *Yi-Ching* was the main source of inspiration for Confucius and the legendary

Lao-tzu (which Jung asserts as a fact).[186]

Emic value judgments in relation to perennial truths very often amount to half-truths, fractional truths, and sheer idiocies of thought and behaviour. The etic holistic does not amount to the diffuse holistic, which constitutes a subtraction of meaning and range of expertise.

One cannot help but feel that Jung would have been wiser to take more heed of such perspectives as that found in a fifteenth century Ming specimen of "Elegant Writing" (*Ku Wan*) by Liu Chi. The latter supplies an anecdote concerning Shao Ping, a nobleman of the early Han era who visited Sze-ma Chi-chu, one of the most reputed diviners of the time. Shao Ping wanted to know the future via the usual consultatory procedure, but the diviner replied: "The divining stalks are so much dead grass; the tortoise-shell (used for divination) is a dead bone. Man has more intelligence than such dead things possess. Why not listen to your (real) self instead of seeking answers in things (outside yourself)."[187]

Jungian themes have tended to gain an eminence that has overshadowed earlier psychological perceptions. The polymathic philosopher Leibniz (1646–1716) had employed the concept of the unconscious. It has been said that he did not in this anticipate Freud in any complete sense. Leibniz used this concept to supplement his exposition of the indestructibility of monads and the distinction between perception and consciousness. He affirmed that a number of unconscious (insensible) perceptions, stored in the mind, can accumulate in such a way as to enter the conscious field. "The present is big with the future and laden with the past," wrote Leibniz,[188] who did not neglect to criticize Cartesian dualism even while rebutting the empiricism of his contemporary John Locke. Leibniz was in some respects ahead of Freud, since the latter was still working under the assumptions of the Lockean *tabula rasa*. Yet not all modern commentators can assess such distinctions, and are unable to concede that the philosophical potential of Spinoza and Leibniz[189] died in the moralism of Hume and Kant.

Though it has been said that Leibniz was concerned with the "unconscious" more than any previous philosopher, this arguably represents a contraction of psychological truth in more perennial vistas. It was not so long ago that it was scholastically pointed out that while most people consider the notion of the archetypal dream to be completely new and revolutionary, in actual fact this notion is not new. Jung's formulation of the archetypal dream can be found in the less well known pages of Muhiyuddin ibn al-Arabi, who was writing seven centuries before Jung.

According to Ibn al-Arabi, there are very different types of dreams. The most common variety is that featuring *khayal*, here using an Arabic term meaning mental images or "imaginings," something neither spiritual nor physical. *Khayal* can provide symbols for hidden realities, but this symbolism may be very flawed. Daily experiences are processed in the dream cycle by *khayal*, and these experiences are then reflected in consciousness ("the inward eye") as the distorted images typical of dreams. These images usually become the symbols or foci of personal desires. Yet there is a second type of dream, of far greater significance, the data for which comes directly from the "Guarded Tablet" (as Arabi sometimes calls it) or Universal Soul (as Landau translates it). In this category of experience, the human consciousness perceives the archetypal ideas contained in the Universal Soul. But even here, imagination (*khayal*) accompanies the received ideas, and distorts them proportionately. Hence the dreamer effectively perceives only the reflections of the archetypal ideas. The symbolism is provided by the dreamer's own imagination, and not by the underlying reality confronted. The purity of the archetypal ideas are thus rendered impure. The dreams accordingly require interpretation, since only the reality behind the symbols is real knowledge.

According to Ibn al-Arabi, there is a third type of dream that is not symbolic at all, but a direct encounter with Reality. These are the truly archetypal dreams, in which the Universal Soul is experienced directly, without distortion. Imagination does not operate at this rare level.[190]

Since the "Universal Soul" of Ibn Arabi's philosophy is a conscious Reality, and not unconscious, there is a pronounced difference between this sufi gnostic explanation and the mysticism of Jungian theory. While Arabi is compatible with the Buddhist *alayavijnana*, Jung is not compatible with either of these Eastern antecedents. While Jung had escaped the clutches of the Lockean *tabula rasa*, i.e., the erased tablet representing the human mind devoid of innate ideas at birth, he missed the realism attendant upon the "Guarded Tablet" of the Spanish Arab.

It may yet transpire that Ibn al-Arabi was being more realistic than both the contemporary theologians of his day and the modern scientific materialists in his "abandonment of the Islamic conception of God as the creator and cause of the universe, in favour of a God who *is* everything."[191] This pantheistic heretic was certainly realistic enough in his depiction of the power of imagination in the human mind even in dreams. Strangely realistic also is an extant reference to *khayal* (imagination) by the sufi philosopher Abdul Karim Jili (*fl.* 1400 A.D.), associated with the tradition of Ibn al-Arabi. In his Arabic work *Al-Insan al-Kamil*, Jili refers to the "seat of *khayal*" in the left and right sides of the human brain; in the left side are stored images which are a facsimile of the "Earth of Misery," and in the right side are stored a contrasting type of images which are a facsimile of the "houris" and other delights of Paradise.[192] The correspondence with brain hemisphere profundities is too close to be dismissed as speculative metaphysics. There is no equivalent reference known to me in the works of Jung or Freud. One might extrapolate that although the brain mediates representations of contrasting polarities of experience, the power of imagination involved is not absolute and is subject to a potentially clarifying effect in personal consciousness.

While the British empiricist John Locke (d. 1704) was influenced by the hamfisted thinker Thomas Hobbes, who asserted that all knowledge was based on sensory perception, others might still prefer aspects of Plato, even though it is customary nowadays to denigrate this Greek as much as possible. A recent Darwinian description of Plato affords the usual derogatory caricature and a literal interpretation of symbolism in the *Dialogues*. If Plato was a wealthy aristocrat who believed that leisure was essential to wisdom, then there must nowadays be some leisurely academics who accomplish less in the way of wisdom for an exorbitant salary. The real point is, of course, that Plato "virtually rejected experiment and even observation;" his argument was that the senses deceive and hence are not to be trusted, since true knowledge comes only from "pure thought, unadulterated by evidence." If the only evidence is sensory, then this might be a fair caricature, but I am not persuaded of either. The interesting fact remains that it was Plato, and not the more empirical Aristotle, who championed the brain as the seat of the soul, even though Darwinists like to stipulate that he only acquired secondhand information about anatomy from the Greek scholars of medicine.[193]

Since leisure and official wisdom were still largely being denied to the working poor even in the supposedly enlightened days of the well-to-do Hume and Earl Russell, I fail to see why Plato should be an exceptional target for empirical distaste. It is not necessary to believe that Plato was the greatest philosopher of all time to find much of interest in the extant corpus attributed to him; one might well deem that Jili and other Asiatics greatly improved upon the brain as the seat of the soul in the qualifications of *khayal* and other subtleties.

A figure who cannot be considered anything of a wealthy elitist was Plotinus (d. 269/70 A.D.), whose ascetic policy included the eradication of all ancestral details. Yet there has been a very marked neglect of Plotinus in the classicist camp; he has been customarily relegated in importance by Platonist "purists" and Aristotelian bigots alike. It was only during the last generation or so that Plotinus has gained a footing of comparative equality in classicist studies, though there is still a wide gulf charted between him and his peers by conservative scholars. Fortunately however, classicists are now able to write that it is generally accepted that Plotinus is not an irrelevant curiosity to be cursorily dismissed by the conventional historian of Greek philosophy in a final paragraph. Instead, it is aptly stressed that critical research has concluded that Plotinus was "one of the last great thinkers of the pagan West."[194] He was clearly very distinct from the aberrant mysticism of the Phibionites.

It is perhaps inevitable that the ensuing Neoplatonist tradition is in general very little understood, in view of the comparatively recent uprating of its contents. Some have remained satisfied with merely noting its differences from Christianity. Hume was an earlier case in point, observing in his *Dialogues concerning Natural Religion* (1779) that "many of the ancient Platonists, particularly Plotinus" specified that reality did not consist in acts of veneration or reverence for Deity, but in "a certain mysterious Self Annihilation or total Extinction of all our Faculties." Hume was distinctively cautious in adding that "these ideas are, perhaps, too far stretch'd."[195] While such ideas (at least insofar as Hume represented them) evidently remained a mystery to rationalists and empiricists alike, Hume disregards them with much less vigour than did the pious Kant. Hume conceivably felt that these ancient ideas were more apt than the prevalent Christian faith.

It is well known to Islamicist scholars that it was not so much Platonism, but Neoplatonism, that was taken up by philosophers in the Islamic world. That is to say, texts of Plato were known to the latter, but the Plotinian perspective strongly coloured the Platonism of *falasifa* (philosophers) like Al-Farabi. Indeed, the Aristotelian tradition amongst the Muslims was, in many cases, very partisan to the *Enneads* owing to a version of Plotinus that was in circulation under the name of Aristotle. The so-called *Theology of Aristotle* (*Aristotalis Uthulujiya*) was translated into Arabic during the ninth century; it was actually a commentary of Porphyry on the *Enneads*, though using an Aristotelian framework.[196] Porphyry was a semi-Aristotelian disciple of Plotinus. His commentary enabled some Muslim Aristotelians to avoid the cul-de-sac of syllogistic logic, since Plotinus inspired in them a more holistic pitch of thought. While for most Latin-speaking scholars, Aristotle was merely a great scientist and logician, to Arabic-speaking philosophers Aristotle was both a great scientist and a great mystic. (This was how Roger Bacon conceived of Aristotle also).

If it be considered a factual error for such a confusion of

entities to have occurred, then it must also be accounted a fact that several leading Aristotelians of the Islamic world were mystics of exceptional calibre in addition to their more empirical and logical achievements.

## The Philosophy of Illumination

One of the trends which maintained an Aristotelian ingredient was the ishraqi tradition of Iran. Henry Corbin's extreme anti-scientific penchant caused him to misrepresent this tradition by referring to it as Platonist.[197] Yet this tag is a very inadequate description here, since not one of the ishraqis can be called a Platonist in the sense that Western classicists apply to the term. Corbin's eschewing of specifically Aristotelian elements is wide of the mark historically. For instance, he virtually ignored the contributions of Qutubuddin Shirazi, who was an excelling scientist and very much an Aristotelian in certain aspects of his approach. In fact, Corbin's perspective on this subject tends to represent the Renaissance humanism of Europe rather than the ishraqi tradition.

Ishraqi method, howsoever ignored by modern scholars, involved a preliminary exegesis in Aristotelian or logical format.[198] The objective was not to become enmeshed in logic, for which reason there was a contrary stress, but a person unfledged in a basic discipline of the mind was not considered amenable to greater flights of the developing human intelligence.

In one of his "Aristotelian" treatises, Shaikh Shihabuddin Yahya Sohravardi Maqtul (d. 1191) informed his reader that he was deliberately restraining the subject matter in order to conform with Peripatetic practice, though commenting that if the treatise was studied carefully, "treasures hidden under a thin veil" would be disclosed. To use the felicitous translation of Corbin, Maqtul added in this passage: "If the half-wit is unable to discover them (i.e. the treasures), the fault is not mine."[199]

In the same Arabic treatise, Maqtul expressed in poetical language the historical (and prehistoric) origins of his philosophy of illumination (*ishraq*). He depicted a confluence of two ancient streams: one Greek, deriving from the legendary Hermes Trismegistus, and the other Iranian, deriving from the legendary Kai Khusrau.[200] The latter is effectively analogous with Zarathushtra in Maqtul's circumspect presentation, which was of pronounced heretical implications in the eyes of Islamic orthodoxy. The Greek pedigree is Neoplatonic and Pythagorean, and elsewhere Maqtul specifically aligns his philosophy of *ishraq* with ancient pre-Islamic Iranian sages who were *not* Magians, and also with the mystical experience of "Plato" and his predecessors.[201] There are two points of basic importance here: (a) that the ancient Iranian sages bore no resemblance to Magians, i.e. Zoroastrian priests, a detail commonly overlooked, and hence leading to ill-founded associations with the clerical superstructure of Zoroastrian tradition; Sohravardi was definitely asserting an ancient Iranian precedent, but one should not look to the orthodox Mazdean scriptural tradition for this link,[202] which will inevitably result in puzzlement (b) the entity described as "Plato" was actually Plotinus, an equation proven by the custom amongst ishraqi authors of attributing to Plato the account of unitive experience (sometimes inadequately described as "ecstasy") found in the *Enneads* of Plotinus. The relevant passage from the *Enneads*[203] was known to them from the "Theology of Aristotle," but the ishraqis knew that it was not Aristotle who had been the author. Maqtul cited part of this passage in his *Kitab Hiqmat al-Ishraq*,[204] which he evidently considered to be one of his more advanced works. So high was the repute of this Plotinian passage in ishraqi circles that Maqtul's commentator Qutubuddin Shirazi wrote out the entire passage, perhaps a memorable penchant for an empirical mystic who knew the limitations of syllogistic logic.

It was Corbin who insisted upon the uneasy rendering of Maqtul's philosophy as "theosophy." This is misleading in its associations and inaccurate in terms of the meaning of words. The key phrase *hiqmat al-ishraq* is more accurately rendered as "wisdom of illumination,"[205] particularly since Maqtul's philosophy deals in part with experiences of "light," which refers to a complex progression of psychological states that have so far been poorly explained by scholars.

In his *Kitab Hiqmat al-Ishraq* (Book of the Wisdom of Illumination), Maqtul describes fifteen types of such *ishraqat* (illuminations), but adds very soberly that: "These photisms mark a half-way stage at which some stop."[206] Corbin did not successfully explain such complexities; phenomenological concern with "mystical" experiences needs to take more account of which ones are really desirable.

Maqtul asserted that he had revived in the last-mentioned treatise the ancient Iranian philosophy of illumination and the illumined experiences of "Plato" and his predecessors.[207] The question of revival in terms of an exact duplication of external characteristics is one of the stumbling-blocks in the conception of a perennial philosophy. Some scholars have expressed scepticism concerning the factor of Maqtul having been the literal heir of ancient Iranian thought. Bearing in mind here that they tend to think of the priestly Mazdean tradition, their scepticism is quite justified, but even if it could be categorically proven which pre-Islamic tradition it was that he was referring to, the literalists might still insist upon known differences of verbal expression.

It should be more obvious than it is that cultural changes in linguistic media impose a limit upon the factor of exact duplication of past verbal formulations. For instance, Maqtul was not writing his technical works in Pahlavi, but in Arabic, and in an allusive style employing heavy symbolism such as would be least offensive to the prevailing custodians of religious law. The Persian language itself had undergone pronounced changes even since Sassanian times; it is not necessary to focus upon the Arabicized revival of Pahlavi here, since the compilation of the *Denkart* amongst Islamic era Zoroastrians reveals the fluctuations of language occurring even amongst the most conservative parties. But far outweighing such considerations is the primary factor of essential philosophy (= love of wisdom) being a matter of experiential expertise; linguistic media afford no reliable register here, since it is only in the realm of verbalized philosophy that finesse can be measured in terms of words. The holistic ingredient in a philosopher like Maqtul is something in addition to the verbal prowess displayed, though the latter ingredient has its own importance and is denied value only by those shallow mystics who have no particular finesse to cultivate in any way. Their version of the perennial philosophy is generally one in which the most simplistic priorities are favoured (and sometimes even no priorities at all).

The orientation of mind implied by the ishraqi convergence of the Greek and Iranian streams of illumination is further complicated for simplistic assessment owing to the specific incorporation of earlier Islamic era sufi entities. There is nothing orthodox in Maqtul's specified pedigree: his human hinge for the Hermetic stream was the sufi mystic (and heretic) Dhu'l Nun al-Misri,[208] while the arch-heretic Hallaj is the intermediary for the Iranian stream,[209] along with the extremely unorthodox Bayazid al-Bistami.[210] These ascriptions do not resemble the standardized "sufi" lineages of the dervish orders, and are given in an altogether wider and more perennial context that ignores religious boundaries.

Maqtul was therefore indicating, in a sophisticated manner, an experiential transmission that could not be confined within any doctrinal format. He does not say exactly how such a transmission worked, but one suspects that, given sufficient scope for a verbal elucidation, his explanation would have been different to that expressed in much popular Sufism. Certainly, there is absent from his writings the insidious dogmatism of the kind which rigidly equates sufis with Islam.[211]

The incorporation of Hermes in the Greek branch of the ishraqi confluence is readily explained by the familiarity of Maqtul with (at least part of) the corpus of Hermetic texts, which had been translated into Arabic. This corpus dates approximately from the era of Plotinus, and though commonly considered as Egyptian in origin, also has strong associations with the Syriac milieu of Harran.[212] The Arabic-speaking savants viewed the legendary Hermes Trismegistus (whom these texts extol) as a very archaic entity, associating him with the archaic prophet Idris mentioned in the *Quran*. Thus Maqtul considered Hermes to have antedated Pythagoras, both entities being closely associated in accordance with the Sabean tradition of Harran. The associations with Idris enabled a certain respectability in orthodox Islamic eyes, but Maqtul was one of those Hermeticists (*haramisah*) whose emphases gained heretical proportions.

A selection of passages from Maqtul's *Kitab Hiqmat al-Ishraq*, long known in English translation, has still not been sufficiently well evaluated in the literature. A review of some emphases found in this selection is relevant here. The statement is found that: "Our master is Plato, especially in his works *Timaeus* and *Phaedo*." This is much more specific of the Arabo-Persian knowledge of the real Plato, not to mention Socrates, who looms particularly large in the *Phaedo*. But further, "we find ourselves in agreement also with Hermes of Egypt." The author specifies that, related to both these ancient philosophies is the wisdom expounded by "the ancient Persians who lived before the Greeks," a wisdom which was *not* the doctrine of the Magians (i.e. Mazdean priests) and nor the teaching of Mani. Though Aristotle was "a great philosopher," his importance should not be exaggerated, urges Maqtul, here expressly criticizing Ibn Sina. Intuitive philosophers of Greece, Persia, and India had experienced perceptions of the "incorporeal lights" in freeing themselves from material restrictions. These "lights," says Maqtul, were referred to by the "virtuous sage and perfect *imam* (leader) Zaradusht of Azerbaijan" in his book *Zend*. This is apparently a reference to the prophet Zarathushtra, who was (mistakenly) believed by the Zoroastrians to have been active in Azerbaijan in north-west Iran; it may not have been the *Zend-Avesta* to which Maqtul was referring, but to one of the later treatises in vogue amongst his Zoroastrian contemporaries. More to the point perhaps, Maqtul asserts that the proof of such teachings does not reside in mere convictions that what "Plato," Pythagoras, and other intuitive philosophers had said was correct; rather, it resides only in the immediate experiential certainty of the illumination(s) signified. In other words, the illuminated philosopher knows the truth with a certainty not possessed by those who merely accept assertions at secondhand, as a doctrine taught by Plato, Plotinus, and others.

Maqtul and his pre-Safavid ishraqi commentators show a clear grasp of the differences between experience and reliance upon faith in matters of mystical philosophy.

The same excerpted passages include a reflection not readily acceptable to some current exegetes of mystical philosophy. Maqtul (approvingly) states that Pythagoras, Socrates, Plato, and Hermes Trismegistus[213] taught the transmigration of souls, as did the ancient philosophers of Egypt, Babylonia, Iran, India, and China.[214] Maqtul inevitably adopted a critical attitude to the subject of transmigration as it was conventionally represented, i.e., the inadequate notion that human souls transferred to animal bodies. In other works, Maqtul rejects the conventional idea of transmigration, but in the *Hiqmat al-Ishraq* he did not repudiate the subject. Possibly because he was on the defensive, he observed that the arguments which sought to disprove transmigration (*tanasukh*) were no more effective than those which supported it (in its distorted form). Some later ishraqis were much more in explicit favour of *tanasukh*.

It emerges here that Sohravardi Maqtul had an unusual affinity with a large number of ancient traditions, a vista which is too broad for some metaphysical digestive systems accustomed to a narrow diet. Pythagorean and NeoPythagorean, Platonic and Neoplatonic, Aristotelian, Zarathushtran, Hermetic, and Indian, is not an exhaustive list of these affinities. In such passages as those mentioned above, there is a striking absence of piety; there is no religious insularism, no dependence upon Semitic prophetology.

Though Maqtul criticized extremist Aristotelians for their neglect of intuitive faculties, it was not the logicians who were the cause of his premature death at the age of only thirty-eight. This event was due to the schemes of the fanatical *ulama*, the Islamic doctors of the law. The scene was Aleppo, in Syria, where the outspoken Iranian philosopher collided with the intolerance of the traditionalist theologians. The official decorum of pious vindictiveness was the order of the day, and the victim was thereafter known as *al-maqtul*, "the murdered." The charges brought against him were for teachings against Islam.

The bigots would not have wished to acknowledge any merits in such statements as that made by Sohravardi Maqtul in the powerful introduction to his *Kitab Hiqmat al-Ishraq*: "The world was never wholly without philosophy and without someone who cultivated it and was declared a philosopher by manifest proofs and facts. This man is the real Caliph or representative of God on earth . . ."[215] This theme of the perennial philosopher is a very sophisticated restatement of the *imam* ("leader") theme, which appears in very different treatments. In its common signification, the *imam* theme is associated with the official Shia doctrine, but this was not what Maqtul was discussing; there are much closer affinities with the Platonist "political science" of Farabi, who had reaccentuated themes found in Plato's *Republic*, in addition to his more Aristotelian achievements. Both Farabi and Maqtul proved that they were far above the sunni versus shia temperament.

One may agree with Nasr that Maqtul considered himself to be the reviver of the perennial wisdom, or *hiqmat al-ladunniyyah*, which he asserted to have existed always, among the Hindus, Persians, Babylonians, Egyptians, and Greeks.[216] Maqtul had not been the first philosopher of the Islamic era to emphasize pre-Islamic wisdom in Iranian channels. The Iranian annalist Miskawayh (d. 1030) had done this in his *Al-Hiqmat al-khalidah*, a treatise which ranges over the thought and writings of many philosophers of the Islamic and pre-Islamic eras, including entities of ancient Iran, India, and the Mediterranean world. But Miskawayh and other writers did not express the same depth perspective as Maqtul, "who considered himself the resurrector of the wisdom of the ancient Persians."[217]

In relation to the Iranian context, Maqtul's philosophy may be considered to have an advantage over the Neoplatonism of his predecessor Farabi, but reflections upon the latter as an Aristotelian have only a partial validity in view of his appreciation of Pythagoras, Plato, and Plotinus.[218]

Another philosopher who was familiar with Porphyry's commentary on Plotinus was Mulla Sadra Shirazi (d. 1640), an ishraqi who admirably repeated Maqtul's claim of a perennial wisdom having existed since the beginning of human history.[219] But Mulla Sadra's presentation notably included scholastic theology (*kalam*) as a salient, and was to mark an increasing formalization of the ishraqi tradition in Iran, rendering it largely sterile in the hands of theologians. Sadra's amalgamation of ishraqi teaching with the new Shi'ite orthodoxy was inevitable owing to his institutional role in the oppressive Safavid milieu; he himself came under accusation of heresy, though not fatally.

Meanwhile, Zoroastrian ishraqis had emigrated from the oppressive Iranian climate to the more liberal zone of Mughal India. This and related events have been rendered needlessly obscure, and also distorted, owing to sheer neglect of the data. For instance, there is no evidence that Azar Kaivan was a priest, as has commonly been asserted. This was a nineteenth century invention of Parsi lore in India, and cannot be traced to the *Dabistan*. Other factors that have obscured events are the result of a scholastic disdain for sociology and any close attention to history, such as typified Corbin's phenomenological approach. The limelight has been bestowed entirely upon Mulla Sadra and a handful of other Muslim philosophers of the era in question. Ignored are such sociological facts as the stigmatization of the Zoroastrian minority by Muslims, and more particularly by Muslim theologians. Even the most brilliant Zoroastrian philosophers in the Greek idiom were ineligible for teaching posts in Islamic milieux. Several of them became small-time merchants in order to maintain themselves, participating in the "underground" trading activities which were cultivated by harassed Zoroastrians who were restricted in their means of livelihood to manual occupations. For Zoroastrian ishraqi philosophers there was a further vocational advantage in trading activities in India, since they were enabled to avoid public exposure of an undesirable kind, the popular Muslim mind having elaborated "alchemical" expectations of making gold in relation to anything Hermetic. The *Dabistan* relates how the Zoroastrian ishraqi Farzaneh Behram ibn Farhad (d. 1624) wore the garb of a small-time trader in order to avoid interruptions from the vulgar, who were liable to identify him as an alchemist. Even then, some thought that he was devoting himself to (literal) alchemy in secret.[220] This was a consequence of the legend which had attributed to Sohravardi Maqtul possession of the "philosopher's stone" and the knowledge of making gold.[221] This attribution had come about as a consequence of the association of ishraqis with the Hermetic tradition, which is a justifiable association only if the nature of Hermeticism is properly understood in its application by illumined philosophers.

## The Western Magi

When the mathematician and occultist Dr. John Dee (d. 1608) demonstrated callow Western enthusiasm for the alchemy and Hermeticism of the European Renaissance, these trends were increasingly removed from their (then) obscure Eastern origins. Even Dee had his good points by comparison with later occultists such as the nineteenth century "magus" Eliphas Levi. Dee was a very passable mathematician by the standards of his time; the same cannot be said for Eliphas Levi, whose magical preoccupations perhaps cannot even be dignified with the Cantabrian stigma of bad philosophy.

The mythology of the Magus (Greek: *magos*) was a peculiarly Western innovation. The Latin plural of magus is magi, the word denoting the priestly tribe or caste of the Medes of Iran; Zarathushtra now appears to have long predated these magi. Greek antiquity had conceived of Zarathushtra as a *magos*, in the sense of hierophant, reputedly the author of alchemical treatises; yet Greek perspectives on Zarathushtra were not as uniform as is sometimes supposed. Some of the Greek writers probably had a more sophisticated perspective on Zarathushtra, the hierophant of the mysteries, than was current in the Italian Renaissance, when the Magus concept was enthusiastically taken up by avowed (Christian) Platonists. In that they were reacting to medieval orthodoxy, one can sympathize with the new spirit of liberality, but the disparities with Eastern events are too marked not to pass without due comment.

The confusing Greek report that Pythagoras had been taught by Zarathushtra, "master of the magi," was less misleading than some emphases of the Italian Renaissance. One inspiration for the latter trend was the Byzantine Platonist Georgius Gemistus Plethon (*c.*1355–1452), who mistakenly ascribed the text known as the *Chaldean Oracles* to Zarathushtra or his magian disciples. This has resulted in the modern scholarly accusation that Plethon had little sense of history.[222] But he was decidedly unusual in medieval Christian annals for elevating the role of Zarathushtra on a par with that of Plato, and for being in defiance of established religious norms. His chief work *The Laws* was assigned to the double patronage of Zarathushtra and Plato, and was anything but an orthodox Christian treatise.

There are still several factors relating to Plethon's life and thought that are unclear.[223] Henry Corbin suggested an affinity between Sohravardi Maqtul and Plethon, even dubbing the latter an "ishraqi" of Byzantium. Corbin thought it possible that Plethon's teacher, the mysterious Jew Elisha, was himself an ishraqi, and compared this obscure entity with another Jew historically known as an ishraqi: namely Sa'd ibn Kammuna, who was an early commentator on the writings of Maqtul. The encounter between Elisha and Plethon is reported to have occurred at the court of the Turkish sultan not long prior to the fall of Byzantium.[224] It seems very feasible that Plethon was acquainted with an ishraqi intelligence, but whether Plethon himself was an ishraqi (in the highly qualified sense) is more debateable.

There are several basic differences discernible between the format of Sohravardi Maqtul and that of Plethon, even though the latter was probably closer to Eastern sources than any of his "Neoplatonist" successors in the Italian Renaissance. Plethon is very strongly implicated in the revival of "Hellenized Magi" concepts, which whatever their value, were amenable to blurred historical perspectives.[225] It should be emphasized that Western scholarship has since disproved various leading attributions made by the Western "Magi" from Plethon onwards, but that these errors did not apply to the ishraqi tradition. Unlike Plethon and his successors in Italy, Maqtul did not conflate Platonism with Zoroastrianism; he did not utilize the *Chaldean Oracles*, and what is even more to the point, he disavowed the magian heritage of the Mazdean priests. Maqtul veered away from theological involvement, he did not reject Aristotelian science as an ingredient of his philosophy. His archaic Hermes Trismegistus was specifiable as the antediluvian Idris, which gives his Hermetic "pedigree" a different chronological framework to the European. In all these matters, his format differed from Italian Renaissance concepts and practice. This leaves only one major similarity: the stipulation of a perennial philosophy in which various antique names figured. Yet he is often strangely ignored in considerations of this latter phenomenon.

Plethon established a school of Platonism at Mistra in the Peloponnese. His teaching received castigation from theological and Aristotelian contemporaries, though his penchant for Greek polytheism did not prevent his participation in the more liberal affairs of the Christian church. In 1438 he acted as an adviser to the Greek delegation attending the Council of Florence, their aim being to negotiate the reunion of the Eastern and Western churches. But he seems to have taken little interest in the proceedings, and while in Italy, is reported to have inspired Cosimo Medici to found his own Platonic Academy. What relation such academies bore to the original is a pertinent question, but they undoubtedly contributed to a new and liberal trend of thought and cultural research.

As a virtual apostate from Christianity, Plethon was a very different figure to that of his liberal contemporary Cardinal Nicholas of Cusa (1401–1464). This German dignitary has gained a mystical reputation, and is often cited as an influence on Leibniz. He attempted to promote a conciliation amongst religious factions, but in a different context of thinking to that of Plethon, Ficino, or Mirandola, who were all deeply concerned with the revival of classical Greek philosophy and other non-Christian traditions.

Plethon's inspiration was a major cause behind the Platonic Academy of Marsilio Ficino (1433–99). But unlike Plethon, he was a priest, and showed more concern for theological orthodoxy than either his predecessor or his younger contemporary Pico della Mirandola (1463–94). He was nevertheless a leading text scholar in this era of "rediscovered" Greek manuscripts from Byzantium; Ficino produced notable editions and translations of the Hermetic corpus, the Dialogues of Plato, and the *Enneads* of Plotinus. Yet his researches in Greek were attended by errors that loom large in the eyes of more recent scholars and philosophers. Like many other Christian Platonists, Ficino believed that Plato had known the Pentateuch, an association which later enabled Steuco to confer the title of *divinus Plato* upon the disciple of Socrates. (By way of comparison, Farabi and other philosophers of the Islamic milieux had called Plato *Aflatun al-ilahi*, "the divine Plato," but they were not theologians).

Ficino followed Plethon in emphasizing the role of Zarathushtra as a master of ancient philosophy, or rather *philosophia priscorium* to use the Latin term (also rendered as *prisca philosophia*). Nasr has affirmed that this designation is "exactly the same" as the *hiqmat al-'atiqah* (ancient wisdom) of Sohravardi Maqtul.[226] This is not intrinsically unreasonable, though there are important differences discernible in the usage of the respective terms. In Ficino's usage, the *prisca philosophia* rather fluently became the *prisca theologia*, which arguably altered the context substantially. Ficino was referring to a lengthy religio-philosophical tradition which he considered to derive from Moses. But Ficino's syncretism was loaded in favour of Christianity; he affirmed that true theology began with Christianity. Somehow supporting this uniqueness in time was the less theological event of true philosophy (*vera philosophia*), which originated with Plato, who was in turn heir to the older wisdom of Zarathushtra, Hermes, Orpheus, and Pythagoras. True philosophy was considered to be the same as true religion in Ficino's view, but one might observe that Plotinus and many other pagan philosophers would have been at acute odds with this equation of Christian Platonism.

Ficino's concept of *prisca theologia* (ancient theology) has been traced back to Plutarch, Diogenes Laertius, Iamblichus, Proclus, and other ancient writers, including even Christians like Augustine of Hippo.[227] A well known statement of Augustine affirms that the Christian religion existed among the ancients, even since the beginning of the human race. This seems to have been a counter to certain pagan philosophers who credited (then) ancient theologians with a knowledge of the truth. The question of precisely which ancient "theologians" are relevant here is still a subject of confusion, particularly in popular literature.

In asserting Christian priorities, it was much easier for Ficino to incorporate an otherwise controversial emphasis: Plethon's elevation of Zarathushtra (or rather Zoroaster as he was known in Greek idiom). In addition to the Hermetic corpus, Ficino also emphasized the importance of the *Chaldean Oracles*, which he firmly believed to have been composed by Zarathushtra. The work generally known as the *Chaldean Oracles* has been dismissed by many scholars as being in the "astrology and magic" category. It was definitely not written by Zarathushtra, who antedated it by many centuries. Even the tag of "Chaldean" is misleading, since modern scholarship has (though not unanimously) deemed it to have been written by two hellenized Asiatics in the time of Marcus Aurelius. Julian the Chaldean and his homonymous son were not typically Platonist, though they did incorporate elements of contemporary Platonist teaching in their much more theurgic treatise. The eminent scholar Arthur Darby Nock commented that it is very difficult to be sure of the meaning of anything in the *Chaldean Oracles*, and there are still current differences of view as to the contents. This is not altogether surprising in view of the fact that this "treatise" consists of fragments.[228]

While European scholars did not discover the Gathas of Zarathushtra for another three centuries, the resources of Arabic and Hebrew were increasingly plumbed (though by no means thoroughly) by scholars like Pico della Mirandola, a contemporary of Ficino who was less orthodox in his approach but short-lived. This advocate of the *philosophia priscorium* researched the philosophers of the Islamic world insofar as these were available to him, and exhibited a penchant for the Jewish Qabbalah. It is easier for some moderns to follow his version of a perennial wisdom than that of Ficino. Several of his theses were condemned by the church. He even sanctioned the *Quran*. Reminiscent of

Muslim philosophers like Farabi, Mirandola favoured the concept of a fundamental unity between Aristotle and Plato; this contrasted with the approach of both Ficino and Plethon, who had emphasized the inferiority of Aristotle (and hence the sciences) in the less Neoplatonic vein.

There is some cause here to assert certain similarities between Mirandola and Roger Bacon. Both of these esotericists were partial to the Arabic and Jewish traditions; both possessed an Aristotelian streak, though Bacon's was actually more substantial. In fact, the heretical Friar Bacon should really be counted amongst the advocates of a perennial wisdom (which some have neglected to do). Though he shows an ignorance of Zarathushtra, and was not so conversant with Greek texts as his Renaissance successors, Bacon did assert an antique and esoteric tradition of knowledge via his glosses to the *Secretum Secretorum*, conceiving of a "universal science" which encompassed all the secrets of nature. This science he conceived as being known to the Hebrews, the "Chaldeans," and the Egyptians prior to its acquisition by Aristotle. Bacon's Christianized glosses here applied to an Arabic treatise which purported to relay Aristotle's advice to Alexander the Great. This "Aristotelian" treatise indicated that the esoteric science was concealed in enigmatic language; Bacon believed that it could be rediscovered by someone morally and mentally qualified to do so. This Arabic treatise appears to have inspired him to leave Paris *c.*1247, where he had been pursuing a mastership in theology. Instead he returned to Oxford, to become an empirical polymath and mystic.[229]

It was a more theological pen than those of Mirandola or Bacon which employed the first discernible use of the term *philosophia perennis*, which has come to represent the concept of a perennial philosophy more than any other Latin designation. The present author cannot see eye to eye with pedantic insistences upon this Latinization, insistences which tend to a markedly ethnocentric perspective.

The work entitled *De perenni philosophia* (1540) was written by Agostino Steuco (1497–1548), who adapted the title from the earlier Renaissance scholars. Steuco was an Augustinian theologian, a Biblical scholar who was a liberal

Roman Catholic but nevertheless anti-Lutheran. This is more understandable when one realizes that he preferred pagan philosophy to the Reformation doctrines; he even found Stoic philosophy acceptable, a point in his favour perhaps by comparison with the pious Kant. Yet Steuco also constrained the perennial in a theological context. Steuco was more erudite than many of his contemporaries, being conversant with Arabic and Hebrew, and acting as librarian of the Vatican library. But it has been aptly stressed that Steuco placed too much confidence in the *prisca theologia*.[230] In his exegesis he relied upon writings which were later proven to be much later than the Renaissance scholars had supposed. The *Chaldean Oracles* and the Hermetic Corpus do not predate the Christian era. The Renaissance did not possess the key to Zarathushtra or to Idris, in addition to other features of non-clarity.

Though scholastics and church orthodoxy opposed Steuco's idea of the perennial, there were many others who attempted a compromise between Christianity and Platonism, including the humanist scholar Erasmus. Yet on the whole, such enthusiasm was heavily weighed down by customary justifications of local doctrines. For instance, Francescus Patricius was the keen editor of the larger recension (1591) of the *Chaldean Oracles*, and wrote that "Zoroaster, first of all people, almost laid the foundations, however rough, of the Catholic faith."[231] Such scholarship is not held in high repute today.

The Christian interpreters identified Zarathushtra with the Old Testament tradition, and hence aligned him with Ezekiel and other Jewish prophets; in this way he could be juxtaposed with Jesus. But this sort of doctrinal assimilation in theology had been occurring long before. From Justin onwards, the Christian apologists had cited Zoroaster and the Magi as being among their witnesses to the truth of Christianity.[232] The theological approach tended to bemuse scholarship for a long time after.

While the *prisca theologia* transpired to be a cul-de-sac, there remained the prospects of wisdom in rejuvenation. But the *prisca philosophia* was set at naught in the writings of Rene Descartes and Sir Francis Bacon, despite the indications of something less inductionist in the latter. Even if Descartes was not influenced by Jesuit thought, as some have suggested, his theological cage was supplemented by an elaborate mathematical device for neglecting all the insistences and nuances of Neoplatonism.

Spinoza had a great deal to renounce in the wake of Descartes, and did not venture into the more encyclopaedic ranges covered by Gottfried Wilhelm Von Leibniz. It was left to the latter polymath to specify the *philosophia perennis* in a famous letter to Remond penned in 1714, in which he observed that truth is more extensive than had previously been thought, and that its trace can be found among the ancients. Aldous Huxley was wrong in asserting that the term *philosophia perennis* was first used by Leibniz; it is much more accurate to deduce with Schmitt that Leibniz seems to have been the first to use the term without referring to Steuco the theologian.

As a rationalist, Leibniz makes a good deal more sense to some than Descartes. Certainly, his defence of the *philosophia perennis* means that the subject is much more valid in Western philosophy than has hitherto been acknowledged by conventional attitudes. Leibniz knew of Steuco's treatise by 1687, much earlier in his career than the letter to Remond. But the influences upon his thinking were much more varied in this direction; Mirandola and Ficino are amongst the more obvious influences which have been detected. Critics have disliked his metaphysical flights, but then they similarly dislike the less empirical side of Newton, the mathematical rival of Leibniz. It may have been a scientific reflection that caused Leibniz to remark in his *Discourse on Metaphysics* that "the opinions of the theologians and of the so-called scholastic philosophers are not to be wholly despised." But he does not deem such opinions to be wholly acceptable. It has been urged that Leibniz may have understood better than any of his contemporaries the importance of accurately evaluating the history of philosophy – involving the ability to discern what is valuable in all systems and all periods of history.[233] One might agree in the context of Western philosophy, though it is perhaps incumbent to state that he may have neglected certain features in the life of Spinoza, despite the fact that his polymathic output vastly exceeded that of his older contemporary.

Though much has been made of the Leibnizian emphasis upon reunion of the churches as a moral goal, at the end of his life Leibniz was stigmatized by the clergy of Hanover as a "believer in nothing" owing to his unorthodox beliefs. He died a virtual heretic.

The subsequent rationalists of Western philosophy left the *philosophia perennis* in total neglect, much as the empirics did. The pious moralism of Kant and the ethnocentric Hegelian philosophy of history were not conducive to an accurate evaluation of the history of philosophy.[234] Even the radical Schopenhauer does not qualify owing to his incomplete excursion into Oriental subjects.

In fairness to later rationalists however, it must be said that Steuconian *theologia* was misleading. Steuco identified the perennial with external religion, which seriously mitigates its philosophical validity. This is still a common error in twentieth century versions. Steuco did not want to think of the reforms needed in the auspices of his contemporary *theologia*. He did not allow for perennial follies.

Further, even Leibniz did not reach an in-depth focus in the *philosophia perennis*, perhaps because he was too weighted with perspectives of the Italian Renaissance. For instance, one looks in vain in the Leibniz archives for an answer to the Zarathushtra problem. Yet this cannot be considered a particular fault of his, since even the leading contemporary specialist in this subject arrived at the wrong answer, and at some length.

## The Kaivani School of Ishraq

Despite the interest in Zarathushtra amongst diverse antiquarians and occultists of Renaissance Europe, throughout the ensuing seventeenth century the humanist scholars remained ignorant of the fact that Zoroastrianism was still existent in Iran and India. Zoroastrian tradition was entirely an event of the past for these savants, who possessed only fractional textual material on this subject from Iran. The first comprehensive history of philosophy achieved its second edition in 1687, when Leibniz was still in the early phase of his polymathic career; this was Thomas Stanley's *History of Philosophy*. It could boast chapters on the "chaldeans" and Sabeans, with whatever accuracy was then current, but its readers were under the impression that everything Zoroastrian was long dead and gone.

Subsequently, a steady trickle of missionaries and travellers in the East contributed various items of information tht remedied this erroneous impression. But clarity was another matter. The Oxford savant (and divine) Thomas Hyde wrote his treatise *De vetere religione Persarum* (Oxford, 1700) still very much in ignorance of very recent Zoroastrian events, let alone more ancient ones. A contemporary Iranist scholar has described Hyde's magnum opus as "the work of an apologist, of a man to whom everything in human history gravitates around Christianity."[235] Hyde's version of monotheism was determinedly opposed to dualism, this being closely associated with the heretical Cathars of the medieval era, who were then still synonymous with the detested Manichees. In some respects at least, Hyde's detour around heresy was equivalent to a travesty of the truth.

Nearly a whole century was to elapse before Sir William Jones discovered the *Dabistan*, though the full significance of this mid-seventeenth century Persian treatise was to be even longer in dawning. Meanwhile, a further chapter in the length chain of perennial achievements had occurred, despite the perennial ignorance in accompaniment. What had occurred amongst Zoroastrians in Safavid Iran and Mughal India was an authentic (as distinct from "Western magi") esoteric variant of Zarathushtran associations – one that was not Magian (i.e. Mazdean orthodoxy), that was of Sabean (= Hermetic) undertones but without any literalist alchemy, that was liberal to a markedly unusual degree, and unpretentious (e.g. no credentials of Platonic Academies). All this has been largely ignored even in the annals of mystical enthusiasm, and even vilified by dogmatists.

The lengthy chapter in the *Dabistan* on Zoroastrianism is

highly unorthodox, to the extent that it is difficult for some to see how the poetical name of the author could reflect anything of a priestly identity. "Mobad Shah," to cite one name of the *Dabistan* author,[236] means approximately "priest-king," and seems almost a sufi pun, particularly when taken in conjunction with its variant of "Mulla Mobad." Since several of Azar Kaivan's Zoroastrian disciples bore the stylism of *mobad*, normally a Zoroastrian sacerdotal title for the priest of a fire temple, one is led to think that this stylism was used in a distinctly unorthodox manner in this school, to which other indications also point. Though my own conclusion is that Mobad Shah was a Zoroastrian by birth, I will not be dogmatic on this point. He could have been a very liberal Muslim of Persian blood. The contemporary latitude of Dara Shikoh and Sarmad, both officially Muslims, is proof enough that such categorizations are inessential in relation to essential philosophy.

The opening sections of Mobad Shah's chapter on Zoroastrianism describe an elaborate version of a symbolic astrology which is reminiscent of earlier Sabean lore. References to mythological "dynasties" (which Sir William Jones construed literally) and to "temples" of the planets (= kings) essentially relate to a developmental sequence in which the "sun" is the apogee. Hence the Kaivanis are designated by Mobad Shah as the Sipasis[237] or "adorers," i.e. of the symbolic sun. The astrological lore is stipulated to be the teaching of the Zoroastrian Sipasis.

The context of this "sun worship" is clearly conveyed in a statement of the Zoroastrian ishraqi Farzaneh Behram ibn Farhad (d. 1624), who wrote in his *Sharistan-i chahar chaman*: "With the aid of Azar Kaivan, I penetrated to the invisible, past the angelic world to the solar world, and hence to the centre of divine reality, attaining this union by means of revelations." This was written by a philosopher with a strong grounding in Aristotelian logic and natural philosophy, and who had trained under Azar Kaivan, the latter being known to his circle as "Lord of the sciences" (*Zhu'l-Ulum*).

This was definitely not theology in the accepted sense of the word, but rather an astral symbolism neutral to various theological traditions. There is to some extent a convergence with earlier ishraqi idioms, which also displayed an affinity with the Sabean lore associated with Harran, a lore which appears to have mediated something of the ancient Babylonian perspective.[238] This "Sabean" semblance lends Sipasi symbolism more of an affinity with ancient Elam[239] than orthodox Mazdean religion. The "sun-worshipping" Sipasi lore was a convenient non-dogmatic shorthand for a cosmopolitan neo-ishraqi grouping which extended to Irani Zoroastrians, Parsi Zoroastrians, Muslims, Hindus, Jews, and even (at least) one Christian. In its extension of the older ishraqi spirit of the antique, the Sipasi lore was a foil to the increasing dogmatism of the new hierocracy of Shi'ite clerics in Safavid Iran. It did strike a strong tangent from Mulla Sadra's compatibility with orthodoxy, though it was in affinity with Sohravardi Maqtul.

Though Proclus might have expressed a high approval of Sipasi formulation, some analysts have expressed annoyance at its obvious lack of resemblance to orthodox Zoroastrianism. There is no reliance upon Mazdean formulae, not even the Gathas. The accusers cannot see what is perennial in philosophy as distinct from doctrinal religion. A variant format of the underlying emphases is supplied in the biographical section of the *Dabistan*, where Azar Kaivan and his disciples are treated with a certain amount of Persian hyperbole.

A Muslim Aristotelian (and keen Plotinian) like Mir Abu'l Qasim Findiriski[240] did not view the lack of orthodoxy amongst the Kaivanis as a shortcoming. Instead he joined them in India as a "sun-worshipper." In such Peripatetic gnosis, the perennial truth was incomparably superior to half-truths and fractions of dogma excluding deeper horizons.

In the chapter on Zoroastrians, the *Dabistan* includes a version of the legend of Zarathushtra, one quite different to the priestly one inherited from the Pahlavi era, but which is very far from being in the Christian image of the *Chaldean Oracles*. But more conventional tastes are pandered to in the latter part of this chapter (not the Sipasi section) by the incorporation of an orthodox Parsi text. This latter is a ritual text, but immediately after reproducing this priestly item, Mobad Shah gives a Sipasi gloss which confers upon this text the status of a preliminary manual of religious law for those unprepared for any deeper truth. This is one reason for the antipathy of conservativist Parsis towards the *Dabistan.* Mobad Shah states that Zarathushtran teaching is "contained in enigmas and parables because, with the mass of society, fabulous narrations, though revolting to reason, excite stronger impressions." He indicates that orthodox Zoroastrian texts come under this category; he was here echoing the Arabic philosophical tradition of Farabi and others, which had given conventional religion a much lower status than philosophy. Here also one should remember that priestly Zoroastrians of the pre-modern era tended to believe that all the texts in their canon were derived from Zarathushtra, and not merely the Gathas. Mobad Shah explains that direct truths merely perplex those unprepared for them, whereas figurative expression meets with their approval. Only a minority of minds comprehend the certainty afforded in philosophy and the abstract truths of religion, while the majority abhor direct truths. "It therefore becomes necessary to clothe the maxims of philosophy in the vestments of law, in order that all classes of society may derive their appropriate advantages from that source."[241]

It is apparent that Mobad Shah was here criticizing the priestly formalists rather than the majority of all classes. A few pages further on, he affirms that philosophy is protected by enigmatic or metaphorical expressions from being misused by the ignorant, while sages can penetrate the metaphor. He mentions that such enigmatic expressions are ascribed to the Magians, but that what survives of this form of speech is only the "Little (*Kah*) Zand," known to orthodoxy. Whereas direct philosophy was expressed in the "Great (*Mah*) Zand," which was lost. This latter is also referred to as the law of Mahabad, the name given to an archaic sage in Sipasi mythology; the context is hence indicative of the great age of the philosophy that was unknown to the orthodox.

Mobad Shah's perspective here should not be confused

with the later interpretation of the Theosophical Society, which saw in Kaivani literature a support for the Western occultist contention that rituals concealed deep truths. The context is not the same. Henry Olcott's version of the *Desatir* (a related treatise) encouraged a preoccupation with ritual; some Parsi members of the Theosophical Society even created new rites. Fetishism tends to be typical of many forms of occultism; the direct truths of philosophy are obscured by ritualism, an inevitable occurrence on the part of those incapable of greater perceptions. Olcott's idea that ritual concealed inner meanings has its amusing dimensions.

In the *Desatir*, an unusual late Persian work exhibiting Kaivani characteristics,[242] a perennial tradition of ancient Iranian sages (or prophets) is depicted, but the anonymous author does not neglect to emphasize that during the interims, a stagnancy perennially occurred which necessitated a revival. Despite the accusations of mythology that have been levelled here, it is still a more satisfying answer in figurative terms than most (if not all) of those proposed by the Western hellenized and/or occultist magi (who can be said to include Olcott).

In the treatise known as *Mukashafat-i-Kaivan* (Revelations of Kaivan), written by a Zoroastrian disciple of Azar Kaivan known as Khuda Jui, it is emphasized that the aspirant on the path of a spiritual development should have certain qualifications. Skill in the medical sciences is advised in order that the practitioner may be able to regulate the fluctuations of his own organism. Further, "he must banish from his mind all articles of faith, systems, opinions, ceremonials." This effectively underlines the Kaivani requisite of non-dogmatism and non-ritualism, despite the tolerance extended to those who thought differently. To be "at peace with all" is another qualification, one reminiscent perhaps of the liberal policy of the Mughal emperor Akbar at the era under discussion, though Akbar himself was influenced by trends of a philosophical rather than monarchical nature. The same treatise advocates an austere contemplation, which will doubtless sound less appealing to some, though it may be that deep-rooted modern opinions on such matters are no more viable than other articles of faith which screen out possibilities of a psychological regulation of the mind and body.[243]

Mobad Shah's version of "peace with all" (Akbar's *sulh-i-kul*) did not mean an absence of criticism, any more than Akbar was amenable to the Hindu custom of *suttee*. The former was charitably adroit in his reflection upon Christian beliefs concerning the Day of Judgment. "Except Christians, nobody else will be found pure and holy,"[244] he comments. The rest of his chapter on Christianity is markedly impartial, and compares extremely well with the biased reporting that many Christian missionaries applied to Asiatic religions and philosophies.

What was it like for a liberally-minded investigator in the encounter with diverse religious traditions? The *Dabistan* reports how Mobad Khushi, a Zoroastrian disciple of Azar Kaivan, met many eminent religious entities prior to his novitiate under the "lord of the sciences." These eminent men included Zoroastrians, Muslims, Hindus, Christians, and Jews. They all wanted him to become a convert to their own brand of doctrine. According to Khushi's own report, all of these doctrinaire entities were prejudiced against rivals, even though each one declared himself as being free of bias.

The subject of reincarnation has met with a very doctrinaire repudiation from the monotheistic religions, and also the dualist religion of Zoroastrianism. The fact is that it was philosophy, and not theology, which championed this subject in countries west of India since the early Christian era. Mobad Shah was one of the Persian-speaking champions in this respect, and his statements tally substantially with those found in the *Desatir*, a slightly earlier Zoroastrian treatise. He can be criticized for not making certain clarifications in the manner of Aziz Nasafi; this may have been a specific flaw in Mobad Shah's understanding of Kaivani lore, though it is necessary to understand that his brief treatment was an advance upon popular Hindu ideas, with which it was in effect competing. The humane aspect of his *ahimsa* (non-violence) theme should not pass unheeded; seldom does any antique treatise stress non-violence to such an extent, and it quite surpasses the Greeks in this respect.

Mobad Shah includes reincarnation in the Sipasi section of his Zoroastrian chapter. His main concern seems to be with the alleviation of animal suffering, and reads more like a medieval version of the RSPCA than a metaphysical elaboration. He concedes that dangerous animals may legitimately be killed, but asserts that the slayer of harmless animals will take on the form of a predatory beast and accordingly receive due retribution (i.e. slaughter). In a similar idiom is his statement that a brutal man is liable to be reborn as an ox ready for the slaughter. This latter assertion does not appear to be made in an allegorical context, though it may be metaphorical. But definite symbolic overtones adhere to a reference to transmigration in the later chapter on philosophers, a reference occurring in a discussion of paradise and hell. The emphasis here seems a much more advanced one, since the "descents" into animal forms are said to comprise hell, i.e., the after-death state of those human entities fixated upon sense-pleasures. Humans who have contracted bad habits gravitate to one of the seven hells, though this is in part to be explained by their feeling of deprivation at the absence of sensual impressions. The base qualities of the soul here assume such guises as that of a serpent or a scorpion, a contrast to noble habits which assume more angelic manifestations in the heaven created by these tendencies. Mobad Shah adds that this is a Peripatetic teaching, though the philosophers he describes are ishraqis and more the Neoplatonic category of Aristotelian.[245]

In the Sipasi section, Mobad Shah writes that while most mishaps befalling humans can be explained as the consequence of past deeds, the fate of a just man is not to be regarded as such retribution, but rather as the consequences of oppression exerted by the temporal ruler.[246] This is a marked improvement upon brahmanical interpretations of the *karma* concept, since the priests of caste India invariably explained away all social anomalies in the light of non-priestly misdeeds. This despotic caste version of *karma* had in its wake such aberrant practices as *suttee* (*sati*), in which wives of caste Hindus immolated themselves on the funeral pyre for no real reason other than perennial habit sanctioned by ritualists.

*Suttee* was one of the Hindu customs disliked by the otherwise liberal monarch Akbar (rgd. 1556–1605), whose policy of tolerance enriched Mughal culture. Indeed, the *Dabistan* devotes a section to Akbar's *din-i-ilahi* ("divine faith"), which was not so much a religion as an eclectic trend of thought, one which has provoked much discussion amongst scholars. Mobad Shah gives due deference to the cosmopolitanism of this trend, which was largely instigated by the liberal Muslim thinker Abu'l Fazl Allami. Amongst its innovations was a prohibition of cow-sacrifice amongst Muslims as a conciliatory gesture to the underdog Hindus, to whom the cow was sacred. Certain Sipasi emphases in defence of harmless animals may have had a close relation to this Akbarian innovation, but not merely in relation to Muslims, since the Parsi priests of India were then still maintaining ritualistic norms via the sacrifice of sheep and goats. Mobad Shah, like the anonymous author of the *Desatir*, was hitting at ritualism in his *ahimsa* emphases.

Though some critics have attempted to depict the Kaivani school as having little or no literal bearing upon Zarathushtra, the irony of such conclusions is that they completely ignore the literal fact that the Gathas of Zarathushtra indicate a critique of animal sacrifice prevalent amongst the sacerdotalists of his uncertain era. A more logical conclusion is that the intervening priestly conservativists had ignored the spirit of the Zarathushtran event.

The philosophical Jew Sarmad was personally known to Mobad Shah, and appears to have been in strong affinity with the unorthodox Kaivani perspectives. He is prominently featured in the Jewish chapter of the *Dabistan*, which is brief and reads in a much more Qabbalistic vein than a rabbinical one. Sarmad had early become a Muslim during his more youthful days in Iran, though he was still sufficiently Judaicized for Mobad Shah to consider him a representative of the Jews. It is evident that Sarmad was nothing of a conservativist. He had early broadened his horizons by studying the works of Abu'l Qasim Findiriski and Mulla Sadra,[247] along with other philosophers, and had later adopted what seemed to Muslim critics a Hinduized ascetic lifestyle. He supplied Mobad Shah with a Persian translation of the opening chapters of *Genesis*, but it is apparent that his perspective on the Pentateuch was not of the conservative rabbinical type. According to the oblique Persian of Mobad Shah, Sarmad said that the spirit of the divine manifests in human entities, that hell and heaven are already experienced in the (pre-death) human state, that the human life is only one day in a total life-span of one hundred and twenty years. There is also a recondite reference to the human entity assuming partly the form of a mineral, partly that of a vegetable, and partly that of an animal, a reference which does not quite fit the Aristotelian perspective of the soul, much less the Talmudic.[248]

Undertones of *tanasukh* would not have added to Sarmad's popularity with the Muslim divines who were influential at the Mughal court. This ishraqi philosopher evidently possessed a biting wit in his criticism of those in high places, and was at acute loggerheads with the theologians who were pressing for a conservative social policy against the Hindus in the attempt to outmanoeuvre the liberal prince Dara Shikoh. Both he and his patron met an untimely end at the juncture of Aurangzeb's rise to the Mughal throne. In brief, Sarmad was executed for heresy.

An earlier Jewish philosopher who is strongly implicated as an ishraqi was Elisha, alias Elisaeus, the teacher of Georgius Gemistus Plethon. Elisaeus likewise met an untimely end, though not before having (at least partially) prepared Plethon in his role as intermediary in the subsequent re-emergence of classical Greek studies in Europe. In 1380 the young Plethon had travelled to the Turkish court at Brusa, where he was tutored by Elisaeus in Greek philosophy and the Muslim commentators. The available record is not sufficiently detailed to reveal ishraqi complexities, though it is thought that Plethon's acquaintance with Zarathushtran lore originated with this early phase. It was *c.*1390 that Elisaeus was burned at the stake by the Turkish authorities, probably for heresy.[249] Like Sarmad, he may have been too bold in philosophy to bend to perennial follies perpetrated in the guise of infallibility.

Sohravardi Maqtul was not the only ishraqi to meet a premature end. Nor was he the only ishraqi to indicate that perennial husks are not the perennial kernel.

The Sabean associations of Maqtul's *Book of the Temples of Light* (*Hayakil al-Nur*) were early commented upon by a French orientalist, who also found ishraqi correspondences with Jewish Qabbalism, Manicheism, and the Neoplatonist "cult of the stars."[250] Manicheism may well be a more apt comparison here than some scholars have thought, in view of the formerly obscure Manichaean theme of the five "lights" which is equatable with the relevant sufi lore of Maqtul's contemporary Najmuddin Kubra. This despite Maqtul's criticism of Mani for maintaining the Magian dualism which he reports as a distortion of Zarathushtra's teaching. This is one of the few points on which Maqtul reflects orthodox Islamic bias, which was inveterately strong against the Manichaeans. But there were differences between the dualism of Mani and the orthodox Zoroastrian equivalent; the finer points in such differences are still being debated by modern scholars. Dualism was a sin in the eyes of Islamic monotheists, who for the most part did not understand the gnostic version of dualism. Maqtul may even have tried to avoid the worst accusations of being a heretical *zindiq* (a term of abuse associated with Manichaeans) by bracketing the Manichaeans (then extinct in the Islamic world) with the Magians.

It is unlikely that the essentials of a perennial philosophy can be found in the straitjacket of theological arguments over theological terms. A gnostic recourse is conceivably nearer the truth, but the subject of gnosticism is so poorly represented in fashionable modern literature that the average reader is liable to completely misunderstand what such recourse amounts to.

Maqtul and others were faced with the problem of clarifying what is generally taken for granted in ancient doctrines. One manuscript of the *Hiqmat al-Ishraq* comments that Plato and his predecessors, and even the Greek Peripatetics, "taught only a one-sided transmigration from man into beast, and not a reverse transmigration into man." This conclusion was evidently based upon only a limited assortment of the Greek texts, though it does reflect common and literalist assumptions. More adventurous is the statement from the same manuscript that Aristotle at first denied transmigration, but later reverted to the teaching of "his master Plato" on this subject.[251] This is contrary to the modern deduction that Aristotle at first accepted transmigration, but later moved away from it.[252] Maqtul was reporting the verdict on Aristotle from another source, and it has been thought that this verdict was arrived at via texts of Pseudo-Aristotle like the much-read *Theology of Aristotle*. Whatever the origin, there are grounds for deducing that Maqtul himself accepted a form of transmigration, since his own declared master was Plato according to the same manuscript.

Also apparent in this manuscript is Maqtul's deference to ancient Zarathushtran teaching. He refers to Jamaspa, Farshadshur, and Buzurgmihr, ancient Persians who lived "before the Greeks." Chronologically, this is two-thirds accurate. Jamaspa and Frashaostra are mentioned in the Avesta as disciples of Zarathushtra. Frashaostra is said to have been the father-in-law of Zarathushtra and a minister of the ruler Vishtaspa, while Jamaspa, another royal counsellor, became a son-in-law of Zarathushtra and is held to have succeeded him as a teacher. But Buzurgmihr was a Sassanian minister of the sixth century A.D., famous for having obtained Indian books for translation into Pahlavi. The link with India was evidently important in ishraqi thinking, and strongly figures in the later Kaivani version of the legend of Zarathushtra, which dramatized the Indian sage "Chengerengacheh" as having contemporary connections with Zarathushtra. Though this may be considered sheer allegory for the archaic era, the Kaivani ishraqis proved the intercultural liberality to the hilt in their own historically tangible activity.

The commentary of Qutubuddin Shirazi (d. 1311) on the *Hiqmat al-Ishraq* furnishes a pertinent historical reflection upon ancient and less ancient Iranian wisdom. This "Aristotelian" ishraqi wrote that Maqtul had revived the philosophy of the ancient Persian sages and harmonized it with the heritage of the Greeks. But long ago misfortunes, and primarily the loss of royal power, had "dug the grave for their wisdom." Alexander the Great had caused most of the

Zarathushtran writings to be burnt.[253] The "writings" would now appear to have been entirely in oral form, but the destruction was real enough via the deaths of a probabilistically large number of Mazdean priests (who preserved the oral heritage) at the time of the infamous Macedonian conquest in the fourth century B.C. Zoroastrian tradition has it that many ancient texts were then lost, though this may already have been the case in respect of intrinsic meaning: modern European investigators found that Parsi mobads in India were in the habit of reciting ancient texts without understanding the words at all. Though practice may make perfect in some instances, in others it may tend to the habitually ridiculous.

Shirazi's remarks make very good sense by comparison with the deduction of David Hume some five centuries later. "The disciples of Zoroaster shut the doors of heaven against all but the Magians,"[254] wrote Hume with sceptical verve. He knew absolutely nothing of Eastern events in the recent past, and in respect of the distant past, he was relying upon Hyde's Christianized reconstruction of the Zarathushtran event. Hence Hume believed that both the early and later Zoroastrians were dogmatic monotheists as distinct from tolerant polytheists; both categories he liked to satirize on the basis of the superior Reason peculiar to Enlightened Europe. The problem for sceptical Reason was that its facts were both sparse and incorrect.

A sceptic who was better informed than Hume on Iranian matters was Voltaire (d. 1778). This *philosophe* had no taste for Christian thinking, and realized that the subject of Zarathushtra was not nearly so simple as some of his contemporaries liked to believe. He seems to have been well up on his European sources, and evidently followed with close interest the arguments that were in progress amongst scholars of the subject. Voltaire reasoned that Zarathushtra provided a weapon of argument against Christianity, since it could now be safely asserted that Moses was not unique and that truth could be found in a non-Christian tradition. Indeed, there is something to be said for Voltaire's standpoint here, but like others, he was misled by the new arguments of the specialists. L'Abbe Foucher was a learned

Iranist of his day, and had revived an older theory found in Pliny, his intention being to solve the discrepancy between various kinds of evidence accumulating. Hence a "second Zoroaster" was postulated and assumed; this new creation of scholarship was the master of Pythagoras and the innovator of Zurvanite teachings (a particular headache for many scholars ever since). In this way, the Christian conception of Zarathushtra was saved. Voltaire gave way to the proposition of a second Zoroaster in his *Essai sur l'histoire generale, et sur les moeurs* (1756), but railed against the theological props. Later, he was disappointed by the scholarly contribution of Anquetil Duperron, whose controversial translation of the *Zend-Avesta* (1771) was the new milestone in Iranist studies. In his preface to this translation, Duperron declared his commitment to humanist scholarship, but in his outlook he remained a steadfast Roman Catholic.[255]

Voltaire died before Sir William Jones located the *Dabistan*, but it was many a moon before this treatise found its way into the clear light of day in an erratic English translation (1843) attended by confusing scholarly deliberations on the *Desatir*, which had emerged even more recently from obscurity. The Hindoos and the Musulmans were not particularly well understood even by the more liberal European colonialists, and it was not sufficient merely to entertain a dislike of Christian theological glosses in order to understand the complexities of Zoroastrian events.

An extreme example of the anti-Christian vogue was the contribution of Friedrich Nietzche (d. 1900). Though not displaying the scholarship of Voltaire, Nietzche produced the only literary work in Europe to use the authentic Persian name of Zarathushtra instead of the Greek rendering. But any resemblance of his *Also sprach Zarathustra* (1885–7) to history ends with the title. Nietzche was not merely desirous of liberating his contemporaries from Christianity, but was anti-moral in his emphases, an error which does not justify inferior forms of iconoclasm. Nietzche used Zarathushtra as a mouthpiece for his own philosophy, and an eminent Iranist scholar has aptly commented that the Nietzchean image of Zarathushtra "is the almost exact opposite of truth." This judgment is not in any way arbitrary, since a statement in Nietzche's subsequent *Ecce Homo* proves that Nietzche was well aware of the disparity between his presentation and the real Zarathushtra. "I should have been asked what the name Zarathushtra means in *my* mouth, in the mouth of the first Immoralist," wrote Nietzche in reference to the failure of his reading public to perceive the irony of his disparate presentation. He affirms that his meaning was "exactly the opposite" of what constituted the "enormous uniqueness of that Persian in history" in "translating morals into metaphysics, as power, origin, aim in itself."[256]

While the Nietzchean version seems to have contributed to much unnecessary confusion in some sectors of thought, a subsequent version of Zoroastrianism from the pen of a specialist scholar is sufficient to send any impartial reader back into sympathy with Voltaire. James Hope Moulton was a Christian missionary in addition to his more humanist role, and acquired first-hand knowledge of the Parsis in India. The results of his fieldwork were published posthumously at Oxford in 1917. In the final chapter of *The Treasure of the Magi*, Moulton concluded that Zoroastrianism is "a religion which for all its high qualities has failed in its mission."[257] His purpose here was to extol the Christian missionaries for their civilizing influence, and to affirm Christianity as "the crown of Zoroastrianism." Many anthropologists of today would wince acutely at such objective appraisal by colonialist apologists. Moulton typically used the New Testament reference to the "magi" as a support for his contention; one feels that even Olcott may have known more about this worn peg than some academics.

Moulton did not even once mention the *Dabistan*, which doubtless was conveniently considered an aberration of the heathen which had failed to meet the requirements of an exclusive claim on absolute truth. Moulton's missionary crown tends to remind one of Teilhard De Chardin's stigmatization of "ancient religions" as being incapable of survival by comparison with the favoured dogma. In the same epilogue to *The Phenomenon of Man*, the statement is made that the metaphysical systems of Plato, Spinoza, and Hegel had not gone beyond the stage of ideology,[258] hence setting a poor standard by comparison with religion. Significantly perhaps, Descartes (of Jesuit associations) is not specified; as the virtual founder of modern Rationalism, his ideology did not gain the maturity of Spinoza's philosophical mysticism, though the Cartesian influence does seem to have curtailed the Spinozan extension of being to the animal species. Though one might agree that Hegel was too ideological, even Hegel had his good points in emphasizing that Kantian doctrine was merely buttressing the theological establishment. Attacks on Plato from a theological perspective look much worse than materialist arguments, and Christian Platonists of comparative discernment might well wonder which is the ideology and which the actual knowledge.

Who would really know which is the perennial philosophy and which the perennial folly in the confrontation of differing axes and ideals that are often worlds apart? Not necessarily the most dogmatic and vociferous defenders of ideologies.

Moulton also penned a more erudite work on Zoroastrianism, one inevitably exhibiting a pronounced monotheistic interpretation. In view of its authorship, one is not surprised to find the bald statement that "there was a singular absence of the mystical element" in the teaching of Zarathushtra. Moulton was not actually against what he called mysticism, but did tend to align this word with the founder of Christianity. Interpretations of what is supposed to have been said in the Gathas are a labyrinth of contradictions, but suffice it to say here that Moulton singled out the absence of (explicit) asceticism in the Gathas, "which cuts him (Zarathushtra) off strikingly from spiritual kinship with India." The reason for this assertion was, of course, that Zarathushtra was therefore of Protestant Christian affinity rather than heathen, again saving the day in the spirit of Hyde for the early prophets prior to the "crown." (The asceticism of the Jewish prophets seems illogically discounted). However, a much more odious reflection was the following: "we may well believe that our Aryan blood was not responsible for a phenomenon (asceticism) safely to be credited to the indigenous population (of India)." Zarathushtra here became an Aryan figurehead related to Christian Europe but much less to the Hindus (it might conceivably have interfered with missionary tactics if the Aryan componency of the Hind had been given due profile). "Zarathushtra never dreamed of any merit in celibacy," we are emphatically told. Scholastic telepathy here gains its main support from the "wedding hymn" in the Gathas, but even Luther is known to have committed the deadly sin of monasticism at one phase in his life. Further proof is derived from the much later Avestan text known as the *Vendidad*, a priestly code which affirms that the married man is superior to the celibate, the man with offspring superior to he who has none, while the man who eats meat is superior to one who fasts. Moulton apparently did not dream that these priestly statements could be used to condone a lax and worldly attitude of gratification and the maintenance of hereditary offices. Ascetics, like the poor, would merely have been potential nuisances to inherited prerogative, as Mani found when he clashed with the sacerdotal powers.

Moulton was typically anti-Manichee, piously alert to matters of heresy, which is the underlying purport of his statement that: "No speculative Gnosticism in Zarathushtra's dogmatics (*sic*) taught the inherent evil of matter." Yet Moulton had to acknowledge the strongly marked dualism of matter and spirit that is detectable throughout the Avesta.[259]

This bias against gnostic elements, elements which are imperfectly understood, loses much weight in the emerging deductions from more recent Iranists that Zarathushtra was expounding a dualism and not a monotheism in the Christian image. To be sure, it was evidently an "ethical dualism," and the preoccupation with this still tends to limit the contextual framework[260] almost as much as conservative ritualism has done for centuries. An ethical dualism is not to be considered antithetical to more "mystical" (i.e. less theological) ingredients. The complexities of the archaic Gathic language still leave many obscurities which may yet divulge generally unsuspected dimensions of meaning.

The major problem with Zarathushtra is pinpointing the context of the Gathas. Their exact age is not conclusively decided upon, and the traditional biography is composed of legendary ingredients. Only half a century ago, a leading Iranist scholar was treating as virtual fact the late Pahlavi record. Williams Jackson wrote that Zarathushtra was currently believed to have lived during the seventh-sixth centuries B.C., and as a native of Western Iran, probably of the Median Atropatene. He gained a revelation at the age of thirty; twelve years later he won a disciple in the ruler Vishtaspa, who became "the Constantine of the faith." The influence of his teaching extended throughout Iran and even beyond its borders, was the extrapolation. Even more debateable is Jackson's conclusion of a "holy war" with Turan (Central Asia) as the consequence of "a vigorous crusading policy." The same scholar was more cautious in stating that Zarathushtra seems to have died by violence at the age of seventy-seven, the Pahlavi texts referring to one Tur-i Bratarvakhsh as his murderer.[261] More recent and critical scholarship would only credit the link with Vishtaspa as reliable, though in what location this occurred is still very much in dispute.

A controversial thesis from the specialist scholar Henrik Nyberg made an acute departure from Christianizing interpretations. This briefly dwelt on *dervish* elements in the Islamic world as being of possible relevance, but despite his ethnographic flair, Nyberg ruined his enterprising book by emphasizing shamanistic practices and (then) recent conjectures on the drug activities of the Scythians reported in Greek annals.[262] Certain influential scholars justifiably criticized this shamanistic perspective, but much less justifiably repudiated the *dervish* relevance.[263] As it was, Nyberg would have done better to focus on the *Dabistan*, which even he ignored, like so many others.

Despite its eccentricities, Nyberg's tangent into an Oriental context of reference was a marked improvement upon the Westernizing vogue so long entrenched in Iranist studies. This trend was at its worst in such deductions as that of Van Wesendonk, who viewed Zarathushtra as a representative of the Occidental attitude, and moreover, as demonstrating the "striving towards the finest spirituality and the urge to struggle with tangible reality" which "pervades all Europe and perhaps shows itself at its clearest in the German."[264]

The finest spirituality is not to be considered an ethnocentric occurrence, which is rather a category of perennial folly, which will invariably waste time on obscurities and distortions at the expense of more tangibly known events.

The spectacle of presumed spirituality is possibly one of the most serious matters in the history of religion and mysticism. One of the precedents which apparently inspired Moulton was the evangelical campaign of John Wilson against the Parsis. Wilson was a Christian missionary from Scotland, and was also President of the Bombay Branch of the Royal Asiatic Society. He was also the author of works castigating Hindu religion, but here it is only necessary to focus upon his pious attack on Zoroastrianism which was published in 1843. The relevant book exhibits a bias that seems incredible by current scholarly standards (though there may of course be exceptions). Wilson devoted several hundred pages to a bludgeoning of the heathen Parsis, using every argument he could muster to prove that their beliefs and interpretations were ill-founded by comparison with his own sanctified calling.

Wilson inserted in this diatribe several thrusts against the "Sipasi Sufis," whom he seems to have envisaged in the same light as the detested Manichees. He scathingly refers to Mani as being "instrumental in corrupting several portions of the early Christian church," a sentiment which is matched by the idiom of his accusation that the *Dabistan* "is the most wretched collection of extravagant fables, fictions, and falsehoods which I have ever perused." This was almost diametrically opposed to the assessment of Sir William Jones. The much less impartial Wilson was irate at Mobad Shah's recognition of the Hindu *kalpas* (which shattered Biblical literalism in chronology), and was censorious of the *Dabistan* reporting which "makes the ancient Iranians supporters of transmigration, which is quite opposed to the

Parsi religion." He complained that the *Dabistan* made the angels, demons, and heroes of the Parsis into "mysteries and parables." It should really be superfluous to add that this is the complaint of a literalist. He triumphantly cites the slightly earlier British scholar William Erskine as remarking that the disciples of Azar Kaivan "have too much the air of conjurors and jugglers," and insists that accounts of them outrage commonsense. It is more likely to dispel missionary commonsense if any impartial reader takes the trouble to check the English translation of the *Dabistan* which appeared in print the same year as Wilson's biased report, since even the imperfect rendition of Shea and Troyer reveals a strange absence of conjuring (though there is some distinctive hagiography). Biblical miracles were of course in a different category. Wilson also found that "the general system of parabolical exposition to which the Sipasis resorted, outrages commonsense." The advocate of evangelical commonsense again invoked a statement of Erskine: "They allegorize the whole of their ancient history; whenever a *div* (demon) is mentioned, understanding by it a wicked man, and the conquest and destruction of the demons they hold to mean only the conquest of man over his passions. In like manner the whole history of Kai Khusrau and Alexander the Great is reduced to a moral and allegorical romance." Bearing in mind that the legendary Kai Khusrau and the allegorical Alexander were part of the Irano-Islamic repertory of classical allusion, the deficit in history does not seem nearly so outrageous as the distortions perpetrated upon historical and allegorical materials by dogmatic literalists. More to the point perhaps, Wilson was outraged that the Sipasi sufis interpreted Satan (Shaitan) of the Muslims and Christians in the same way they interpreted the Ahriman of Zoroastrian dualism, i.e., as an inner or psychological principle of distortion in man. To Wilson unorthodoxy was blasphemy, and he narrowly described the sophistication as "the utmost violence to the meaning attached to the word by these (orthodox) communities."

Another evangelical accusation against the *Dabistan* was that its references to Zarathushtra were culled expressly from the *Sharistan* and *Zartusht-Namah*, the former being a Sipasi work and the latter a thirteenth century Persian work. Wilson meant to imply that there could not possibly be any historical relevance here owing to late sources, but his argument is undercut by the parabolical usage of such material which he himself points out, i.e., the Sipasis did not intend their Zarathushtra legend as literal fact. He opined tht the Sipasi philosophers had never seen or studied the *Vendidad* or any other text of the *Zend-Avesta*, and added, with typical charity, that the *Dabistan* author "was quite incapable of interpreting them (Avestan texts), or commenting upon them."[265] It is quite true that Sipasi (= Kaivani) writers show little interest in the texts of the *Zend-Avesta*, and do not rely upon them for data. But the reason for this neglect requires a deeper appraisal than a conversion drive is capable of. Several, or even most, of the Zoroastrian Kaivanis may not indeed have been very conversant with the Avesta; they were not practising priests, they were not liturgists, but instead they were ishraqis. As ishraqis they were not concerned with conventional doctrines, but with the formulae and metaphor of an inner development, and with a philosophy much broader than the religious ideologies afforded. In their view, the Avestan texts amounted to a literary corpse, the tool of theological literalism, part of a priestly milieu in which the Gathas were interpreted in the same context as the ritualistic *Vendidad*. Even the Gathas would not have been important to their philosophy; even when the German philologist Martin Haug discovered by the 1860's that the Gathas were more archaic than the rest of the Avesta, this revelation did not for some time lift the veil of distortion imposed by both Zoroastrian priests and European exegetes. Even today, it is still being debated as to what the Gathas mean, and for all anyone definitively knows, the Kaivani-ishraqis may have been right to ignore conventional interpretations.

The infallible Wilson was treating the *Vendidad* as the words of Zarathushtra; he was perhaps a millenium in error here, and would have done better to be more allegorical. Wilson would perhaps have suffered apoplexy if he could have read the more recent and much more erudite thesis of

Marijan Mole, which opted for an "allegorical" interpretation of the Gathas that has been a source of controversy amongst Iranists. The problem with Mole's interpretation is that it tends to mitigate the factual dimensions of Zarathushtra;[266] in this respect, the Sipasi section in the *Dabistan* compres very favourably, since it includes factual biographies of the Kaivanis which lend a solid basis for historical comparisons and extensions. (Not all of the Sipasi section is allegory; indeed, Mobad Shah expressly stipulates that allegorical interpretation is resorted to only after reason is exhausted).

The bible-punching Wilson also ventured a critique of the *Desatir*, more understandably than his denunciation of the related *Dabistan*. The reason why this attack was more pardonable is because a learned Parsi, one Mulla Firuz, had not long ago attributed a substantial antiquity to the *Desatir* on account of its Pahlavi-style format. This treatise has the complexity of a text and commentary in two different languages, the former being composed in a unique adaptation of various scripts that is perhaps best described as an Indo-Iranian polyglot. European scholars had much to say about it at the time of its appearance in print in the early nineteenth century. It is probably no older than the sixteenth century, but Mulla Firuz considered it to be an authentic work of Iranian antiquity. This gave European scholars the opportunity to vent a pronounced critical spleen; they tended to overdo this at the expense of evaluating the philosophical contents. Wilson cited the British scholar Norris in the *Asiatic Journal* of 1820, who had concluded that a substantial part of the hybrid language was "nothing more than Dari disguised," Dari being a late Persian dialect used by the Zoroastrian minority in Iran. Wilson also invoked Erskine once more, who had attributed the *Desatir* to the Sipasi philosophers. This was good scholarship, but was merely used as proof of Zoroastrian error. Wilson remarks sneeringly that Alexander the Great is made into a Zoroastrian convert by the *Desatir*, and that the Greeks are represented as becoming Zoroastrians in the days of Vishtaspa (Gushtasp), Zarathushtra's royal patron. But even here Wilson's jibe is out of context,[267] and not merely because he conflated different references to the Greeks.

The Persian commentary to the *Desatir* text relates a story of a debate between Zarathushtra and a Greek (Yunani) philosopher, with the consequence that the latter becomes a follower of the Iranian sage, and converts the inhabitants of his native land to the prophet's teaching. But this story appears in juxtaposition with an ishraqi theme, again involving Greeks but in a context that has an obvious transpositional value (obvious, that is, to those sufficiently educated in the themes). The text is relaying purported words of Zarathushtra, who affirms that the "sect of inner illumination" will arise among the Greeks in addition to that of reason. The commentary adds that the "sect of Gushaspians" (i.e. the illuminated, the *ishraqiyyun*) of Iran and Greece is a nexus between the illuminated and the rationalists. When Sikandar (Alexander) came to Iran, he found that the Gushaspians had the most wisdom, and were even able to leave the body when they pleased. There was also another sect in Iran who sought to discover the real nature of things by reason and meditation. Yet there was no such group in Greece. Alexander collected all the books of this rationalist sect and had them translated into Greek. He made his prime minister the head of this rationalist sect, which consequently prevailed amongst the Greeks.[268] This is an unusual anecdote which amounts to a neo-ishraqi explanation of Aristotelian origins. Alexander's prime minister is here Aristotle, in accordance with the belief of the Arabs and Persians of the Islamic era. The rationalist sect is that of the Peripatetics, who hence transfer to the West, leaving the illuminated sect in the East. This is a play upon standard ishraqi symbolism of the division between the "occident" and "orient," between the methodologies of the (logical) Peripatetics and (intuitive) ishraqis. These methodologies lead to different results until their eventual liaison (as predicted here by Zarathushtra, and as depicted in the anecdote of the "converted" Greek philosopher). Hence the folly of missionary literalism in assuming that the Greeks were thought to have been converted to orthodox Zoroastrianism.

Wilson was not the only one to believe that Zarathushtra represents orthodox religion in this passage. Williams Jackson was another scholar who missed ishraqi dimensions in the *Desatir*, despite his more liberal concessions to the Sipasi literature. He assumed that the conversion of the Greeks was on similar lines to the story of the Indian sage "Cangranghacah" (Chengerengacheh) in the *Cangranghacah-Nama*, a Persian poetical work of the thirteenth century.[269] In this latter, a brahmin of India becomes a disciple of Zarathushtra at Balkh and afterwards converts many of his compatriots to the new teaching. This story is repeated in the *Desatir*, but the conversion of the compatriots is omitted: the Indian sage merely returns to the Hind. Some Western scholars early surmised that this story refers to the Vedantic philosopher Shankara (owing to the name "Senkerakas" supplied in the text of the *Desatir*), implying an intention to exalt the triumph of an Iranian over a major Hindu philosopher. But such nineteenth century interpretations ignored ishraqi undertones. A more definite Hindu sage of great fame appears in a story of similar format that is included in the *Desatir*. This sage is named as "Bias," which is feasibly a rendering of Vyasa, the sage reputed as a redactor of the Vedas and believed to have authored the *Mahabharata*. Again there is no mass conversion of Hindus in accompaniment.[270] Only the husk of these stories was assimilated by text analysts accustomed to the interpretations of orthodox religion.[271] In the more obvious context, the inclusion of Indian sages in the train of Zarathushtra was one literary method of underlining the affinities with the "perennial" tradition of ancient Iranian sages depicted in the *Desatir*, who (together with the allegorized Alexander) had continually revived a continually atrophying impact upon human events. In a more implicit context, the linkage of Iranian, Greek, and Indian traditions was a distinctive feature of ishraqi philosophy. Azar Kaivan is stated in the *Dabistan* to have early in his life achieved affinity with the wisdom of India in an illuminative experience that transcended time and cultural barriers. In his early years in Iran he had learnt the sciences of the Greeks, Indians, and Iranians; this appears to have been part of the signification involved in his title of *Zhu'l-Ulum*, meaning "master of the sciences."

Mir Findiriski is also known to have devoted much attention to the Indian heritage, conceivably under Kaivani inspiration. In his *Risala-i-Sana'iyyah* (*Treatise on arts and sciences*), Findiriski affirmed that those philosophers who are correctly tutored in Iranian wisdom (*hiqmah*), Hindu wisdom, and the *Theology of Aristotle* (i.e. Plotinus and Porphyry) will perceive these diverse expressions of wisdom to hold the same essential and perennial meaning. He did not say that all representatives of the nominal wisdom exhibit a perennial value, which in general is the meaning currently adhering to the debased concept of a perennial philosophy.

In the pages of John Wilson's missionary tirade against the Parsis, there is no understanding of even the most elementary ishraqi concepts. He ended his tract with such doctrinaire statements as: "Wherever it (Christianity) is unknown and unacknowledged, there is ignorance, superstition, cruelty, oppression, and immorality." More than slightly insulting was the christianly cruel remark: "It is almost degrading to contrast it (Christianity) – not to speak of comparing it – in these respects, with the Parsi religion."[272] It is for posterity to judge how this bias compares with the magnanimous coverage of the *Dabistan*, which so offended missionary insularity. But it is perhaps incumbent to pose a salient question here: what can any researcher seriously expect in terms of impartial accuracy from the multitude of dogmatically righteous attacks that have been perpetrated against heretics and unbelievers in past eras?

What seems even more objectionable in retrospect than the missionary zeal is the fact that Wilson's diatribe was launched under the credentials of impeccable scholarship. In 1784 Sir William Jones had founded the Asiatic Society of Calcutta, a venture which had stimulated a new interest in studies of oriental subjects amongst the European literati. By 1843 Wilson was President of the Bombay Branch of the Royal Asiatic Society, and deviating markedly from the example of Jones. Wilson can in fact be considered anti-

Asiatic; he not only flouted the ideals of humanist scholarship, but also provided a striking example of the colonialist mentality. On the title page of the abovementioned diatribe, he inserted a sentiment of the Bombay Government (with an explicit acknowledgment): "The course of argument and fair reason cannot be impeded." But it was, and for many decades.

Bias in scholarship may not always be so obvious as in Wilson's offering, on account of which the claims of fair reason should be duly emphasized in sectors tending to a truncation of arguments and unfair representation.

One aspect of Iranian repertories which has received a curiously blunted profile in scholastic literature is that known as Zurvanism. The Sipasi philosophers can be aligned with a late form of Zurvanite approach. Zurvanite trends have (very) obscure antecedents in the Achaemenian era, and in later Iranian eras constitute a complex array which has puzzled some conventional (religious) scholars by its simultaneous "monotheism" and "dualism." In the Sipasi repertory, it is not nominal Zurvanism that is represented, but there are certain indications that link with Zurvanite concepts amongst medieval Zoroastrians of Iran, and which can be traced to the more unorthodox specimens of Zoroastrian literature. It must be stressed thsat the Zurvanite phenomenon was nothing of a uniform or regular occurrence – for instance, the Sassanian situation of Zurvanite clerics versus Zurvanite Manichees poses acute problems for a facile perennial philosophy of Zurvanism. Owing to the evident differences amongst Zurvanites, it is even possible to ask if Zarathushtra was an inherent proto-Zurvanite, with the additional question as to which aspect of the "broken pattern" he most accurately fits. Reformers and dissidents are more likely allies for the more radical Zurvanism than priestly hierarchies, always allowing for marked differences in the assimilation of essentials – in which respect deficiencies can speedily transform the esoteric into the exoteric.[273]

## Etics/Emics of the Universal

One of those scholars who derided the concept of a perennial philosophy was the late R.C. Zaehner, reputed as an expert on Iranian and Indian religion. He understandably expressed an aversion for Aldous Huxley, and characterized the dismissed concept as "All is One and One is All." This is not inapplicable for the amorphous popular approach to the theme of the perennial, but Zaehner failed to provide an etic clarification to the content of his own studies. One can agree that the banal perennial has been invoked as a testament to the truth of every kind of religious syncretism. Zaehner made the more uncommon criticism that Engels used the perennial concept to transform the economic thinking of Marx into a new kind of "mysticism and incomprehensible transcendentalism" in the *Dialectics of Nature*. The same scholar accused Teilhard de Chardin of transforming Christianity into a "Platonic *mischmasch*." The reader might deduce from this that Zaehner was an orthodox Christian who was averse to mysticism. That judgment is only partially correct, since Zaehner was here taking the opportunity to repudiate the claim of philosophy to an ultimate truth. Hence, in opposing Plato, he used Aristotelian science to buttress the implicit claims of orthodox religion, in the spirit of Aquinas. Philosophy can only be a relative truth, not Truth, urges Zaehner.[274] In the hands of an Aquinas, one can agree that philosophy has distinct limits. The fact that Zaehner is still considered one of the leading experts on Zurvanite philosophy is no encouragement to treat his conclusions on that subject as any ultimate guideline.

"Zurvanism seems to offer nothing"[275] was Zaehner's catholic conclusion on the subject. He was unable to make sense of his own research, which did (if nothing else) reveal that Zurvanism as it had survived in the Pahlavi books had very largely been tapered to suit the orthodoxy of the Zoroastrian clergy. Zurvanism would assuredly not be the only tradition to have suffered contusion and deformation at the hands of dogmatists, a phenomenon which is evidently a perennial occurrence afflicting philosophies.

It has been aptly observed that the "perennial philosophy" has been a popular term since *circa* 1900, and that it has since been common practice for people of various persuasions to appropriate the concept in order to lend their own views a higher status. Looked at from this perspective, the only claims of reasonable validity would be those antedating the twentieth century. But Charles Schmitt, for instance, went to the other extreme in pinning the concept down to Steuco only. This was a literal conclusion based upon usage of the term *philosophia perennis*, and this preference for the Latinization displayed a similar ignorance to that of Aldous Huxley in respect of Iranian emphases concerning the perennial that are extant in the works of Maqtul, Findiriski, and the Sipasi philosophers. Neither Leibniz nor Steuco deserves sole copyright for a concept that was elsewhere expressed more clearly and with more qualifications.

It was more appropriately emphasized by Schmitt that the "perennial philosophy" had found twentieth century representatives in the varied ranks of Thomistic Scholasticism, Scholasticism in general, modern Platonism, Huxleyan mysticism, positivism, naturalism, and Roman Catholic philosophy – a list that is by no means exhaustive. Schmitt wryly added that he had not yet seen scepticism referred to as the *philosophia perennis*, but that he expected this addition any day. He observed that the relevant concept did not appear in the pre-twentieth century scholastic tradition, and emphasized that it did not have any particular affinity with the philosophy and theology of Thomas Aquinas.[276]

It is obvious enough that a great deal of the recent identifications and affiliations are categories of emicism, i.e., deficient evaluations of a phenomenon imperfectly represented. The objective should now be to clarify the factor of etic possibilities, i.e., to ascertain which are the more emic or deficient contours in perennial trends and which are more accurately to be deemed of etic or intrinsic validity. This is really an elementary exercise, but I have very seldom seen it acknowledged that there are such differences in historical events pertaining to a "perennial" philosophy.

A major influence upon the version of Aldous Huxley was

the more scholarly contribution of Ananda K. Coomaraswamy (1877–1947). Despite the pronounced influence of the latter, he has comparatively seldom been investigated in any detail by fans of the perennial, since much of his writings were in the form of articles for learned journals, some of which proved difficult to locate even for specialists. Coomaraswamy identified *philosophia perennis* with the *sanatana dharma* (eternal religion) of Hinduism, and added the suffix of *et universalis* to the increasingly well known Latinization. Under his influence many religionists in various parts of the globe have identified "tradition" with the perennial philosophy. Huxley was one case in point, but there have been some who were and are far more dogmatic than the eventual devotee of mescalin. This traditionalist emphasis has resulted in a type of comparative religion in which orthodox theology ousts philosophy as the salient perennial.

The conflation of the "universal" in philosophy with all types of religion and dogma is not conducive to accuracy, only to another trend of perennial folly.

The element of the traditional cannot be excluded from philosophy, providing this is qualified in terms of an adaptable tradition. For instance, there is some justification for inclusion of the *sanatana dharma* in perennial perspectives, providing that this is sufficiently clarified in relation to orthodox Hinduism. The same considerations apply to other traditions and religions.

One of the flaws in the expositions of Coomaraswamy is his failure to evoke sufficiently the depth element in Vedantic and related Indian philosophies, and his replacement of this vital factor with an acute degree of convergence with Thomism.

The son of a Ceylonese aristocrat and a wealthy Englishwoman of a mercantile family that had formerly engaged in the "India trade," Coomaraswamy did not fashion his career in the mould of a guru, but was instead known as a connoisseur of art and a polymath. During the period between 1917 until his death in 1947 he was on the staff of the Boston Museum of Fine Arts, and he found time to write some three hundred learned articles in addition to his much more well known books. His career as an art historian is not under discussion here. Some have deduced that he became more of a philosopher in his later years, but a more relevant consideration here is that he is classified as a theologian. He came under the influence of the Neo-Scholastic movement resurgent since the late nineteenth century, a movement harking back to the medieval schoolmen, chiefly Aquinas.

The centennial report of the Boston Museum of Fine Arts (founded 1870) describes Coomaraswamy as "a philosopher and theologian who spoke the language of Yoga and of Thomas Aquinas with unconscious transition between East and West."[277] It seems incongruous to some that he should have given such disproportionate attention to Aquinas; he might more consciously have transited to philosophies of a different complexion if less theological priorities had been discerned.

A recent biographer has written of Coomaraswamy that his emigration to America "more or less" isolated him from India, where lived a number of teachers whom he trusted, Ramana Maharshi (d. 1950) being the best known amongst them. Coomaraswamy was refreshingly honest in maintaining that he himself was not a guru, only a toiler on the way. Yet he perhaps tended to underemphasize the importance of finding a competent teacher – this, after all, is a traditional reminder, and Coomaraswamy was a traditionalist. Though he had come to accept Ramana Maharshi as a genuine saint – this entity demonstrating a remarkable indifference to publicity – Coomaraswamy did not attempt to seek out Maharshi at his ashram in South India. He did write that he knew of no Ramana Maharshi living in Europe. This was in a letter dated August 1947, on the eve of his decease, an epistle in which he added that he did not trust any of the missionary swamis, and "not even Vivekananda, were he still alive; were Ramakrishna himself available, that would be another matter."[278] Coming from such a noted traditionalist, this seems something of an invidious comparison between Vivekananda (d. 1902) and his teacher Ramakrishna of Dakshineswar (d. 1886). That Coomaraswamy distrusted Western Vedantists seems more appropriate. Some think that he became too accustomed to Western ways and attitudes, and neglected some of the more important Eastern sources that were known to him. Yet his version of the perennial philosophy has gained unquestioning acceptance from a remarkably large number of enthusiasts, most of them via the Huxleyan grapevine.[279]

Coomaraswamy was noted for his critique of Western lifestyles, a critique not without justification. He did not always mince words about the false sense of ethnic superiority possessed by Westerners. He was a sharp critic of American materialism, and earned a certain amount of resentment owing to his emphasis that: "the higher the standard of living, the lower the culture." He continually exhorted fellow Indians in America to emulate Gandhi's example of simple living. An Indian professor of demography has remarked that Coomaraswamy perhaps failed to stress that while man does not live by bread alone, he nevertheless needs bread in order to live. Sripati Chandrasekhar points out in this respect that traditionalists often forget that those who seek higher values in life are often those who have already acquired the basic requirements of civilized existence. In this respect, critics have been able to emphasize that Coomaraswamy enjoyed all the many comforts and amenities with which America could provide a scholar working under museum auspices.[280] One cannot but remark here on the comparison with Vivekananda, who notably did emphasize the factor of crucial bread at the Chicago Parliament of Religions in 1893, and who maintained a traditional lifestyle of austere simplicity. But then Vivekananda is considered a "modernist" by the more dogmatic traditionalists. He certainly emphasized the necessity for the jettisoning of brahmanical norms long before Gandhi entered his less conventional phase.

Coomaraswamy has been described as the first scholar to substantiate the continuity between pre-Aryan India, Vedism, Brahmanism, and Buddhism. This argument has notably been championed by Eliade, though others have been more critical. I do not deny implicit elements of perenniality with regard to these diverse cultural phases, but neither Coomaraswamy nor Eliade have successfully clarified the explicit emic accumulations from more etic occurrences.[281]

It should be more obvious than it has been to some that Gautama Buddha is only equatable with the more etic features in the brahmanical milieu. Extensions of this anthropographic argument mean that a great deal of emic flotsam is non sequitur in any consideration of continuum intrinsics. Events, personages, and accoutrements sometimes deemed as of great significance may have a much lower etic status that is actually equivalent to nil. For this reason, it is simplistic rhetoric to continually stress the common metaphysical basis of all religions.

In certain respects it is evident that Coomaraswamy's generous references to Roman Catholic saints served to assuage insular religious grievances against foreigners. One can concede his position as a liberal Hindu in this respect, but it is notable that his predecessor Vivekananda did not bow to scholastic theology – though Vivekananda did respect the asceticism of the more mystical Catholic saints. In a lecture on Ramakrishna and religious tolerance delivered at New York in 1936, Coomaraswamy made no mention of Vivekananda, which perhaps tends to accentuate the difference between a scholastic traditionalist and a mystical modernist. In this lecture Coomaraswamy laboured with his recurrent theme of comparative religion, and used several quotes from Aquinas. "Even St. Thomas admits that some of the Gentiles who lived before Christ's temporal birth may have been saved." This reflection is not likely to excite the less theologically minded. The audience were conceivably not as broad-minded as they could have been, but one does not have to agree with Coomaraswamy's assertion that it is "perfectly legitimate" to feel that a given religion is more adequately true than another, e.g., that Catholicism is more valid than Protestantism, or that Hinduism holds more truth than Buddhism. One is relieved to find the follow-up assertion that real distinctions can be drawn. Coomaraswamy points out that Christianity maintains that metaphysics, though the highest of the other sciences, is inferior to "the sacred science of theology;" in contrast, Hinduism is primarily metaphysical, "and only secondarily religious." Therefore, adds Coomaraswamy, "however much a Hindu may find himself in enthusiastic agreement with the angelic and celestial doctors," i.e. Aquinas and Bonaventura, he is more in rapport with Christian mystics whose orthodoxy is suspect, e.g. Eriugena, Eckhart, Boehme, and Blake, "and more at home with Plotinus than with the representatives of Christian orthodoxy." It is to be regretted that Coomaraswamy did not make such qualifications more often; Plotinus receives a much fainter profile in his writings than Aquinas does.

In the same lecture, Coomaraswamy made an unusually strong point (for him) against orthodoxy that is more reminiscent of Vivekananda. He pointed out that the activity of Christian missions still endorsed a conversion by force: "the force of money, expended on education and medical aid bestowed with ulterior motives." He accused Christian missionaries of transgressing the commandment which enjoins against bearing false witness of one's neighbour; there were no worse offenders in this than the missionaries, he stated.[282] Over forty years earlier, Vivekananda's fame had inspired the jealousy of missionary interests which fanned the gossip concerning the primitive savages of India; the detractors of the heathen were perhaps galled the more on account of the fact that they now had in their midst a scientifically-oriented modernist monk from the Hind. Coomaraswamy seems to have preferred the theologized science of Aquinas for some strangely conservative reason.

One very striking feature of Coomaraswamy's traditionalism was his firm repudiation of reincarnation. This is definitely not in the spirit of the *sanatana dharma*, and would appear to strongly reflect Coomaraswamy's partiality for Christian doctrine (which was much more pronounced than his appreciation of Islam or modern science). In an article of 1939, he did in fact conflate reincarnation with the Christian doctrine of preexistence in Adam and the inheritance of original sin. An extremely dogmatic statement here was: "No doctrine of reincarnation . . . has ever been taught in India, even in Buddhism – or for that matter in the Neoplatonic or any other orthodox tradition." One is led to the conclusion that Coomaraswamy's scholarship is not always sound when it comes to a conflation with orthodox traditions. He correlates the *Brahmanas* with the Old

Testament in respect of emphasizing the archaic aphorism that those who have departed from this world have departed forever. The *Brahmanas* were priestly texts of the Vedic era, and the notion of their part in the continuum from the Indus civilization to Buddhism is frankly not complimentary to the prowess of any perennial philosophy, but traditionalism frequently moves in a backward arc of response to mysticism. He slightly relaxes his dogmatism to concede: "I do not say that a belief in reincarnation has never been entertained in India," but one suspects that if Indian history had been even more hazy than it is, then Coomaraswamy would have been eager to attribute the rejected belief to a nineteenth century origin. He insisted that any such belief could only have resulted from "a popular misinterpretation of the symbolic language of the texts." Coomaraswamy's literalism might have confused some of the more orthodox pundits, but even they might have smelt a rat in the corollary extended: "If you ask how such a mistake could have arisen, I shall ask you to consider statements of Saints Augustine and Thomas Aquinas." The Thomistic *sanatana dharma* then declares reincarnation "an impossibility, for good and sufficient metaphysical reasons,"[283] which sounds like a joke even to hardened materialists who would logically accept metempsychosis in the raw rather than submit to eternal damnation.

In a later article appearing in 1944, the dogmatism is unabated on this subject. Coomaraswamy's point of departure is Shankara's dictum: "There is no other transmigrant but the Lord." Coomaraswamy interprets this with a bald literalness that would do credit to the most rabid monotheistic bible-punchers rather than the pantheistic nuances of Advaita Vedanta. His view is explicitly in agreement with the absence of reincarnation in Christianity, from which one might infer that comparative religion gone mad is not a universal truth, but merely an error of interpretation. Scholastic literalism has never been an enlightening factor in philosophy save by comparison with something more perceptive. Coomaraswamy made further extreme difficulties for his exegesis in denying that Plato was referring to the individual soul in a well known passage of the *Meno*.[284]

Plato reports Socrates as affirming that "the soul of man is immortal," and the context is discernibly one of reincarnation via such wordings as "the soul . . . has been born many times."[285] The Coomaraswamian attempt to theologize is not at all convincing here, though it might have pleased the more orthodox Christian Platonists.

It is very interesting to compare this theologized version of reincarnation with the views of Vivekananda. In an article written in America in 1895, this leading disciple of Ramakrishna had defended the Vedantic teachings on this subject, teachings which were prone to attack from his Christian detractors in America. By that time, Vivekananda had felt the full sting of missionary animosity for some eighteen months, but with typical resiliency, he used contributions of Western scholars to augment his heretical position in the midst of the godly. He starts off with an affirmation that there never was a time "when some race, or some individuals" had upheld the truth concerning "the real meaning of the divinity within." He adds that advanced intellects had given up the search for truth in the face of "the vagueness of many schools and sects" and "the violent superstitions of organized priestcraft." He observes that belief in an immortal soul, or in the pre-existence of the soul, had been nurtured even amongst thinkers placed in the milieux of religions hostile to such ideas. This was the foundation of Hinduism and Buddhism; the educated classes amongst the ancient Egyptians had similarly adhered to it, and also the ancient Persians; the Greek philosophers had made it the corner-stone of philosophy, and "the sufis among the Mohammedans almost universally acknowledged its truth." This might be taken as a precedent for the twentieth century concepts of a perennial philosophy, though it was only indirectly his concern to stipulate such a basic consideration. He distinguishes the Indo-Aryans from other races in respect of the specific belief in metempsychosis, and quotes Karl Heckel's conclusion that the doctrine of transmigration was "entirely foreign to the popular Egyptian religion," and that elements of affinity in the mystery teachings of antiquity were not inherent in the Osiriac doctrines, but were instead derived from Hindu sources. He also cites Brugsch and Maspero on an early Egyptian text which is conventionally considered to reflect the "materialism" of the Egyptian views on the after-life. Thus he emerged with the conclusion, tailor-made by the scholars, that the ancient Egyptians, Babylonians, and Assyrians had entertained primitive ideas about the independence of the soul from the body. This meant that transmigration themes had first arisen in India, though some modern scholarship would today be prepared to question this. Vivekananda cites the Greek story of Pythagoras being instructed upon reincarnation by the brahmin priests of India, which is by no means definitive in a historical context. Via the Egyptians, the Jews also were here viewed as deriving themes of reincarnation from India. In an exegetical manner, Vivekananda was in effect contrasting the Judaeo-Christian religious attitude with the Indian, and to the greater credit of the latter. One does not have to agree with various features of Vivekananda's exegesis to concede with David Hume (who is also quoted) that: "The Metempsychosis is therefore the only system of this kind that philosophy can listen to."[286]

Whether or not Hume had any secret thoughts about his ultimate destiny or antecedents, Vivekananda himself did not clarify the controversial subject of regression into animal forms that his compatriots widely believed in. This is a particular failing of his exegesis, but he did clearly state his view that the *Deus ex machina* recourse of the Christian theologians was "quite irrelevant; it amounts to nothing less than a confession of ignorance." Here he was siding with the "eternal time" theory in a new variant of the old philosophical contest against "creation from nothing," once so powerfully argued between the Neoplatonists and the Christian theologians. Nearing the end of his article, he unleashes a direct thrust against his opponents: every theory of the creation of the soul from nothing "inevitably leads to fatalism and preordination," responsible for the idea prevalent amongst both Christians and Muslims "that the heathens are the lawful victims of their swords." This accusation of predatory beliefs was a stock one used against the Muslims by Christian exegetes, but Vivekananda did not so obligingly distinguish between different versions of colonialism. Instead he favoured an argument of the Nyaya tradition of logical philosophy, which reasoned that reincarnation was confirmed by karmic impressions (of actions) remaining latent or unperceived when unexpressed, and reappearing in their effect as experiential tendencies (*pravrittis*). This argument is conceivably more sophisticated than that which predestines to an eternal hell.

Vivekananda had a further relevant twist to his defence. Unlike the Christians, he was not at loggerheads with the new Darwinian theory in respect of a human evolution from animal forms. But as he pointed out, there was a strong difference in the interpretation given to the phenomenon of evolution by Hindu philosophers and Western materialist thinkers respectively. The former explained it by the conscious efforts of individual souls and the storing of experiential residues as tendencies in the individual mind; whereas the materialist evolutionists explained it by hereditary physical transmission and the theory that the brain is the subject of all actions. This was the real issue to be fought out, he urged; only if cellular (genetic) transmission is the all-sufficient explanation can materialism be regarded as inevitable.[287] As posterity should now be aware, even many scientific materialists no longer accept genetic rationales as all-sufficient explanations,[288] and technical theories of brain function have shot into mentalist vistas – theories which might ultimately prove to widespread logical satisfaction what mental impressions really are.

It is possible to assert that Vivekananda was much more of an "Aristotelian" in the scientific sense than Coomaraswamy, who was more aesthetically and scholastically oriented. Ironically perhaps, despite his aversion to Vivekananda the modernist, the genesis of Coomaraswamy's theories on Hindu art derived from Vivekananda, though this was not acknowledged. This is not difficult to ascertain, since Coomaraswamy had been a personal friend of Margaret Noble, alias Sister Nivedita (d. 1911), a British disciple of Vivekananda who had renounced her former role in life to inaugurate an educational programme for Indian women in Calcutta. She possessed a keen knowledge of

Indian art which was one of her legacies from Vivekananda. It was Coomaraswamy who undertook to complete the last two-thirds of Nivedita's book *Myths of the Hindus and Buddhists* (London, 1913) at her death, and it may be that his elaborations on the Indian art heritage were in a similar proportion of originality. Nivedita had championed Vivekananda's criticism of the theory of Hellenic influence on Indian art, which was a strongly entrenched theory amongst Western savants, who were often slow to recognize the genius of anything Indian.[289] The counter-theory had been expressed by Vivekananda at the Paris Congress of the History of Religions in 1900. The context of this event was perhaps proof enough of the limitations imposed by religious orthodoxy.

The Congress was originally intended to be another Parliament of Religions like that held at Chicago seven years earlier, but the function was changed into a scholarly venue that did not permit any discussion of direct "sectarian" views. The Roman Catholic world had influentially opposed a Parliament, fearing that Oriental ideas might place orthodox Christianity in jeopardy. The outcome was that Vivekananda was reduced to debating with Western orientalist scholars on the pedestrian question of whether the Vedic religion was the consequence of nature-worship. He was drawn up against the German scholar Gustav Oppert, who attempted to trace the origin of the Shiva-linga to "mere phallicism." Vivekananda doubtless wondered how long it would be before concealed religious bias let in more light on the history of religions and philosophies, despite his former extravagant praise of the Sanskritist Max Muller. Rather patiently perhaps, he contested the ideas of the eminent that Greek culture had influenced Indian literature, Indian art, and Indian sciences. Some of the Sanskrit scholars agreed with him,[290] but in general the classicist and theological biases were slow to diminish.

Half a century later, Coomaraswamy had obscured much of the light thrown upon the *sanatana dharma* by opting for a drastic conciliation with Thomism that strongly coloured his innovation of *et universalis*. To his credit, he emphasized that he had never wished to establish a new school of thought (though in effect he can be said to have done so). "Perhaps the greatest thing I have learned is never to think for myself," he said in 1947, just prior to his death. By this he meant the unity or "One World" that applied to the *philosophia perennis*. While respecting his wish not to be self-intrusive, it is difficult not to feel that the realm of *philosophia perennis* was invaded by aliens in Coomaraswamy's interpretation which so markedly glossed disparities and eschewed some vital elements. A representative list of the names he most favoured in this "One World" were Buddha, Plato, St. Augustine, Plotinus, Shankara, Ramanuja, Aquinas, Meister Eckhart, and Boehme.[291] Hence orthodoxy, mysticism, and philosophy have no boundary lines; in practice, Aquinas dominated all the others listed. The less orthodox, and the non-orthodox, will beg to think for themselves in case they ever find themselves in jeopardy of the inquisitorial torture-chambers which Aquinas (d. 1274) effectively defended in his role as a Dominican theologian who was perpetually concerned to defeat the doctrines of heretics and heathens.

One of the supporters of Coomaraswamian perennial tradition has written that "a true gnostic would be the first to realize the immense importance of Thomism." Seyyed Hossein Nasr also suggests that Aquinas "himself may have also been a Christian gnostic when he put his pen down and chose silence."[292] Much would here depend upon definitions of Christian gnostics perhaps, but the Cathars of France were arguably much more gnostic than their Dominican persecutors who mounted an incredible feat of judicial massacre in the bloodstained gowns of pious tradition. While Aquinas was writing down his arguments to shore up the faith against the Saracen philosophers, his fellow Dominicans were the active agents of the newly created pious horror known as the Inquisition.

According to the same scholar, the perspective of the Muslim Peripatetics was "in many respects close to that of St. Thomas."[293] But this is an undue conflation of Thomism with the *mashsha'iyyun*. The only similarity exists in the fact that the "Angelic Doctor" frequently quotes his Muslim rivals; his intention was to appropriate Aristotle in the manner of an apologist for the church, a very different tactic to that of the Aristotelians in Islamic countries.

The confusion between gnostics and traditionalists is typical of the Coomaraswamian vogue for the perennial philosophy. In much the same way, sufis are conflated with orthodox Islam and a non-Muslim sufi is deemed a heretic by the advocates of "tradition." Orthodox tradition is justified the world over in this vogue, and no account is taken of the disparities of diabolical bloodshed, conquests of empire, pogroms, and the inequalities of social classes. All tradition is defended in the name of the sacred; all wrongs become right in the name of a transcendent unity of religions which is committed to ignoring historical details. No wonder that gnosis has become such a meaningless word in the modern era.

Coomaraswamy and his followers have selected Meister Eckhart (d. *c.*1328) as another example of the greatest mysticism. He was another Dominican, though excommunicated by the Pope at the time of his death, being considered a heretic by the Inquisition. One can concede that he had outgrown the diabolical extensions of tradition, but in the anthropographic view, the comparatively neglected Roger Bacon is a more suitable candidate for perennial honours. Bacon is still held in abhorrence by modern theologians for his critique of the thirteenth century theological situation. But modern biographers of Eckhart can still write: "In defence of the Inquisition, the duty of whose officers it was to check the irregular movements, there is much to be said."[294] The preoccupation with glamourizing sordid episodes is not convincing. Bacon did the opposite in repudiating the role of the contemporary orders of friars; he himself had joined the Franciscans but was considered one of the heretics in this movement, heretics who were in general severely dealt with. That Thomas Aquinas was a mere "ignorant boy" in Bacon's view has seemed blasphemous to the champions of tradition. Bacon was more mature in his "esoteric" Aristotelianism, though his writings do reveal Christianizing glosses in the moralist vogue that set pagans on a lower footing than the anointed. Bacon's version of the perennial philosophy was careful to include the Hebrews among the first custodians of the "universal science," though this Biblical association is not to be found in the *Secretum Secretorum*, only in Bacon's glosses to this Latin translation from the Arabic. Nevertheless, Bacon was much more "Arabic" than Aquinas, and may in fact have been a true gnostic beneath the veneer of piety.

It is much easier to agree with Nasr on the subject of John Scottus Eriugena, in that the latter's *Periphyseon* has been inveterately neglected by Christians owing to its association with Cathar circles in the thirteenth century. But Nasr complains that orthodox attempts have been made to reduce this treatise to a "simple Neoplatonist or pantheist" position, and instead affirms it as "a witness of something essential to the sapiential dimension of Christianity."[295] One might comment here that pantheism is not so reductionist a stance as monotheistic orthodoxy, and that the esoteric is not so readily to be transformed into the exoteric by a distortion of tradition. Eriugena was writing from the perspective of early Irish Christianity in addition to Neoplatonist sources, and this ninth century Irish philosopher still possessed the punch of his Irish predecessors in confronting orthodox doctrines with alternatives befitting more expansive minds than those filled with pious sawdust. But this Irish tradition was afterwards snuffed out, and it was the Cathars who aptly inherited Eriugena's exegesis, in addition to other streams of Eastern thought conveniently dubbed "Manichaean" by stigmatizers of heresy.

One of the twentieth century vicissitudes befalling the term *philosophia perennis* has been its rewording as *religio perennis* (perennial religion). This substitution was made by the Christian theologian Frithjof Schuon, who has deemed it to more accurately reflect wisdom. Others incline to think that *sophia perennis* would be more apt, though conceivably the vogue for Latinizations in this field has ceased to have any meaning or usefulness. Schuon has been influential in stressing the religious content of perenniality, and has gone to the extreme of dismissing the view that metaphysics is a branch of philosophy. For Schuon, metaphysics is a branch of religion only. Hence the dogmatic affirmation that "*all* (italics mine) philosophy suffers from certain limitations which, even in the most favourable instances . . . exclude a completely adequate appreciation of metaphysic."[296] So once again dogmatism has appropriated the fruits from less dogmatic sectors, dislocating historical facts in the general decline since the Coomaraswamian emic generalizations. Perennial religion is now the order of the day in some interpretations, and heretics are duly chastised by the perennial priests of infallibility.

It is very easy to agree, however, with the Schuonite statement that: "Religion translates metaphysical or universal truths into dogmatic language."[297] That is an apt observation, and one reason why perennial religion excludes a completely adequate appreciation of metaphysic.

The transcendent unity of religions has given Schuon the excuse to express an incredibly pious and "spiritual" denigration of Vivekananda, together with an odiously infallible critique of Ramakrishna, who is deemed to have been hopelessly wrong in marking out his chief disciple as a spiritual genius. Ramakrishna, we are told, attributed to Vivekananda "a genius for ontological and plastic realization which he neither had nor could have." This omniscience is accompanied by the more approximate deduction which attributes to Ramakrishna "something like an unconscious usurpation of the prophetic function." Vivekananda is criticized for his "powerful, proud nature," yet the conclusion is logically legitimate that unctuous traditionalist critics are the most proud and vindictive "spiritual" snobs in their assumption of all graces and sacred airs. "Under no circumstances," it is unequivocally asserted, "could he (Vivekananda) have been a *jnani* who had perfected his realization (*sadhana*) in a previous existence." Now irrespective of whether or not one believes in reincarnation, this statement is in flat contradiction to the "traditional" contention of Ramakrishna, who was most explicit concerning the young Vivekananda. It is evident, therefore, that when the "unity of religions" is transcendently emphasized, this simply means according to a particular traditionalist interpretation which is at more or less total variance with other traditions; free play for arbitrary distinctions is still allowed and indeed (divinely ?) sanctioned.

Schuon's underlying accusation against Vivekananda is that he was a modernist; this is a term of abuse indicating heretical innovations from tradition, very much in the spirit of the many generations of righteous divines who castigated the (genuine) sufis for their departures from orthodox norms of habit and thought. Schuon clearly thinks that Vivekananda was "deformed by false education in school." This is a reference to the latter's Westernized education at Calcutta University where he read British philosophers and scientists like Hume, Mill, Comte, and Spencer – and all of whose interpretations he soon rejected. But he did not neglect to turn his back likewise upon the thoroughly anachronistic structure of brahmanism and its caste taboos, which he derided as a "kitchen religion," a reference to the traditionalist aversion to priestly food being contaminated by contact with untouchable outcastes and low caste persons. Traditionalists are in an extremely unenviable position in the humanitarian sense (irrespective of their divine affiliations) in stigmatizing Vivekananda. But undaunted, Schuon affirms in relation to Vivekananda's career that "Ramakrishna could not foresee effects the causes of which he had not conceived," a reference which at the most, proves the traditionalist bias against secular education at the expense of respecting mature Hindu philosophy. Ramakrishna conceivably knew that there would be at least one witness after him to the essential *sanatana dharma* in the Kali-yuga of traditional and modern ignorance.[298]

In order to prove Vivekananda's errors, Schuon selects some statements from Vivekananda's works. These statements are described as absurdities. The very first statement revealingly pinpoints the social position of women, but then sociological matters are customarily blanketed by traditionalists, who often have no wish to change anything for the better in matters of social inequality. In a collection of impromptu class talks, Vivekananda is reported as saying that Jesus was imperfect because he did not allot women an equal place with men, i.e., none of his women disciples were given the status of an apostle. This disparity is attributed to Jewish custom, by which even Jesus was bound. This was treated by Schuon as blasphemy, in the typical manner of the heresiographer. Like most heresiographers he quotes out of context; this particular collection of talks contains numerous very favourable references to Jesus, and in the very next sentence, Vivekananda asserts that Jesus was "the greatest character next to Buddha," which was high praise. Even Buddha was not fully perfect, he adds, though the Buddha did recognize the equality of women in religion. Vivekananda's stress on the lack of perfection was part of his caution against making men into gods, since the consequence of this can be undue adulation of customs which may be imperfect. "We ought to criticize these great ones," he says accordingly, since "we too must become Buddhas and Christs."[299] This is far more humane and a far more esoteric teaching than those which stress total belief in every recorded saying or deed of some figurehead from whom the individual supplicant is forever removed under pain of heresy.

Likewise heretical to *religio perennis* was Vivekananda's remark in his *Karma Yoga* that the Buddhas and Christs commonly known are inferior to those greater examples of which the world knows nothing. Hundreds of these unknown exemplars had lived in every land, he added. This makes a great deal of sense in respect of a *philosophia perennis*, which is continually obscured and distorted by popular treatment – which has diminished the status of various known Buddhas through discernible hindsight (Vivekananda often subscribed to the notion that Buddha had taught a no-soul doctrine, which was a common interpretation of Theravada Buddhism and Western scholarship). His own teacher Ramakrishna has frequently received mediocre treatment despite factual indications to the contrary.

Extremely revealing is Schuon's stigmatization of a statement quoted from a letter of the heretic to Sister Nivedita. The English translation of Schuon renders this as: "The totality of all living beings is the personal God." It is therefore pantheism that is considered to be modernist, in which case Advaita Vedanta has been very modern since at least the time of Shankara well over a thousand years ago, at the most conservative estimate. The transcendent unity of religions professed by heresiographers might well be considered parochial in the sense of an antiquated and bigoted intolerance.[300]

Moving from the emics of perennial religion, it is pertinent to pick up the traces of the Coomaraswamian trend in its more philosophical guise. Probably the best representative of this was Sir Sarvepalli Radhakrishnan, whose presentation of Indian philosophy is frequently very sophisticated, and whose standpoint did not always converge with that of Coomaraswamy. But even he tended to be amorphous in reference to the perennial philosophy. Following Coomaraswamy, he stipulates the *sanatana dharma*, "the eternal religion behind all religions," as perennial philosophy. He quite reasonably affirms that different verbal expressions of this are determined by the environment and the climate of thought prevailing, and there may indeed be much truth in his view that those who overlook the perennial wisdom and instead "cling to outward forms and quarrel among themselves are responsible for the civilized chaos in which we live."[301] But though he urges that it is necessary to return to this "fundamental wisdom which has been obscured and distorted in the course of history by dogmatic and sectarian developments,"[302] he does not clarify that this will not be achieved by an opting for the "unity of religions" concept which is an elementary cultural obligation and the field of *religio perennis* as distinct from the more advanced requirements of *philosophia perennis*. Radhakrishnan unfortunately incorporated the error of conflating these two categories of *perennis*, which is clearly visible in his quotations from Plotinus and St. Augustine, which are placed directly on par, as if no basic distinctions between the traditions represented had ever existed.

The abovementioned quotation from Plotinus is that in which he affirms that his teachings on the hypostases were not new – "they do not belong to the present time, but were made long ago, not explicitly." Plotinus remarks that he has interpreted them afresh, relying upon Plato's Dialogues as evidence for the antiquity of these views. The latest translator of Plotinus adds that this belief in the "non-explicit" character of traditionally authoritative writings was held in common by both pagan and Christian traditionalists of the first centuries A.D., and also adhered to by later Christian traditionalists.[303] Yet it is obvious enough that very different interpretations were given to what was less explicit in earlier times.

The abovementioned quotation from Augustine of Hippo (354–430) reflects the orthodox Christian appropriation of antique associations at a time of increasingly formal codification of church dogmas. Radhakrishnan quotes Augustine's assertion that the Christian religion existed among the ancients, and "never did not exist, from the beginning of the human race until Christ came in the flesh, at which time the true religion, which already existed, began to be called Christianity."[304] But this dogmatic ascription of perenniality was used to screen out all other rivals to ancient truth. The ascription is only admissible if it was an esoteric Christianity that was being exposited, but Augustine was orthodox, and much less esoteric than the Manichees whom he had left while still in their outer circle, confused by contrasting arguments from Christians. Some of the Coptic ascetics might conceivably have been in the right to make such an extensive claim,[305] but Augustine was one of those instrumental in blanketing out less clerical trends amongst early Christians. Though Christian commentators have been fond of the claim that "during the patristic period all that was best in the spirit of Neoplatonism flowed into the veins of the Church,"[306] what was "best" in the interests of orthodox consumption amounted to a straitjacketing of the Neoplatonist dynamic.

The style of Coomaraswamy has more recently blanketed the significance of Plotinus. Many twentieth century writers have read the latter in quotation, but demonstrate not the slightest comprehension of his teaching. It is very fashionable nowadays to list Plotinus as one of the exponents of perennial philosophy, but until the list is more etically qualified, he will remain an effective blank in the annals of emicism. In perusing current emic formats, the average reader will have no suspicion, for instance, that Plotinus engaged himself in a loaded dispute with the "gnostics." What Plotinus would have thought of some of the current enthusiasts who link his name with "perennial philosophy" would probably not be complimentary, and may well have merited an even stronger critique of pretenders to gnosis.

A recent "transpersonal" version of the perennial theme has not yet caught up with the fact that it was not Leibniz who coined the phrase "perennial philosophy," and does not even mention that it was a Latin term that was then under consideration. This is rather typical of the continuing Huxleyan idiom of ahistorical penchant. Plotinus is early quoted as one of the inventory of great names, but the thesis is not geared to historical dimensions, save perhaps by analogy. As usual, the statement is found that the perennial philosophy forms the esoteric core of Hinduism, Buddhism, Taoism, Sufism, and Christian mysticism, in addition to "being embraced, in whole or part, by individual intellects" varying from Spinoza to Jung. But there is little or no further qualification expressed other than the reflection of "in whole or part." Instead, there is the usual simplistic definition of the perennial philosophy as in essence constituting the "ground" or "suchness" or reality of all things and events. [307] This reflects the Eckhartian formula = Buddhist void = anything else vaguely pantheistic in the neo-Huxleyan continuation of simple catchphrases. Perhaps that is why Jung has not yet been drastically corrected in the light of early Mahayana teachings, to select only one of the glaring disparities in the vogue for perennial emics.

It has been remarked that many scientists "have always flirted with, or totally embraced, the perennial philosophy . . . even Isaac Newton." [308] The sense of flirtation seems peculiarly apt, though not at all to be restricted to scientists; on the contrary, this superficial sense of familiarity should be recognized as the norm of interest in this subject. Newton's fascination for a secret tradition going back to Pythagoras was probably a great deal deeper than most of the current alliances and dalliances with a subject that is ridiculously easy to canvas and exploit in its amorphous formats.

Flirtation with the perennial philosophy on the basis of the inadequate premise of pantheism (despite its relevance) is equivalent to the mere postulation of a metaphysical factor such as is the norm in some forms of academic philosophy. It is not a sufficient gauge of the perennial philosophy; it does not make the flirter into a (working) philosopher, whatever the perennial auspices that might be appropriated and advertised.

Etic analysis of this subject requires the minimal stipulation of a shallow version of the perennial philosophy that far outnumbers anything authentic in respect of the statistics dividing flirters from philosophers. Flirters very frequently become premature gurus, a current commercial habit greatly facilitated by the ahistoricists who are not exacting even in elementary matters of scholarship and experiential specifics. The fashion in Huxleyan and neo-Huxleyan circles is one of using a small selection of "experiential" concepts in the loosest possible sense that in practice requires no familiarity with sources or with standards explicit in some of the traditions customarily nominated. Such circles are rarely interested in historical details, but instead prefer fantasy, which in general is accompanied by undisciplined lifestyles. It is no wonder that many critics give no credence to such loose treatments; the literary imbecile is proffered concepts in the idiom of the "hidden teaching beyond yoga" and "kundalini beyond the chakras," i.e., sheer novelty value for jaded palettes. The truth is rather that shallow copyists and distorters perennially wriggle out of meeting finer standards, instead opting for easy substitutes and garish diversions. The present author cannot blame any critic, in the absence of consulting source materials, for thinking the whole subject to be a commercial hoax of the narcissistic vogue. This vogue includes diverse bandwagon gurus following on from "beat zen" and related amusements, a thoroughly Western species of fraud who specialize in sensation, showmanship, fantasy, and more indescribable exercises in obscurantism that have a curious affinity with four-letter word occultism.

Californian zen is well known amongst the literate for its "instant illumination" which actually amounts to "do as you like." Anything goes for the fake gnostic, as Plotinus perceived in the more exacting perspective of the perennial philosophy. A developed discriminative wisdom is not reducible to the diffuse holistic deficiency unless psychology is compressed into a cage convenient for cretins.

In his biography of Plotinus, Porphyry (233–*c*.304) reports that his teacher had frequently attacked the position of those identified as "gnostics," and had finally written the treatise *Against the Gnostics*. Porphyry identifies these gnostics with numerous Christians who had abandoned the old (Greek) philosophy. These renegades declared that Plato had failed to discern the truth, and they concocted various revelations which were circulated in the name of Zoroaster (Zarathushtra) and also other names then famous in initiatory lore. Porphyry adds that he himself had shown that the corpus attributed to Zoroaster was spurious, and only recently written by the gnostics in order to give an impression of antiquity for their doctrines (as against those of Plato).[309] Different scholarly attitudes have been expressed on this topic,[310] and very often the main point has been missed. Plotinus has certain affinities with gnostic milieux, and his literary attack on the Christian gnostics is strong enough to warrant the inference here that it was much more than mere secession from Platonism that he was opposing. He himself was a very unorthodox Platonist, though one thoroughly opposed to Epicureanism in the forms then current. It may be that, in his Egyptian antecedents, he was familiar with a proto-Phibionite gnostic trend amongst the diverse groupings who are lump-classified as "gnostic."

The Plotinian attack on Gnosticism was radically different from that of the Church fathers, and there is only a very superficial resemblance in the matter of the accusation that the gnostics wrongly despised and hated the material universe and denied the goodness of its creator. In point of fact, Plotinus was as much opposed to Christianity as he was to Gnosticism. As Vivekananda was much later to do, he viewed "creation from nothing" as irrational, instead maintaining the eternal and panpsychist nature of the unvierse, i.e., the "World-Soul." The Plotinian reverence for the planets, metamorphosed as "gods," was also incomprehensible to the orthodox Christians, though the Sipasi philosophers would have found no difficulty with the more elastic pagan equations (much vulgarized in the Roman world).

Since there appear to have been gnostics amongst the friends of Plotinus (friends resistant to his neoplatonism), it is feasible that there was more than one type of "gnostic" that he was referring to. He accuses gnostics of perverting the ancient Platonic teaching into a fantasy, for the purpose of bloating their delusions of spiritually elite status. He himself cannot so easily be accused of this common failing, since he was defending the gradual and exacting study of truth which the gnostics were in haste to avoid in a more instantaneous achievement. He accordingly accuses them of a false claim to constitute a privileged class, who do not rely upon salvation by their own efforts but instead claim a dramatic form of divine intervention. He was here referring to the inexplicable nature of *gnosis* (as it was generally portrayed), in the sense of a secret knowledge which had the power to "save." But this could be variously interpreted, and one of the accusations of Plotinus was that the imagined prerogative of gnostics led to excuses for immoral conduct.[311] One should not deduce that this was true of all gnostics, any more than one should believe that Plotinus was fabricating. It is very unlikely that he was making the charge without foundation; if modern sequels are anything to go by, then he is more likely to have been understating in respect of those committed to a quick and easy route to "spiritual" honours, or rather megalomania.

Plotinus refers to the gnostic lack of clarity on the subject of virtue, insinuating this deficit as an Epicurean affinity. The inference is that these gnostics were too much in love with physical pleasures; though he does not say so, this flirtation with gnosis was in contradiction to the more advanced gnostic ideals (particularly those in the non-Christian sector of Manichaeans, an embryonic grouping at that time). He remarks sarcastically that those who already had the *gnosis* should pursue basic requirements of conduct in conformity with the characteristics of a spiritual nature, "for that nature is aware of (inner) nobility and despises the pleasure of the body."[312] This type of emphasis is anathema to flirters; modern Western gurus of the flirtatious variety rely upon the pleasure-loving nature of their sycophants in order to bemuse them into a state of continued torpor and atrophydom of mental and spiritual faculties.

In opting for the course of a neo-Phibionite sensationalist, Aldous Huxley was yet a mild and civilized version of the more outlandish extravaganzas of perverted perenniality that were to follow.

Just as one sometimes finds glossed reports of modern gnostics who were and are demonstrably flirters with debased wisdom, so also one too often finds glamourized reports of the Alexandrian era gnostics. Plotinus is much less romantic than the comparatively illiterate exponents of today's commercial occultism. For instance, he criticizes the gnostic claim to control the higher powers by magic, and to cure diseases by casting out demons. He gives the neglected information that gnostics were in the habit of writing out magical chants for their theurgic procedures, and that gnostics assumed that diseases were evil spirits. This vogue of spells and charms is appropriately contrasted with the procedure of the philosophers, "who free themselves from diseases by temperance and orderly living."[313] This ancient psychotherapy should be clearly distinguished from current NeoReichian Gestalt tactics, which are probably a cause of some diseases in their advocacy of physical pleasures in immoderate doses.

Porphyry, the "toughest" of the later Greek Neoplatonists, continued the anti-gnostic stress of his teacher Plotinus; his "Aristotelian" treatise was later to find a new and commodious home in the tradition of the Muslim Aristotelians and Neoplatonists. The Christian scholar R.C. Zaehner tried to find proof that Shaikh Sohravardi Maqtul was a protester against monism, i.e. pantheism, and made a misleading reference in a long tradition of scholarly incompetence in ishraqi matters. Zaehner has it that Maqtul "categorically denied the possibility of the soul ever becoming one with God."[314] Plotinus might have smiled down the centuries if foreknowledge was within reach of pagans, since Maqtul approvingly quoted the Plotinian statement of unity with "the One" in his *Kitab Hiqmat al-Ishraq*. The affirmation of Plotinus (IV.8.1) that he had "come to identity with the divine"[315] was perhaps an ace card in his struggle against Christian gnostics; this affirmation is not made in any sensational manner, and he carefully qualifies it by providing a context in which he does not remain in this exalted condition permanently.

Zaehner's monotheistic gloss should read that Sohravardi Maqtul did not claim any supreme gnostic prerogative of the kind that was misused by flirters with wisdom. But Zaehner was concerned to undermine the concept of a pantheistic perennial philosophy, and could not tell the difference between the simplistic Huxleyan idiom and more vintage sophistications. The Christianizing Zaehner referred to his own interpretation as a "theistic interpretation of the monistic type of mystical experience in which the mystic claims identity with the 'One.'"[316] Hence Zaehner was attempting to combat the axis of the philosophy of Plotinus. He was thorough enough in his efforts, in that he mitigated horizons in Iranist studies, Sanskrit studies, and Islamic era studies. The confusion he wrought has been longlasting.

Though modern theologians have continued to disfigure the history of philosophy and mysticism, beneath the guise of scholarship there are usually clear errors of scholarship in their exegesis. Zaehner neglected to inform his reader that Maqtul explicitly acknowledged the Iranian sufi Bayazid al-Bistami (and not Junayd of Baghdad) as a key link in the transmission of ancient Iranian wisdom that contributed to the confluence of *ishraq*. Zaehner sides with the "orthodox" Junayd (d. 910) against Bistami (d. *c.*874), though his version of Junayd is typically truncated. Zaehner's theistic bias caused him to attribute the monism (or rather pantheism) of Bistami to a Vedantic influence from India. This enabled him to castigate the "monist tide" unleashed by Bistami (and checked by Junayd) as a lamentable aberration from true mysticism. For Zaehner, the authentic feature in Sufism (to use a Western word) was the "love of God," a phrase clearly in line with Christian preferences. He cannot bear to define monism as "identity with God," but instead opts for a less shattering "oneness of the self." Theological modifications are often distinctly parsimonious, though whether they are scientifically oriented is very disputable.

After trying to compress Junayd into a theological thimble, Zaehner resigns this attempt in relation to the later burgeoning of Sufism that was comparatively unrestrained by fears of orthodox condemnation. He follows the anachronistic caricature of Iranian philosophy and mysticism that had been promulgated by much earlier Western scholars, and laments the supposed fact that so "little effort of systematization" was made in Iran – though Zaehner means this in a very narrow theological sense. After Ghazzali (d. 1111), we read, the mystical stream "got lost in the sands of religious syncretism in which monism, pantheism, and theism were inextricably mingled." This heresiography is accompanied by the afterthought that although "so maddening to the intellect," this syncretism created "a poetic flowering that has seldom been equalled."[317] This concession to aesthetic considerations is rather typical of the muted appreciation of Iranian thought during the medieval period that has been widely expressed by specialist scholars. What is so maddening to Western intellects (of the theological variety or no) is not to be so easily dismissed by a recourse to the delights of poesy, along with metrical cogitations equivalent to whether "tool" rhymes with "fool." Later medieval Iranian philosophy and mysticism may well amount to getting lost in the sands of misunderstanding on the part of complete aliens in that field of thought, but it is not on this account to be considered a write-off by more competent scholars and less flirtatious philosophers.

Highly suspicious in terms of interpretive standards is the Zaehnerian description of the teaching of Muhiyuddin ibn al-Arabi (d. 1240) as "theoretical monism."[318] This aspersion is typical of the general orthodox reluctance to concede any validity to the *wujudi* (pantheist) perspective in sufi philosophy; even very recently, the writings of Ibn al-Arabi have been banned in certain conservative locales.

Similarly stigmatized by theism are the Mevlevi followers of Jalaluddin Rumi, who are styled as "theologically indifferentist."[319] Whatever dire sins were being implied here, readers should know that Rumi's bardic expressions have elsewhere been scholastically revealed as defying definition as a product of any particular culture. His unusual poetical format in the *Mathnavi* manages to evade orthodox literalisms despite its larding with well known Islamic themes. Rumi was taught by the unorthodox Iranian dervish Shams-i-Tabriz, who does not appear to have been in any favour with the orthodox divines.[320] Zaehner's theism would perhaps have seemed as backward to Shams as Eckhart must have deemed the reprovers with whom he was confronted when he was required to answer the charges of the Inquisition, one of the worst bodies of crushing bores known to history. The "love of God" can assume some very strange twists in dogmatic flirtation.

Zaehner was pleased to find the Iranian dervish Najmuddin Razi, alias Daya (d. 1256), defending Islamic orthodoxy, and interprets him as criticizing monism. Though there are complexities in his *Mirsad al-Ibad*[321], Daya discriminates against philosophers and Hindu brahmins in the fashion of "orthodox" Sufism, which represented more insular characteristics than the *wujudi* trend. This orthodox variant was closely connected with the dervish orders, which began to mushroom at this time. This "popular Sufism" of the orders exhibited many emic features of approach, and is often mistaken for the entire sufi phenomenon. But it should be clearly distinguished from "high Sufism," to use a convenient phrase of recent coinage. This matter throws into relief the importance of discerning etic features of sufihood, but traditionalists find this concept difficult. The suggestion that many so-called "sufis" were not anything of the kind is often met with incredulity by the less critical. It is perhaps rather similar to the problems which some Christians have in distinguishing Francis of Assisi from St. Bonaventura.

Zaehner also found an anti-monist emphasis in Ibn Tufayl (d. 1185) of Spain, but very much less convincingly for his purposes than in the case of Daya. Ibn Tufayl was a philosopher whose scepticism of orthodox norms railed against the indoctrination associated with the concept of revelations. He was definitely not one of the more rigid Aristotelian logicians, and expressly refers to advanced psychological experiences in the introduction to his distinctive classic *Hayy ibn Yaqzan*. He affirms that what can successfully be expressed in words and books amounts to a discursive introduction to the experience of the "oriental philosophy" mentioned by Ibn Sina (Avicenna). But it is very rare, he qualifies, for this to be done properly, owing to the difficulty in "mastering even the most trifling part of the experience." He further stipulates that even those who do master a part of this experience "speak of it publicly only in riddles," as a consequence of orthodox bias. Even more specific in its allusion is his remark that if he (Ibn Tufayl) told the reader of the highest levels he had himself reached without first dwelling on preliminary steps, "it would do you no more good than blind faith."[322]

Theistic attempts at reductionism are not therefore even slightly convincing.

Ibn Tufayl was referring to some of the same philosophical sources used by his contemporary Sohravardi Maqtul, and their qualifications made in experiential description can be closely aligned in certain respects. In many ways, the later work of Farzaneh Behram ibn Farhad (d. 1624) was of similar intent, in that the *Sharistan* was in effect an introduction to the revelatory union with the "empyrean world" of solar symbolism which is closely related to the "oriental philosophy" of the ishraqi tradition. The Sipasi philosophers would have felt quite at home with the planetary associations known to Plotinus, who was "oriental" in the ishraqi sense. However, such subtleties were entirely lost upon Zaehner, who evidently assumed that it was irrelevant to investigate post-thirteenth century developments in Iranian philosophy, having proved (he thought) the aberrancy of monism. In the light of his treatment of comparatively well documented exponents, what encouragement is it to accept the Zaehnerian version of the more ancient Manicheanism and the more archaic Zarathushtra?

A major problem in the Zaehnerian interpretation is the facile interpretation of *baqa* (stabilization of expanded consciousness) as theistic, and the failure to grasp that there is a series of states (and not just one) implied by this (very) popularized term appropriated from early Sufism. It might even be said that the consciousness signified is the real etic perennial of advanced philosophy, closed to obscurantist scholars and simplistic holistic freaks alike. While scholarly exercises of belief inevitably arouse disdain in the "let-go" camp, the atrocious versions of the perennial found in free-and-easy holistica amount to an introduction to perennial folly.

Unable to resist extending his theistic interpretation to the Sanskrit field, Zaehner produced a matching explanation for the *Bhagavad-Gita*, a major classic, and part of the voluminous Sanskrit epic known as the *Mahabharata*. The theistic specialist contended that the modern commentators on the *Gita* were conditioned by the most ancient of the medieval commentators, i.e. Shankara,[323] who was an exponent of the Advaita (non-dualist) Vedanta, which has been closely associated with the much earlier teaching of the Upanishads. In some respects, Zaehner's contention is accurate here, since Shankara is much more well known than the later commentators on the *Gita*, Vedantists like Ramanuja and Madhva. If Zaehner had merely defended Ramanuja's Vishishtadvaita (qualified non-dualism) or even Madhva's Dvaita (dualism), his exegesis would not be so debateable, but as it is, his overall theistic assumptions can be discerned as missing the point of the *bhakti* (love) ideal in the best versions of this. Zaehner was perhaps conditioned by too inadequate a register of associations to explicate the finer points of the sufi ideal of *mahabba* (love) and the Hindu *bhakti* (or *parabhakti* in its deeper connotations). *Bhakti* is often confused by traditionalists with a sentimental devotion, and there are perhaps too many confusions with the more decadent forms of Krishna-*bhakti* to facilitate a concise redefinition of the term. Perhaps what one should say most of all is that, unlike Zaehner's despising of monism, it will not do to deride the preparatory love for a personal God, but biased conceptions which stress the love of a personal God as the crown of the "unitary experience" are not to be regarded as equivalent to the Upanishadic *moksha* (liberation). The personal deficit might merely amount to one of the erotic Tantric love-trysts so popular in contemporary Californian guruism.

The theist theory that Bayazid Bistami was influenced by Advaita Vedanta was intended as an aspersion upon both. Zaehner might ironically be compared to Coomaraswamy in attempting to annul the panpsychist dimensions of the *Gita* teaching on transmigration, in which it is specified that the reincarnating soul casts off worn-out bodies and acquires new bodies.[324] This verse comes from the second chapter, which presents teachings discernibly related to the (now obscure) Sankhya and Yoga traditions of the classical Sanskrit era. One scholarly theory has been that the *Gita* was originally a Sankhya-Yoga treatise which was taken over by Krishna sectarians, but this and other theories of origin have transpired to be inconclusive.

The *Gita* is a poetic work of some seven hundred stanzas. It is sometimes described as an eclectic treatise in which apparently conflicting doctrines are harmonized. Aldous Huxley referred to it as "one of the clearest and most comprehensive summaries of the perennial philosophy ever to have been made,"[325] though he typically neglected to clarify contextual details. In extending Coomaraswamy's definition of the *Gita* as "the focus of all Indian religion," Huxley elaborated a simplified pantheism which places Aquinas on an equal contemplative level with Shankara;[326] this is a logical flaw in which Zaehner emerges as a proof of disparity.

Perhaps the major factor to be emphasized is that the metaphysics of the *Gita* are traditionally recognized to go hand in hand with a necessary preparation for apprehension via rigorous discipline.[327] This can be regarded as an etic feature in tradition which renders void the pretensions of those shallow modernists who seek an easy alternative to discipline in much the same way as many of the more ancient pretenders did. But the desired discipline does not mean the straitjacketed conformity that produced and abetted the Inquisition, since it is easy to condition any reflex into a behaviouristic nightmare of custom.

Shallow modernist monists limit themselves to an unenviable confusion between the materialist and non-materialist categories of monism. The Advaita Vedanta is not materialist, and nor is it even remotely equivalent to the neo-materialist conflation of the mind and body expounded by NeoReichian Gestalt. NeoReichian liberation is even further removed from *moksha* than the Cartesian mind-body split.

Academic philosophy might still confuse *advaita* with the idealism of Bishop Berkeley, but then academic philosophy is frequently cast in a customary mould of traditionalist theory that is rooted in the biases of eighteenth century Rationalism and Empiricism.

At the Paris Congress of the History of Religions (1900), Vivekananda aired the complaint that the *Mahabharata* had not yet been properly read by Westerners (though he thought the same of Hindu pundits also). The *Gita* is very much shorter, but the same complaint can still be aired in general concerning this component treatise. Its date of composition is still in dispute, though Radhakrishnan assigned its origins to the fifth century B.C. One can disagree with certain Hindu traditionalists in their uncritical approval of the *Gita* reconcilement of the Vedic cult of sacrifice with other schools of thought like the Sankya and Yoga, together with the Upanishadic emphasis on the *Brahman-atman* identity. Shankara (*c*.788–*c*.820) was an atypical brahmin who ventured the interpretation that Vedic rites were intended only for those who are encumbered by ignorance.[328] Though the *Gita* and other texts were frequently given forced interpretations by the Vedantic commentators, this particular qualification seems of an etic validity. The problem with Shankara's overall view is that he conceded the eminence of the brahmin stratum and function in Hindu society. Yet at the same time, he undermined the pernicious belief that the upper classes had an exclusive right to salvation. One is obliged to classify these half-measures as an emic limitation, despite the admirable sentiment expressed in the Shankara text *Manisapancaka*: "He who has learned to look upon the phenomenal world in the light of *advaita* is my true teacher, be he an outcaste or a *dvija* (twice-born, of the higher castes)."[329] By comparison, Ramanuja seems to have aligned himself much less with caste traditions in the eleventh century, though he too was a brahmin. His theistic teaching closely reflects the medieval *bhakti* tradition in some respects, though it is also in affinity with the so-called "theistic" texts amongst the Upanishads (which are the primary textual support of the Vedantic tradition).

In many ways, two recent Hindu exponents have provided an updated version of Shankara and Ramanuja respectively. Neither Vivekananda or Mahatma Gandhi were brahmins, but both were expositors of the Vedantic tradition. Vivekananda was a low class *kayastha* by birth, and Gandhi a *vaishya*; the disparity in social status by comparison with the famous expounders abovementioned may even have been matched by a greater discernment on the part of the modern sequels. Vivekananda primarily regarded himself as an advaitin, while Gandhi is more associative of theistic Vedanta, though in a very distinctive sense. How much these two resembled sages of the vintage Upanishadic era is perhaps liable to different interpretations, but both of them concluded that it is folly to rely totally upon inherited wisdom.

Though Gandhi did not become a modernist until the last years of his life, he had much earlier concluded that something was amiss in the conventional Hindu interpretation of the *Gita*. Gandhi first read this classic in 1888–9, while he was studying law in England. Though it was Sir Edwin Arnold's poetic English translation that he perused, it was apparent to the young Gandhi that the *Gita* was not a work of history. He understood it to be an allegory; in contrast, his orthodox compatriots interpreted the text in a very literal manner, assuming it to be an historical description of a battle in which the warrior (*kshatriya*) Arjuna tried to avoid slaying his kinsmen on the field of war, but was reminded by his charioteer Krishna to discharge his caste duty. Krishna figures in the *Gita* as an *avatar* (incarnation) or proto-*avatar*, and hence is synonymous with divine counsel. Gandhi interpreted these features in terms of a perennial struggle in the psychology of mankind, a struggle in which the spiritual principle (Krishna) aids the higher impulses (Arjuna) on the battle-field of the soul. In 1929 Gandhi wrote an introduction to his Gujerati translation of the *Gita* in which he conceded that the letter of the text allows a possible interpretation of warfare as being consistent with renunciation, but he contested the usefulness of such interpretation on the basis of his own experience.[330] Not long afterwards, he became increasingly less conservative in his attitude to caste norms.

Several decades earlier, Vivekananda had taken a much less conciliatory attitude to the caste question in his initial confrontation with Vedantic classics. Caste taboos and priorities of all kinds were anathema to his way of thinking from the inception of his career, and he was always prepared to criticize the disparities evident in traditionalism. Though an upholder of Upanishadic teachings, he referred to "the mazes of many irrelevant subjects" in these prized texts of the Vedanta, in addition to the more inspiring passages they contain. This quote comes from a class-talk he gave at Calcutta in 1897, in which he compared the haphazard compilations of the Upanishads unfavourably with the more consistent arrangement of the *Gita*. But he expressed an applicable criticism of the traditional assumptions of historical context for the *Gita*, and ventured the possibility that the whole of its supposed historicity might be proved absolutely false. But this would not be any loss, since historical research did not apply to the real Vedantic aim of an advanced consciousness. Yet he added that historical research had its use, because "it will not do for us to remain bound by wrong ideas born of ignorance." Indeed, he lamented the lack of historical inquiry amongst his compatriots, and went on to criticize the many sectarians who believed that there was no harm in telling an untruth if this was beneficial or facilitated preaching. Hence many of the Tantric scriptures commenced with the fanciful ascription: "Mahadeva (Shiva) said to Parvati." But it is necessary "to believe in truth only," he affirmed in opposition to this tendency. Faith in antique traditions, without inquiry into the truth of such traditions, injuriously "keeps men bound hand and foot," so that even some great men adhered to superstitions. "Shun all superstitions completely," was his stern warning in the face of Brahmanism and other beliefs.

Vivekananda evidently considered it a rational possibility that the framework of the *Gita* was an allegory,[331] in much the same way as Gandhi was later to express. A few years later, he encountered the superstitions of Western savants at the Paris Congress, where the erudite President of that convene disagreed with him over his assertion that the *Gita* was an integral part of the *Mahabharata*. The only reason adduced as proof to the contrary was that Western scholars were mostly of the opinion that the *Gita* was not integral to the Epic.[332] Majority views do not always constitute the truth, whether in scholarship, science, religion, or philosophy. Yet more important than dates is the nature of content, which is very often outdated owing to the different mentality sets demanding new linguistic media and angles of expression for truths and opinions.

More recently, Zaehner has also concluded that the *Gita* was originally conceived as an integral part of the *Mahabharata*,[333] thus helping to offset earlier views of the "German" school associated with R. Garbe, and also other theories assuming a disparate authorship. This does not rule out the possibility of oral embellishments to the original, though it is perhaps unnecessary to conjecture that the *Gita* statement (18.42–44) in support of caste vocations was an interpolation. The *Gita* takes this issue for granted, though elsewhere in the *Mahabharata*, the matter of caste obligation is questioned by the main hero Yudishthira, the elder brother of Arjuna. Though virtues were traditionally correlated with the castes, it was evident to the more perceptive that purported virtues were frequently in abeyance.[334]

Despite reflections upon Epic poetry, Zaehner's convergence with Vivekananda is superficial. In a general survey of Hinduism, the theistic advocate grudgingly described Vivekananda as having "performed the extraordinary feat of breathing life into the purely static monism of Shankara."[335] Zaehner was correct enough in observing that although Vivekananda adopted a tolerant attitude of "each to his own" in religion, it is clear that he did not consider all religions to be equally true, since this Advaitin maintained that religions are only valid on a relative plane – in that religions are paths leading to "the One." This was a cause of alarm to Zaehner, who went to the unjustifiable extent of comparing Vivekananda with Nietzche in undermining the Christian obsession with sin and its corollary of absolute dependence on the grace of God. While it is true that both Vivekananda and Nietzche viewed orthodox Christianity as a debilitating set of beliefs, their overall perspectives were more or less diametrically opposed. If the history of religions cannot accurately chart such disparities, then the history of philosophy should attempt to make up the deficit.

In Zaehner's view, Vivekananda "laid the foundations of Neo-Vedantism in America which later captivated Huxley" and other famous literary personalities. His pointed review of Vivekananda's achievements is actually a critique, setting the latter at variance with the "theism" of Ramakrishna. The theistic argument here was that in "developing philosophically in a purely monistic direction," Vivekananda was adopting a position "which would seem to falsify Ramakrishna's actual experience." This is attended by the conclusion that "Ramakrishna was by nature a bhakta, not a jnani, a worshipper of God rather than an introspective seeking the One within himself."[336] The real crux is that Zaehner could not assimilate Vivekananda's repudiation of a Personal God, a concept which this Advaitin believed to apply only to human teachers who fulfilled a completed role in the cosmic process. This is logical enough if one concedes that all souls are potentially divine, *avatar* theories apart.

The fundamental difference between Vivekananda and his teacher was not mentioned by Zaehner. Ramakrishna compared the followers of "left-hand Tantra" with those who use a defiled entrance to the edifice of spiritual aspirations; there was a suitable qualification here, since the "dirty path" is contrasted with more direct routes of entry such as the "front door". Nevertheless, he stressed that this was still an entrance, albeit very crude and inferior to other avenues.[337] In contrast, Vivekananda repudiated "dirty path" aptitudes, dismissing them as apathetic and liable to errors too serious to patronize.

In repudiating the drug advocacy of Aldous Huxley, Zaehner was merely doing what Vivekananda would have done more knowledgeably if allowed to speak for himself in alien climates of opinion. Drugs are linked to "left-hand" practices (which specialize in a sensual element), though slaphappy moderns frequently cannot tell which hand it is that requires amputating in the envisaged transpersonal surgery of the "New age."

Revealing of the scholarly attempt to silence Indian reformists are the reflections of Professor Mircea Eliade, an advocate of "left hand" Tantra who refers to the "suave, moralizing writings of Vivekananda." One gleans from this that Vivekananda was not anything of a Nietzche after all. But further, Eliade considers Vivekananda's "popularization" of the Vedanta to be "hybrid and non-Indian," which reflects the curious desire of some traditionalist exponents to view intelligent Hindus as foreigners to their own soil. Modernism is inconvenient for those having tantric nostalgias for the ahistorical past.[338] Vivekananda was not a moralizer in the customary sense; the Eliadic pique is a reaction to the Vedantic eschewing of orgiastic tendencies.

Reverting to one of the less discerning moralists, to the end Zaehner remained truculently theistic[339] and historically distorting. His last book has been deemed markedly idiosyncratic even by its sympathizers. Idiosyncrasy is not proof of error, but there are glaring blindspots in Zaehner's argument, which is an attack upon Eastern pantheism. This argument is more strident than his earlier criticism of Huxley's justification of mescalin usage. Zaehner had formerly made some very valid criticisms of drug advocates like Timothy Leary, who had myopically confused the expansion of consciousness expounded in Eastern mysticism with the new usage of LSD. But in *Our Savage God*, Zaehner extended this criticism as support for his pet theories on the history of religious progress.

The Zaehnerian epitaph insinuated (very strongly) that Huxley's perennial philosophy had lead to the situation of Californian murderers (literally) who had interpreted Eastern mysticism in the sense that killing and being killed amount to the same thing. He focussed upon the sinister episode of Charles Manson and the Sharon Tate murders which made headlines in 1969; a certain American professor had suggested to him that these murders had been inspired by Eastern mysticism. Zaehner appears to have been rather eager to confirm the case, though it would not sound convincing in a court of law. Reminding his readers of the moral ambivalence in modern Western Zen, he uses this as a moral excuse to attack the monist Vedanta, or rather Neo-

Vedanta. Huxley's mescalin here tends to become confused with the entire heritage of monistic Vedanta. The classical Upanishads are duly singled out for opprobrium – these texts are monistic in contrast to the later "theistic" category, though datings are very approximate. These key texts are correlated with the PreSocratic philosophers Heraclitus and Parmenides, much to the disadvantage of all parties specified, since they are all considered primitively pantheist and/or morally ambivalent. Yet even more obscurantist than the disdained Presocratics is Mahayana Buddhism, for which Zaehner seems to harbour an especial venom, or rather scholarly aversion. The march to the glories of theism was married by the monistic monster of the perennial philosophy. Zaehner triumphantly seizes upon the well known fact that modern Zen and the guru-cults stigmatize discursive thought as the arch-enemy of mystical experience, and he provides an antidote, since the hero of his book is Aristotle, who regarded discursive thought as a necessary training for the contemplation of the enlightened human. But Zaehner's Aristotle is not so much the Greek philosopher as a theistic saviour. In his introduction, he clearly states that "the God of the philosophers, then, is the God of Aristotle as interpreted by St. Thomas Aquinas."[340] This invests the whole thesis with an inverted quality equivalent to putting the cart before the horse.

This Neo-Scholastic thesis reads rather like a more up to date analogue of Hegel's less theistic, but nonetheless confused, lectures on the philosophy of history, in which Western achievements are lent an air of unsurpassed victory. In Zaehner's version, Socrates and Plato appear to be credited with an inchoate religious sense, but are capped by Aristotle, who holds in check the "perennial philosophy" of the West. Any earlier religion or philosophy seems to be consigned to effective oblivion – always remembering that Zaehner favoured the conservative traditional dating for Zarathushtra. Yet even if the latter is not considered anything of a Presocratic, he would not fare very well in the scheme, since even the Judaic origins of Christianity are chastised as a testament to the primitive (Zaehner appears to have believed in being literal at all costs, though he is not alone in this feat). More justifiably, he berates the Huxleyan vogue for stringing together statements from varying sources as proof of the same teaching, but he goes to the opposite extreme in assuming that there can be no fair comparison made between Eckhart or John of the Cross and the early Upanishads – which were too early in Hindu philosophy to have achieved the theistic maturity of the *Gita* (which, to Zaehner, was synonymous with Ramanuja and not the detested Shankara).

The Zaehnerian version of *religio perennis* seems as much bent upon the emic employment of reason and discrimination as some of the modern cults which have been confused with ancient and less ancient precedents. One might turn to the obscure fragments of the hapless Heraclitus with a sense of profound relief at escaping the totalities of modern knowledge.

The scholastic folly which affixed the Manson case to the entire "monistic" spectrum is another tedious example of the bias inherent in religious perspectives. It is obvious to intelligent people that cult values can produce abnormalities; even dime novels pick up on this theme in the interests of current literary consumerism. There were murder cases in America during the 1920's that were then being discussed (with more justification) as the consequence of the availability of the translated books of Nietzche; this was quite apart from any influence in nazi circles.[341] It is quite unnecessary to blame murder vogues on Eastern mysticism, which in general teaches the exact opposite. While Aleister Crowleys abound, it is incumbent for Western misdemeanours to be attributed to their real source in Western atrophydom, just as much as it is necessary to stigmatize the barbarities of the Inquisition instead of glossing pious horrors with traditionalist theories of progress.

If Zaehner had possessed the non-theological faculties of a modern Aristotle, he might have discerned a very elementary point: the worst of the modern Western cultists correspond to the "left hand" tantric substrate of the *sanatana dharma*, a substrate which is to be clearly distinguished from traditions like Vedanta. The cultist extremes include diverse Thugs and Phibionites, primitive literalists and sensationalists who are actually no worse than literalist Inquisitors who launch pogroms (and in some respects actually superior). These extremes have nothing whatever to do with viable philosophy. It eluded Zaehner's mystical theism that Western followers of Nietzchean slogans like "beyond good and evil" (the title of a book by Nietzche) are equivalent to the "dirty path" in Hindu Tantra that was dismissed by Vivekananda as an aberration. Many modern cultists are so illiterate that they would not know the difference between Nietzche and Zarathushtra, but it is necessary to remember that they are quite frequently misled by tinsel opportunists of the Western commercial media. Those preferring back doors to front doors in the quest for wisdom pay a heavier price of admission, which is that of enslavement to the standards of the network of exploiters who trade in those who cannot think for themselves.

It remains incumbent to remind both the highly educated and the less literate of the travesties of scholarship sometimes committed by eminent Professors and literary entities. As regards an applicable endeavour to go beyond good and evil in a sane sense, if the "good" Zaehners and the "evil" Huxleys are alike avoided as interpreters, the would-be philosophers might begin to see what is perennial in terms of real achievements and banal follies. They are likely to require just as much discrimination as intuition.

*Conclusion:*

The etics of the *philosophia perennis* are much more complex than is generally assumed. Various writers who have expressed opinions for and against the subject have omitted clarifying clauses, a neglect that renders their extrapolations misleadingly emic. It is not sufficient to state the subject in terms of its perenniality, since follies are not generally distinguished. Nor is it sufficient to emphasize the universality of the phenomenon, since this is frequently so generalized an emphasis as to be meaningless. It is first necessary to pinpoint the essentials of philosophy, which transpire to be exacting in perspective and performance. For a greater operational accuracy in terminology, one would require a phrase like, e.g., etic perennial essential philosophy, but such a cumbrous stylization is unlikely to prove popular.

In the face of prevalent confusions in popular idioms, I propose to chart the subject on a more extensive scale according to anthropographic criteria. This is a daunting project, but the complexities of the subject fully justify the effort at greater clarity.

There is tangible evidence to prove that at least some persons in recorded history cultivated the view that a perennial wisdom was in occurrence which relates neither to orthodox theology nor formal philosophy, but to an experiential encounter with reality and its continuum in human lives. This should not be confused with the current mania for experiential "exercises," many of which are likely to tie the candidate in an experiential knot if he or she is not sufficiently wary. Similarly, to harp upon the mere unity of religions is irrelevant in this subject, since that theme gives no guide to intrinsic experiential content independent of forms and doctrines. One criterion of philosophy is to see through and behind forms and appearances, an ability in which theology is not particularly expert. Philosophy should first teach the analysis of superstition and dogmatism, though not according to the Cartesian method of doubt. The fundamental is the dynamic of experience, but this is so little understood in general that a preparatory programme is vital in order to better distinguish what kind of experience it is that is being referred to.

The researcher into, and exponent of, this subject is at all times obliged to distinguish, as much as possible, the etic from the emic. The reason for this is that otherwise what is recovered from history is liable to constitute the emic perennial as distinct from the etic perennial.

These factors are not at all unrelated to scientific thinking as is sometimes imagined and declared. On the contrary, the subject of philosophical perennialities is intimately related to a science of culture, one that furthermore encompasses a variety of disciplines too often divided in current curricula. In the anthropographic view, perennial etics/emics necessarily relate to features of, e.g., the rise and fall of cultures, ethnic vicissitudes, linguistic programming, and minority/ majority foci in learning. While these and other features are customarily ignored by partisans of a "perennial philosophy," the picture will inevitably be incomplete, unconvincing, and subject to an amorphous tendency to unduly abridge, excise, and conflate.

The anthropographic extension of axis to a science of culture includes etic/ emic particulars relating to the hard sciences. A relevant exercise in this respect has been essayed elsewhere, and has to date met with an almost total non-comprehension from the typical partisans of a "perennial philosophy." One of the points I wished to make (non-explicitly) in *Psychology in Science* was that it is possible to verbalize aspects of the perennial philosophy in an "Aristotelian" and sceptical format for educational purposes. The responses have been predictably mixed in view of the implicit cues. It is applicable here to draw attention to the postcript in that book, in which I declined to identify with either the "mentalism" or the "dualism" of Roger Sperry and John Eccles respectively. Some think that my alternative of "monism" was rather enigmatic. Let me clarify this point in a non-dogmatic manner: Ecclesian dualism amounts to the Judaeo-Christian theology of creationism and attendant orthodoxy in a sophisticated scientific guise. Sperry approximates to another "perennial" philosophy of a kind compatible with mentalist perspectives, though in the last analysis, he is a modern experimental empiricist in outlook. But my version of monism is equivalent in the last analysis to a panpsychist perspective (though a very qualified one).[342] All three of these differing views might be considered "perennial" in the rather glib (emic) sense now reserved for the catchphrase by critics. I therefore leave the reader with an etic/emic choice, and not one dogmatically asserted by me: which is the etic perennial?

It is relevant to add that in the abovementioned essay I repudiated four letter word occultism, (neo)Reichian "tantra," showbiz guruism, drugmania, and various other "perennials." I trust that it is not necessary to put such shallow varieties of emicism to the question for readers who are still reasonably literate.

# NOTES

1. Spinoza, *On the Improvement of the Understanding*, trans. R.H.M. Elwes (New York: Dover, 1955), p. 6. Spinoza distinguishes these acquisitions in the sense of means and ends, and is repudiating the latter.
2. See Paul Feyerabend, *Against Method* (1975; fourth imp., London: Verso, 1982).
3. Cf. Karl R. Popper, *Realism and the Aim of Science* (London: Hutchinson, 1983), pp. xxxi ff., on Thomas Kuhn's theory which Popper feels to have unjustly implicated him as a "naive falsificationist." Popper's critical rationalism, often dubbed falsificationism, is not subscribed to by all philosophers of science.
4. For some of Sperry's research conclusions, see R. Sperry, *Science and Moral Priority* (Oxford: Basil Blackwell, 1983).
5. K.R.D. Shepherd, *Psychology in Science: Towards a Universal Science of Human Progress* (Cambridge: Anthropographia Publications, 1983), including a more detailed review of the brain hemisphere issue.
6. See J.C. Eccles, *The Human Psyche* (Heidelberg: Springer Verlag, 1980), pp. 5 ff. This modification was a result of Sperry's continuing research.
7. R.E. Ornstein, *The Psychology of Consciousness* (first edn, 1972; second edn, New York: Harcourt Brace Jovanovitch, 1977).
8. See, e.g., R. Puccetti, "Brain Bisection and Personal Identity," *British Journal for the Philosophy of Science* (1973) 24: 339–55; *id.*, "Rigterink on Mental Division," *Canadian Journal of Philosophy* (1982) 12 (1): 75–6.
9. M. Kinsbourne, "Biological determinants of functional bisymmetry and asymmetry" (3–13) in *idem*, ed., *Asymmetrical Function of the Brain* (Cambridge: Cambridge University Press, 1978), p. 11.
10. Colin Blakemore, *Mechanics of the Mind* (Cambridge: Cambridge University Press, 1977), pp. 165–7, criticizing Ornstein's position.
11. Carl Sagan, *The Dragons of Eden: Speculations on the Evolution of Human Intelligence* (London: Hodder & Stoughton, 1978).

12. S.P. Springer and G. Deutsch, *Left Brain, Right Brain* (San Francisco: W.H. Freeman, 1981).
13. Colin Wilson, *Frankenstein's Castle* (1980; Bath: Ashgrove Press, 1982). Wilson constructs his interpretation on the basis of Ornstein (note 7 *supra*) and J. Jaynes, *The Origin of Consciousness in the Breakdown of the Bicameral Mind* (Boston: Houghton Mifflin, 1976). The latter lacks the empirical element in Ornstein's treatment. For a criticism of the anthropological theory of Jaynes, see my *Meaning in Anthropos*, n. 97; *Minds and Sociocultures*, introduction.
14. Anthony Stevens, *Archetype: A natural history of the self* (London: Routledge, 1982).
15. O. Mannoni, *Freud: The Theory of the Unconscious*, trans. R. Bruce (London: NLB, 1971), p. 55.
16. *The Collected Works of C.G. Jung, Vol. 9 Pt 1: The Archetypes and the Collective Unconscious*, trans. R.F.C. Hull (London: Routledge, 1959), pp. 43–4.
17. Rupert Sheldrake, *A New Science of Life* (1981; London: Granada, 1983), p. 27.
18. C.G. Jung, *op. cit.*, pp. 75–6.
19. *Ibid.*, p. 76.
20. Liliane Frey-Rohn, *From Freud to Jung: A Comparative Study of the Psychology of the Unconscious*, trans. F.E. Engreen and E.K. Engreen (New York: C.G. Jung Foundation for Analytical Psychology, 1974), pp. 121 ff.
21. See Kenneth Ch'en, *Buddhism in China: A Historical Survey* (Princeton, N.J.: Princeton University Press, 1964), pp. 320–3, for an interpretation of Chinese extensions. On Asanga, see A.K. Warder, *Indian Buddhism* (Delhi: Motilal Banarsidass, second edn 1980), pp. 436 ff. Asanga is said to have founded the Yogacara (Vijnanavada) school of philosophy. The subject of *alayavijnana* receives fullest treatment in the *Mahayanasamgraha* (*Compendium of the Mahayana*), a text attributed to Asanga. *Alayavijnana* is here described as the cause of defilement, receiving the traces (of *manas*) and retaining the "seeds." Warder interprets "seeds" as latent ideas, but impressions is an alternative. Warder translates *alayavijnana* as "home consciousness." For a translation of the *Mahayanasamgraha*, see Etienne Lamotte, *La Somme Du Grand Vehicule D'Asanga*, 2 vols (new edn, Institut Orientaliste Louvain-La-Neuve, 1973).
22. Alexander Lowen, article in David Boadella, ed., *In the Wake of Reich* (London: Coventure, 1976), p. 40.

23. J.J. Blom, *Descartes: his Moral Philosophy and Psychology* (New York University Press, 1978), pp. vii, 1.
24. *Psychology in Science* (1983), p. 33.
25. Arthur Koestler, *The Lotus and the Robot* (London: Hutchinson, 1960), p. 282.
26. Cf. *ibid.*, pp. 281 ff.
27. Cf. *ibid.*, p. 280.
28. A. Koestler, *The Ghost in the Machine* (London: Hutchinson, 1967), pp. 335–6.
29. A. Reza Arasteh, *Growth to Selfhood: The Sufi Contribution* (London: Routledge & Kegan Paul, 1980), pp. 132, 113.
30. *The Oxford English Dictionary Vol. 1* (Oxford: Clarendon Press, 1933; repr. 1970), p. 361 column one.
31. *Ibid.* I have taken the liberty of rendering some words in modern English in order not to unduly confuse readers.
32. See my *Meaning in Anthropos: Anthropography as an Interdisciplinary Science of Culture.*
33. A. Ruhe and N.M. Paul, *Henri Bergson: An Account of his life and philosophy* (London: Macmillan, 1914), biographical introduction.
34. *Psychology in Science*, p. 150.
35. *Ibid.*, pp. 3 ff.
36. *Ibid.*, pp. 160 ff.
37. Paul K. Feyerabend, *Against Method: Outline of an anarchistic theory of knowledge* (London: NLB, 1975), p. 28.
38. *Ibid.*, pp. 32–33, 33 n. 4, 21 n. 12.
39. *Ibid.*, p. 189.
40. Paul Feyerabend, *Science in a Free Society* (London: NLB, 1978), p. 39.
41. *Ibid.*, p. 105.
42. Shepherd, *Psychology in Science* (1983), pp. 169 ff.
43. Feyerabend, *Science in a Free Society*, p. 31.
44. Marvin Harris, *Cultural Materialism* (New York: Random House, 1979), p. xii.
45. *Ibid.*, pp. 27–8.
46. *Ibid.*, p. 10.
47. *Ibid.*, pp. 262 ff.; Harris, *Cannibals and Kings* (Glasgow: Fontana/Collins, 1978), pp. 75 ff. Cf. Shepherd, *Psychology in Science*, p. 162, top paragraph.
48. Harris, *Cultural Materialism*, pp. 315 ff.
49. Herbert Wendt, *From Ape to Adam*, trans. S. Cupitt (London: Thames and Hudson, 1971), pp. 250–1.
50. See Desmond Morris, *The Naked Ape* (London: Jonathan

Cape, 1967), incorporating errors which include a stress upon aggression in human evolution.

51. *Psychology in Science*, pp. 149 ff., citing Alexander King, "Economy, Energy, Environment: The Need for a Trandisciplinary Approach" (365–388) in V. Mathieu and P. Rossi, eds., *Scientific Culture in the Contemporary World* (Milan: Scientia, 1979).
52. Aurelio Peccei, *One Hundred Pages for the Future* (Oxford: Pergamon Press, 1982), foreword. For a pointed commentary, see my *Psychology in Science*, pp. 160, 164 ff.
53. Glen Schaefer, *Universe with Man in Mind: The New Paradigm* (Cranfield, Beds.: Translational Press, 1982), pp. 26 ff.
54. James E. Lovelock, *Gaia: A New Look at Life on Earth* (Oxford: Oxford University Press, 1979), p. 148.
55. Erik Dammaan, *The Future in Our Hands* (Oxford: Pergamon Press, 1979), p. 111.
56. *Ibid.*, p. 160.
57. *Ibid.*, pp. 36 ff., 151, 153, and citing Professor Georg Borgstrom, *Flykt Fran Verkligheten* (*Flight from Reality*) for the information on world forecasts.
58. C.D. Darlington, *The Little Universe of Man* (London: George Allen & Unwin, 1978), pp. 268 ff. On Darlington's Darwinism, see further my *Psychology in Science*, pp. 130 ff.
59. *The Complete Works of Swami Vivekananda Vol. 1* (twelfth edn, Calcutta: Advaita Ashrama, 1965), p. 20.
60. For the anthropographic rectification of this Darwinian (and neo-Darwinian) tendency, see my *Vivekananda: his life and teaching* (forthcoming). I have felt under no obligation to tailor the subject to Darwinian (or neo-Darwinian) dimensions.
61. Marvin Harris, *Cannibals and Kings: The Origins of Cultures* (1978), p. 209.
62. For arguments in favour of alternatives see, e.g., Larry Dossey, *Space, Time, and Medicine* (Boulder and London: Shambhala, 1982). Cf. Peter Medawar, *Pluto's Republic* (Oxford University Press, 1983).
63. Colin Wilson, *Frankenstein's Castle* (1982), p. 67.
64. Fritjof Capra, *The Turning Point* (London: Wildwood House, 1982), pp. 460–2.
65. *Ibid.*, pp. 318–319.
66. *Ibid.*, p. 411.
67. *Ibid.*, p. 329.
68. *Ibid.*, pp. 377 ff.

69. S.H. Nasr, *The Encounter of Man and Nature* (London: George Allen & Unwin, 1968), p. 38. See also *Psychology in Science*, p. 179 n. 87.
70. Nicholas Rescher, *Al-Farabi: An Annotated Bibliography* (University of Pittsburgh Press, 1962), p. 11.
71. See further my *Psychology in Science*, pp. 73 ff. Cf. S.C. Easton, *Roger Bacon and his Search for a Universal Science* (Oxford: Basil Blackwell, 1952), for an orthodox approach that theologically confuses the facts.
72. See chapter seven of Shepherd, *Sufis, Batinis, Scientists and Philosophers of the early Islamic era* (forthcoming).
73. For a view on this, see Frances A. Yates, *The Rosicrucian Enlightenment* (London: Routledge & Kegan Paul, 1972), pp. 155 ff.
74. Richard S. Westfall, *Never at Rest: A Biography of Isaac Newton* (Cambridge University Press, 1980), pp. 286 ff., 530–1, 299 ff.
75. Aristotle, *The Metaphysics Bks I–IX*, trans. Hugh Tredennick (Cambridge, Mass.: Harvard University Press, *Loeb Classical Library*, 1933), p. 147.
76. *Ibid.*, pp. 159–61.
77. *Ibid.*, pp. 155–7.
78. *Ibid.*, pp. 181–3.
79. See Paul Feyerabend, *Science in a Free Society* (1978), pp. 9, 28. Modern Protagoreanism is not without its sophistication, though I beg to disagree strongly. I believe that a more enlightened education and democracy require different guidelines, though I do strongly agree with Feyerabend that a more enlightened education is necessary for the benefit of the lay population.
80. *The Oxford English Dictionary Vol. VI* (Oxford: Clarendon Press, 1933; repr. 1970), p. 386 column two.
81. Cited approvingly in A.J. Ayer, *Hume* (Oxford University Press, 1980), p. 96.
82. John Bricke, *Hume's Philosophy of Mind* (Princeton, N.J.: Princeton University Press, 1980), pp. 25–6, 153. The argument here is not that Hume was anything of a Cartesian dualist, but that "a bundle dualist may be an interactionist," referring to Hume's conception of the self as a bundle of impressions.
83. H. Bergson, *Matter and Memory*, trans. N.M. Paul and W. Scott Palmer (London: George Allen & Unwin, 1911).
84. Algot Ruhe and Nancy Margaret Paul, *Henri Bergson: An*

*account of his life and philosophy* (1914), p. 33.

85. *Ibid.*, pp. 41, 40.
86. Shepherd, *Psychology in Science*, p. 110, also referring to "metaphysical speculation" in this sense, which is difficult to understand only for those who do not concede the difference between the First Philosophy and counterfeit. Some have tended to think that I agree with all Einstein's later views on science, though this is not the case if the relevant terminology is correctly decoded, and the overall format of my essay taken into due consideration as underlining psychological priorities. My reference to the danger of "acceptance of only part of the epistemological validity that extends to both man and the universe" (*ibid.*, p. 110) can be taken as referring to both Einstein and Schrodinger, amongst others. The more subtle and polite critique appears to be lost upon casual readers.
87. Henri Bergson, *An Introduction to Metaphysics*, trans. T.E. Hulme (London: Macmillan, 1913), pp. 78–9.
88. Bertrand Russell, *Unpopular Essays* (London: George Allen & Unwin, 1950), pp. 75–6.
89. *Ibid.*, p. 64.
90. *Ibid.*, p. 65.
91. Bertrand Russell, *Sceptical Essays* (London: George Allen & Unwin, 1928), pp. 65–6.
92. *Ibid.*, pp. 71–2.
93. See A.F. Parker-Rhodes, *The Theory of Indistinguishables: A Search for Explanatory Principles Below the Level of Physics* (Dordrecht: D. Reidel, 1981).
94. David Bohm, *Wholeness and the Implicate Order* (London: Routledge & Kegan Paul, 1981), p. 22.
95. David Bohm and Rupert Sheldrake (interview), "Morphogenetic Fields and the Implicate Order," *Re-Vision* (1982) 5(2): 41–8.
96. Ilya Prigogine and Isabelle Stengers, *Order Out of Chaos* (London: Heinemann, 1984), p. 312.
97. See J.C. Eccles, *The Human Mystery* (Heidelberg: Springer Verlag, 1979); *id.*, *The Human Psyche* (1980). Cf. Shepherd, *Psychology in Science*, pp. 119 ff.; *id.*, *Meaning in Anthropos*, chapters 1, 4 and 10.
98. Joseph Silk and John D. Barrow, *The Left Hand of Creation* (London: Heinemann, 1984), p. 208.
99. Fred Hoyle, *The Intelligent Universe* (London: Michael Joseph, 1983), p. 249.

100. *Ibid.*, p. 190. Cf. my remarks on the earlier version of Hoyle's steady-state theory in *Psychology in Science*, pp. 111 ff.
101. Bertrand Russell, *Sceptical Essays* (1928), p. 64. Cf. Henri Bergson, *Creative Evolution*, trans. A. Mitchell (London: Macmillan, 1911).
102. Teilhard de Chardin, *The Phenomenon of Man* (London: Collins, 1959), p. 31.
103. *Ibid.*, pp. 324–5.
104. *Ibid.*, pp. 182 ff.
105. Joseph Head and S.L. Cranston, eds., *Reincarnation in World Thought* (New York: Julian Press, 1967), pp. 251, 249, and citing Cudworth's *The True Intellectual System of the Universe* (1678).
106. *Ibid.*, p. 257.
107. Meher Baba, *God Speaks: The Theme of Creation and Its Purpose* (New York: Dodd, Mead & Co., 1955). This work received a favourable review by the Tibetological scholar E.Y. Evans-Wentz, but was otherwise ignored, and possibly through sheer indifference rather than owing to the messianic associations of the author. The work contains a devotional introduction by an editorial hand that seems out of keeping with the contents, which are markedly impersonal in tone.
108. Gershom Scholem, *Kabbalah* (Jerusalem: Keter Publishing House, 1974), pp. 344 ff., adopting a conventional scholarly interpretation, which despite whatever deficiencies it might have, is vastly superior to the vulgar versions of Qabbalah in vogue in the West.
109. See my *From Oppression to Freedom*, Part Two, for a treatment of Sarmad and Mir Findiriski.
110. Fazlur Rahman, *The Philosophy of Mulla Sadra* (Albany: State University of New York Press, 1975), p. 247.
111. See my *Sufis, Batinis, Scientists and Philosophers of the early Islamic era*, chapter seven.
112. Reynold A. Nicholson, *Rumi, Poet and Mystic* (London: George Allen & Unwin, 1950), p. 103.
113. *Ibid.*, p. 187 n. 1.
114. Head and Cranston, eds., *Reincarnation in World Thought*, pp. 146–7.
115. See my *Meaning in Anthropos*, chapter twelve.
116. Cf. Fritz Meier, "The Problem of Nature in the Esoteric Monism of Islam" (149–203) in *Spirit and Nature: Papers*

*from the Eranos Yearbooks*, trans. R. Manheim (London: Routledge & Kegan Paul, 1955), pp. 193 ff. On Nasafi, see also my *Survey of the Sufi Phenomenon.*

117. R.A. Nicholson, *op. cit.*, p. 24.
118. Head and Cranston, *Reincarnation in World Thought*, p. 146, quoting from Ibn al-Arabi's lengthy treatise *Al-Futuhat al-Makkiya.*
119. Arthur Koestler, *The Ghost in the Machine* (1967), pp. 68–9, 213.
120. *Reincarnation in World Thought*, p. 145, citing Nadarbeg K. Mirza, *Reincarnation and Islam* (Madras, 1927), pp. 57–8. The main scholarly source on the Hallajian poetry is Louis Massignon, ed. and trans., *Le Diwan d'al-Hallaj* (third edn, Paris: Paul Geuthner, 1955), but the editor was not partial to the subject of reincarnation. For more on Hallaj, see chapter eight of my *Sufis, Batinis, Scientists and Philosophers of the early Islamic era.*
121. David Shea and Anthony Troyer, trans., *The Religion of the Sufis* (London: Octagon Press, 1979), p. 67. The translation is clumsy, and comes from Vol. 3 of the unabridged 1843 trans. of the *Dabistan.*
122. See A. David-Neel, *Initiations and Initiates in Tibet* (London: Rider, 1931); *id.*, *With Mystics and Magicians in Tibet* (London: Bodley Head, 1931).
123. Karl Popper, *The Self and Its Brain* (Heidelberg: Springer Verlag, 1977), p. 68, whose review of panpsychism is both biased and misleading, and mirrors a logical positivist perspective.
124. See Arthur Schopenhauer, *The World as Will and Representation*, trans. E.F.J. Payne, 2 vols (New York: Dover, 1969).
125. On Dara Shikoh, see my *From Oppression to Freedom*, Part Two. On the Upanishads, see my *Minds and Sociocultures*, Part Three.
126. Robert T. Clark, Jr, *Herder: his life and thought* (Berkeley: University of California Press, 1955), pp. 286–7, a biased account that deems the transmigration hypothesis "both unnecessary and inadequate."
127. Isaiah Berlin, *Vico and Herder* (London: Hogarth Press, 1976), pp. 163–4, 174–5.
128. Popper, *op.cit.*, pp. 53–4.
129. Henri Bergson, *Creative Evolution* (1911), p. 187.
130. For a formulation in compact modern terms that owes in-

spiration to this perspective, see my *Meaning in Anthropos*, chapter five.

131. See the ingenious theory in Rupert Sheldrake, *A New Science of Life* (1981), a development of organismic perspectives.
132. Cf. Karl Popper, *Unended Quest* (rev. edn, sixth imp., London: Fontana/Collins, 1982), pp. 187, 236 n. 299.
133. See the editorial introduction to A.J. Ayer, ed., *Logical Positivism* (Glencoe, I11.: Free Press, 1959), in which the famous antimetaphysical credo of David Hume is cited with approval.
134. Herbert Marcuse, *One Dimensional Man* (London: Routledge & Kegan Paul, 1964), pp. 186–7, and citing Bertrand Russell, *Unpopular Essays* (1950), p. 76, for the Papal episode.
135. John Davy, "The Evidence for Life after Life," in *The Observer Magazine*, April 8th and 15th, 1979.
136. Margot Grey, "The Near-Death Experience," *Internationale Zeitschrift fur Psychiatrie und Psychoanalyse* (Berlin 1982) 15: 129–147, pp. 130, 141–2, citing Karl H. Pribram, *Languages of the Brain* (1971). See also Pribram, *Consciousness and the Brain* (New York: Plenum, 1976).
137. *Sunday Times*, 5th February, 1984, p. 44.
138. Fritjof Capra, *The Tao of Physics* (1975; London: Fontana, 1983), pp. 23–4.
139. See Shepherd, *Sufis, Batinis, Scientists and Philosophers of the early Islamic era*, chapter seven.
140. See *ibid.*, chapter eight. On Massignon, see the biographical foreword by Herbert Mason in the latter's translation of Massignon's *The Passion of Al-Hallaj Vol. 1* (Princeton, N.J.: Princeton University Press, 1982). Mason remarks that it is difficult to say when Gandhi's influence upon Massignon commenced. They met only once, towards the end of Gandhi's life, but the influence of pacifism and vegetarianism was evident earlier in Massignon's career (pp. xxxii–xxxiii).
141. Annemarie Schimmel, new introduction to Margaret Smith, *Rabi'a the Mystic* (1928; repr. Cambridge University Press, 1984), p. xxix.
142. *Ibid.*, p. xxviii.
143. Margaret Smith, *Rabi'a the Mystic*, pp. 111 ff., esp. p. 126.
144. For some remarks on the Bektashis and shamanism, see Appendix Five of my *Ancient Cultures in Flux*. Still a major source on the former is J.K. Birge, *The Bektashi Order of Dervishes* (London: Luzac, 1937).

145. For a biography of Babajan, see my *A Sufi Matriarch: Hazrat Babajan* (Cambridge: Anthropographia Publications, 1986).
146. For a treatment of the Kaivani groups, see my *From Oppression to Freedom*, Part Two.
147. Apart from his editing and translation feats, Corbin's magnum opus is considered to be *En Islam Iranien*, 4 vols (Paris: Gallimard, 1971–2). This work has met with varying reactions from Iranist scholars. The second volume focusses upon the ishraqis.
148. Cf. Seyyed Hossein Nasr, *Islam and the Plight of Modern Man* (London and New York: Longman, 1975), pp. 146–7, observing that Corbin was early influenced by Martin Heidegger, and that it was through Corbin's translation of Heidegger's *Sein und Zeit* that Sartre was first attracted to existentialism.
149. See Paul Fenton, trans., *The Treatise of the Pool by Obadyah Maimonides* (London: Octagon Press, 1981); Shepherd, *Sufis, Batinis*, introduction.
150. David Shea and Anthony Troyer, trans., *The Dabistan*, Vol. 3 (Paris: Oriental Translation Fund of Great Britain and Ireland, 1843), p. 220.
151. Louis Fischer, *The Life of Mahatma Gandhi* (1951; London: Granada, 1982), pp. 416 ff.
152. Sarvepalli Radhakrishnan, *Indian Philosophy Vol. 2* (second edn, London: George Allen & Unwin, 1931), p. 780.
153. Shea and Troyer, trans., *The Dabistan*, Vol. 2 (Paris, 1843), pp. 289–92. This translation is clumsy, but remains the only complete one.
154. Christmas Humphreys, *Buddhism* (third edn, Harmondsworth: Penguin, 1962), p. 189.
155. For one Tibetan view, see Thubten Jigme Norbu and Colin Turnbull, *Tibet: Its History, Religion and People* (1969; Harmondsworth: Penguin, 1972), pp. 342 ff.
156. See Shea and Troyer, *The Dabistan*, Vol. 2, pp. 268 ff. For a modern treatment, see W. Owen Cole and Piara Singh Sambhi, *The Sikhs: Their Religious Beliefs and Practices* (London: Routledge and Kegan Paul, 1978). See also W.H. McLeod, *The Evolution of the Sikh Community: Five Essays* (Oxford: Clarendon Press, 1976).
157. Mill's essay *On Liberty* (1859) has produced differing interpretations. See, e.g., Gertrude Himmelfarb, *On Liberty and Liberalism: The Case of John Stuart Mill* (New York: Alfred

Knopf, 1974), esp. pp. 169 ff. on the subject of women in Mill's thought, and concluding that *On Liberty* was "the case of women writ large." The view here is that Mill's lack of reference to the feminine issue in his major essay was owing to caution in the face of public opinion. Yet in other respects, *On Liberty* was much less temperate than the more traditional liberalism found in other works of Mill. Himmelfarb comments that although modernity has so far favoured the more extreme liberalism in Mill, this situation may yet be reversed in favour of more temperate dimensions (*ibid.*, p. xxii). Cf. Maurice Cowling, *Mill and Liberalism* (London: Cambridge University Press, 1963), esp. p. 104, affirming that Mill was attempting in *On Liberty* to protect the elite from domination by mediocrity – far from being an attempt to free men from the constraints of *all* doctrine, this provocative essay was rather an attempt to free men from customary and habitual doctrine.

158. Arthur Waley, "Anquetil Duperron and Sir William Jones" in *id.*, *The Secret History of the Mongols and Other Pieces* (London: George Allen & Unwin, 1963), pp. 25, 27.

159. Cf. Mary Boyce, *Zoroastrians: Their Religious Beliefs and Practices* (London: Routledge & Kegan Paul, 1979), p. 195, favouring Zoroastrian orthodoxy.

160. For a more detailed treatment of Zarathushtra and early Iranian religion, see Part Two of my *Minds and Sociocultures* (forthcoming). Appendix One of that work includes data on the Mazdakites of Sassanian Iran. On Zarathushtra and Zurvanism, see also my *Ancient Cultures in Flux.*

161. On the *Desatir*, see Shepherd, *From Oppression to Freedom*, Appendix One. Cf. the discussion on this distinctive treatise in Troyer's introduction to Shea and Troyer, *The Dabistan*, Vol. 1 (Paris, 1843).

162. Cf. Marijan Mole, *Culte, mythe et cosmologie dans l'Iran ancien* (Paris: Presses Universitaires de France, 1963), pp. 12 n. 1, 283, 286, 311, 349, 457, in brief and passing reference to the school of Azar Kaivan, which Mole describes as sufi-ishraqi eclecticism in Mazdean disguise. Mole was one of the few Iranists to cover the Islamic era of Sufism. He tried to evade the "Semitic prophet" interpretation of Zarathushtra, but produced an unsatisfactory conclusion to otherwise daring research. Had Mole paid closer attention to the *Dabistan*, he might have learned more about sufi history, which could have prevented his aversion to an historical Zarathushtra.

163. See Mary Boyce, *Zoroastrians* (1979), omitting explicit reference to the Kaivani school.
164. Mary Boyce, ed. and trans., *Textual Sources for the Study of Zoroastrianism* (Manchester: Manchester University Press, 1984), p. 11, which is the most recent date ventured by Boyce at the time of writing, and a conservative one by past standards of the same scholar.
165. See R.C. Zaehner, *The Dawn and Twilight of Zoroastrianism* (London: Weidenfeld & Nicholson, 1961).
166. Aldous Huxley, *The Perennial Philosophy* (London: Chatto & Windus, 1946), p. 7.
167. *Ibid.*, p. 299.
168. Aldous Huxley, introduction to *The Song of God: Bhagavad Gita*, trans., Swami Prabhavananda and Christopher Isherwood (London: Phoenix House, fifth revised imp., 1956), p. 7.
169. See Mircea Eliade, *Autobiography Vol. 1: 1907–1937*, trans. M.L. Ricketts (San Francisco: Harper and Row, 1981), chapter ten. See also note 338 *infra*.
170. M. Eliade, *The Quest: History and Meaning in Religion* (Chicago: University of Chicago Press, 1969), pp. 35–6, 50 ff., 130 ff.; *id., Occultism, Witchcraft, and Cultural Fashions: Essays in Comparative Religions* (Chicago: University of Chicago Press, 1976), pp. 13 ff., and affirming that Levi-Strauss "is fundamentally a philosopher."
171. Eliade, *The Sacred and the Profane*, trans. W.R. Trask (New York: Harcourt, Brace, 1959), pp. 206–7.
172. On the subject of Indian ascetics and orgiastics, see the introduction to my *Vivekananda: his life and teaching*.
173. Cf. Mircea Eliade, "Spirit, Light, and Seed," *History of Religions* (1971) 11: 1–30, reprinted in *id., Occultism, Witchcraft, and Cultural Fashions* (1976), esp. pp. 109 ff., 99 ff., 114, 103–4, and citing G. Tucci on the Tantric tradition. Eliade maintains the erroneous spermatic associations of *khvarenah* in his *A History of Religious Ideas Vol. 1*, trans. W.R. Trask (London: Collins, 1979), pp. 315–16.
174. Cf. Fritjof Capra, *The Tao of Physics*, p. 103, for a "left-hand" interpretation of the Upanishads that is typically misleading in the permissive climate of popular mysticism.
175. On this subject, see Marijan Mole, ed. and trans., *La Legende De Zoroastre: Selon Les Textes Pehlevis* (Paris: Librairie C. Klincksieck, 1967). A very antiquated translation of Zarathushtra's hagiography culled from the *Denkart* and the text of Zadspram is E.W. West, *Pahlavi Texts Pt. V*

(Oxford: Clarendon Press, 1897, *Sacred Books of the East*).
176. Henrik S. Nyberg, *A Manual of Pahlavi Pt. 1: Texts* (Wiesbaden: Otto Harrassowitz, 1964), p. XVII.
177. David Hume, *The Natural History of Religion*, ed. by A. Wayne Oliver (Oxford: Clarendon Press, 1976), p. 72.
178. *Ibid.*, pp. 94, 93, 95.
179. J. Perez-Remon, *Self and Non-Self in Early Buddhism* (Berlin: de Gruyter, 1980), p. 304.
180. See, e.g., C.A.F. Rhys Davids, *Sakya or Buddhist Origins* (London: Kegan Paul, 1931), pp. 235 ff.
181. See, e.g., V.P. Vharma, *Early Buddhism and Its Origins* (New Delhi: Munshiram Manoharlal, 1973), pp. 155 ff., describing the Rhys Davids thesis as fantastic and ridiculous.
182. Christmas Humphreys, *Buddhism* (third edn, 1962), pp. 20–1, 85 ff.
183. For a translation of the *Yi-Ching*, see James Legge, *The Sacred Books of China: The Texts of Confucianism, Pt. II: The Yi King* (Oxford: Clarendon Press, 1882, *Sacred Books of the East*, Vol. XVI), who expressed disapproval of the oracle function in his introduction. Legge also had cause to observe that only occasionally had any Confucian critic ventured to doubt that the text and commentarial Appendices of the *Yi-Ching* formed one homogenous whole, or that all the ten Appendices were from the hand of Confucius. These fragmented commentaries are known as the Ten Wings, and at least eight of them were early ascribed to Confucius by the fourth century after his death. Legge concluded that the Appendices attributed to Confucius were actually written some time after his death, probably between 450–350 B.C. Cf. Richard Wilhelm, trans., *The I Ching or Book of Changes* (third edn, London: Routledge & Kegan Paul, 1968), who did not express disapproval of the oracle function, and who thought it highly probable that the commentary known as *T'uan Chuan* was the work of Confucius (p. lix), but who did not fail to observe that the commentaries comprising the Ten Wings "differ greatly with respect to content and intrinsic value" (p. lx). Cf. Alfred Douglas, *The Oracle of Change: How to Consult the I Ching* (Harmondsworth: Penguin, 1972), favouring the divinatory usage of the text, and referring to the Legge translation as an "Oriental curio" (p. 16).
184. This is a clarification of what some have deemed an enigma-

tic comment on the *Yi-Ching* in my *Psychology in Science*, p. 11. For a more detailed clarification, see my *Chinese Philosophers* (in preparation).

185. C.G. Jung, Foreword to the Richard Wilhelm trans., pp. xxviii–xxix. Dated 1949.
186. *Ibid.*, pp. xxxiii–xxxv.
187. This anecdote has been available in the Legge translation of the *Yi-Ching* (p. 41 n. 1) for a century, and reflects the more enlightened views of the Chinese literati and sages.
188. Daniel N. Robinson, *An Intellectual History of Psychology* (revised edn, New York: Macmillan, 1981), pp. 275–6, citing *New Essays on the Understanding* (1765), a work of distinctly posthumous fame.
189. For a more detailed treatment of Spinoza and Leibniz, see my *History of Philosophy* (in preparation).
190. Rom Landau, *The Philosophy of Ibn Arabi* (London: George Allen & Unwin, 1959), pp. 40–2.
191. *Ibid.*, p. 27.
192. Reynold A. Nicholson, *Studies in Islamic Mysticism* (Cambridge: Cambridge University Press, 1921), p. 125 n. 1. See also Shepherd, *Psychology in Science*, pp. 66, 199.
193. Colin Blakemore, *Mechanics of the Mind* (1977), pp. 11–12.
194. Michael Atkinson, *Plotinus: Ennead V.I* (Oxford University Press, 1983), p. v.
195. David Hume, *Dialogues concerning Natural Religion*, ed. by J.V. Price (Oxford: Clarendon Press, 1976), p. 179. Hume was evidently utilizing a passage in Colin MacLaurin, *An Account of Sir Isaac Newton's Philosophical Discoveries* (London, 1748).
196. See F. Dieterici, ed. and trans., *Die Sogenannte Theologie des Aristoteles*, 2 vols (Leipzig: J.C. Hinrichs, 1882–3), for the Arabic text and a German trans.
197. E.g., Corbin, *The Man of Light in Iranian Sufism*, trans. N. Pearson (Boulder: Colorado: Shambhala, 1978), referring to it as "neo-Zoroastrian Platonism." Even this avant garde designation leaves something to be desired.
198. It was this precedent that contributed to the stylization of my *Psychology in Science*, and not merely current social science as has perhaps been too readily imagined in some quarters.
199. H. Corbin, *Spiritual Body and Celestial Earth: From Mazdean Iran to Shi'ite Iran*, trans. N. Pearson (Princeton, N.J.: Princeton University Press, 1977), p. 119.

200. Sohravardi Maqtul, *Kitab Mashari w'al-Mutarahat* (*Book of Conversations*) in H. Corbin, ed., *Opera Metaphysica et Mystica de Sohrawardi*, Vol. 1 (Istanbul: Maarif Matbaasi, 1945, *Bibliotheca Islamica 16*), pp. 502 ff.

201. The relevant passage from *Kalimat al-tasawwuf* has been translated into English by Earle Waugh in the latter's critical review of Corbin's *En Islam Iranien* in *History of Religions* (1975) 14: 322–34, p. 324. Waugh makes some apt criticisms of Corbin's phenomenological method, and accuses Corbin of having supplied a "metahistory operating in a realm transcending the historical and only obliquely related to it" (p. 323). Waugh is critical of Corbin's analogical arguments for solid connections between the traditions claimed by Sohravardi Maqtul, but phenomenological exegesis apart, there need be no confusion about these traditions if they are evaluated in accordance with the actual historical and manuscript data.

202. I have provided an answer to this problem in *Sufis, Batinis, Scientists and Philosophers of the early Islamic era*, chapter nine. One need go no further back than the Sassanian era to find the initial solution to what some have approached as a problem. Chronologically therefore, this solution tallies with the Neoplatonic-Hermetic phase.

203. *Ennead* IV.8.1. The most recent version of this passage is A.H. Armstrong, ed. and trans., *Plotinus: Enneads Vol. 4* (Cambridge, Mass.: Harvard University Press, 1984, *Loeb Classical Library*), pp. 396–401. Plotinus begins with a brief description of his personal mystical experiences that is unique in the *Enneads.*

204. The Arabic text can be found in H. Corbin, ed., *Opera Metaphysica et Mystica de Sohrawardi*, Vol. 2 (Paris: Librarie D'Amerique et D'Orient, 1952, *Bibliotheque Iranienne 2*), with a French introduction that is not totally clarifying for various reasons.

205. This is the case even if one agrees with Corbin's interpretation of an "Oriental philosophy" being continued by Maqtul in succession to Ibn Sina. The scholarly debate over a certain Arabic phrase used by Ibn Sina need not be projected in a way that changes philosophy into theosophy. Corbin's contribution was an improvement upon more conventional interpretations, but his analysis of the link between Maqtul and Ibn Sina remains awkward.

206. Corbin, *Spiritual Body and Celestial Earth*, p. 126, for a very apt translation.
207. Even if one corrects the Plotinus-Plato identity in accordance with the demands of scholarship, Plato is quite legitimately implicated amongst the predecessors owing to Maqtul's references to works and themes of Plato, e.g., the Platonic Ideas.
208. On this important figure, see the relevant sections in my *Ancient Cultures in Flux* and *Survey of the Sufi Phenomenon*.
209. An investigation of the copious data available tends to bear out this contention; the problem has hitherto been the disproportionate assessment of Iranian traditions. See my *Sufis, Batinis*, chapter eight.
210. The less well known Al-Kharaqani (d. 1029) is also specified by Maqtul. For both of these ishraqi forbears, see the relevant sections in my *Survey of the Sufi Phenomenon*.
211. It is to be regretted that the otherwise liberal Seyyed Hossein Nasr has affirmed that "because Sufism is the esoteric and inner dimension of Islam it cannot be practised apart from Islam." See Nasr, *Living Sufism* (London: George Allen & Unwin, 1980), p. 152. It is evidently this attitude which caused him to discriminate against the Kaivani school of ishraqis (*ibid.*, p. 121), since he does not associate them with "Islamic gnosis."
212. There have been numerous misconceptions about the Hermetic tradition, which was of variable content. For an attempt to rectify various misconceptions, see Shepherd, *The Hermetic Discontinuum* (in preparation).
213. Also listed here are Empedocles and Agathos Daimon. The former is actually Pseudo-Empedocles, while Agathos Daimon is another deific entity, one associated with the Sarapis cult of Egypt. Archaeology reveals Agathos in the form of a sacred snake with the head of Sarapis, but it is uncertain whether Agathos was of Greek or Egyptian origin. He was already a deified figure in the Hellenistic period, as patron and symbol of Alexandria. This is confirmed by the "Potter's Oracle," an example of Egyptian folk literature extant in a Greek translation. On this, see M. Pietrzykowski, "Sarapis-Agathos Daimon" (959–66) in *Hommages a Maarten J. Vermaseren Vol. 3* (Leiden: E.J. Brill, 1978).
214. Walter Scott and A.S. Ferguson, *Hermetica Vol. 4* (Oxford: Clarendon Press, 1936), pp. 264 ff., giving a translation of

passages from Max Horten, *Die Philosophie der Erleuchtungnach Suhrawardi* (Halle, 1912). Horten's work was an abridged trans. of a copy of the *Hiqmat al-Ishraq* lithographed at Tehran (1895–8), and which included a commentary by Qutubuddin Shirazi and later glosses by Mulla Sadra. The Constantinople manuscript earlier used by Baron Carra de Vaux supplies variant readings, which is typical of textual complexities in this field.

215. O. Spies and S.K. Khatak, ed. and trans., *Three Treatises on Mysticism* (Stuttgart: W. Kohlhammer, 1935), p. 15. This work presents three of the allegorical writings of Maqtul, which follow a completely different format to his more discursive works.

216. See S.H. Nasr, "Shihab al-Din Suhrawardi Maqtul" (372–98) in M.M. Sharif, ed., *A History of Muslim Philosophy Vol. 1* (Wiesbaden: Otto Harrassowitz, 1963). It is the more difficult to understand, therefore, why Nasr should have referred condescendingly to the Kaivanis as a "curious eclectic movement" (*ibid.*, p. 397 n. 73). The bias against describing the Kaivani school as ishraqi seems unduly orthodox.

217. S.H. Nasr, *Knowledge and the Sacred: The Gifford Lectures 1981* (Edinburgh University Press, 1981). pp. 68, 89 n. 22.

218. Cf. *ibid.*, pp. 44, 72. Nasr credits Farabi as being more liberal than modern philosophers, but relegates him to the status of a Peripatetic who merely saw a relation between philosophy and revelation. This is in contrast to Nasr's former evaluation of Farabi as a sufi. Cf. Nasr, *Science and Civilization in Islam* (Cambridge, Mass.: Harvard University Press, 1968), p. 47. It seems that some commentators become less liberal in becoming more theological.

219. Nasr, *Knowledge and the Sacred*, p. 72, observing that in almost every discussion of his magnum opus *al-Hiqmat al-mutaaliyah fi'l asfar al-arba'ah*, Sadra refers to pre-Islamic philosophies in addition to the Islamic variety, and takes for granted the perspective of a perennial philosophy. See also S.H. Nasr, *Sadr al-Din Shirazi and his Transcendent Theosophy* (Tehran: Iranian Academy of Philosophy, 1978). Cf. Fazlur Rahman, *The Philosophy of Mulla Sadra.*

220. For more on the Zoroastrian ishraqis, see Shepherd, *From Oppression to Freedom*, Part Two. The report of Farzaneh Behram comes from the Sipasi section of the *Dabistan*. Cf. Shea and Troyer, *The Dabistan Vol. 1* (1843), p. 110.

221. O. Spies and S.K. Khatak, *op. cit.*, p. 10, also observing that

Maqtul was legendized in the popular shi'i manner as an imam who had not been killed but had merely disappeared.

222. J. Duchesne-Guillemin, *The Western Response to Zoroaster* (Oxford: Clarendon Press, 1958), p. 4.
223. This despite the detailed study of Francois Masai, *Plethon et le Platonisme de Mistra* (Paris: Societe D'Edition "Les Belles Lettres," *Les Classiques de l'Humanisme*, 1956).
224. H. Corbin, *Avicenna and the Visionary Recital*, trans. W.R. Trask (London: Routledge & Kegan Paul, 1960), p. 275.
225. An erudite work which has received criticism from some Iranists is Joseph Bidez and Franz Cumont, *Les Mages hellenises: Zoroastre Ostanes et Hytaspe d'apres la tradition Grecque* (2 vols, Paris: Societe d'editions "Les Belles Lettres," 1938). This work reviews many Greek sources. On Plethon see Vol. 1, pp. 158 ff.; Vol. 2, pp. 251 ff.
226. S.H. Nasr, *Knowledge and the Sacred* (1981), p. 89 n. 23, and adding that it cannot yet be answered as to whether there was a historical link between the respective formulations, or simply a repetition of the same truth.
227. Charles B. Schmitt, "Perennial Philosophy: From Agostino Steuco to Leibniz," *Jnl of the History of Ideas* (1966) 27: 505–32, p. 509.
228. See the lengthy study of H. Lewy, *Chaldean Oracles and Theurgy* (Cairo, 1956; new edn, Paris: Etudes Augustiniennes, 1978).
229. Cf. A.B. Wolter, "Bacon, Roger" (240–2) in *The Encyclopaedia of Philosophy Vol. 1* (New York: Macmillan, 1967), p. 240. Wolter does not do justice to Bacon's unorthodox tangent. He describes the *Secretum Secretorum* as a study in kingcraft which gives much astrological advice and hints at the occult properties of numbers.
230. On Steuco, see Charles Schmitt, *art. cit.*, pp. 515 ff.
231. Cited in Duchesne-Guillemin, *The Western Response to Zoroaster* (1958), p. 4, who omits the date of the recension.
232. *Ibid.*, p.5.
233. Cf. Schmitt, *art. cit.*, pp. 532, 530–1, and stressing the influence of Nicholas of Cusa on the ecumenical views of Leibniz.
234. Cf. Jacob Needleman, *The Heart of Philosophy* (London: Routledge & Kegan Paul, 1983) for a liberal neo-Kantian evaluation which stresses the contribution of Kierkegaard.
235. J. Duchesne-Guillemin, *The Western Response to Zoroaster*, p. 12.

236. On this topic, see Shepherd, *From Oppression to Freedom*, Part Two, note 43.
237. There are actually several terms used in the *Dabistan* for the same Kaivan school, the others being Azar Hushangi, Abadi, and Yazdani. I propose to subsume all of these terms under Kaivani-ishraqi, which is more explicit.
238. See D. Chwolsohn, *Die Ssabier und der Ssabismus* (2 vols, St. Petersburg: Buchdruckerei der Kaiserlichen Akademie der Wissenschaften, 1856) which is still a valuable source of information owing to its sheer bulk. Its 1500 pages include translations of texts bearing upon elusive subjects. For a treatment in more compact form, see chapter seven of my *Sufis, Batinis, Scientists and Philosophers of the early Islamic era.*
239. On this obscure sector of Iranian archaeology, see Walther Hinz, *The Lost World of Elam*, trans. J. Barnes (London: Sidgwick & Jackson, 1972). For more recent references, see my *Ancient Cultures in Flux.*
240. The name of this Aristotelian sufi was inaccurately translated by Shea and Troyer as "Mir Abulkasim Fandaraski" (*The Dabistan*, Vol. 1, 1843, pp. 140–1). Findiriski has a definite identity with the Kaivanis, though this is often neglected.
241. Shea and Troyer, Vol. 1, pp. 351–3. The two quotes seem apt enough, though the English trans. is often clumsy in its rendition.
242. See Shepherd, *From Oppression to Freedom*, Appendix 1, for a summary of the *Desatir* contents.
243. The relevant passage is cited in the Sipasi section of the *Dabistan*. Cf. Shea and Troyer, Vol. 1, p. 76. Khuda Jui is another bearing the title of *mobad*, but one would tend to think that this is metaphorical. His treatise is also known as *Jam-i-Khaikhushru*, and is a commentary on Kaivan's poetry.
244. Shea and Troyer, Vol. 2, p. 312. Mobad Shah relates that he met several learned *tarsa* (Christians), apparently Portuguese Catholics.
245. For a treatment of the *Dabistan* chapter on the philosophers, see my *History of Philosophy* (in preparation). Several of these philosophers were of Zoroastrian background.
246. See Shea and Troyer, Vol. 1, p. 69.
247. The *Dabistan* reference to these two influences on Sarmad is extremely brief, and it is difficult to be certain of specifics,

though it has been deduced that Sarmad was a pupil of these philosophers. See S.A.A. Rizvi, *A History of Sufism in India Vol. 2* (New Delhi: Munshiram Manoharlal, 1983), pp. 475 ff.

248. Mobad Shah's chapter on Jewish religion is more of a spotlight on Sarmad than a survey of Judaism. Yet he writes with typical objectivity that he did not take seriously those accounts of this religion that were written by biased non-Jews. Several of Sarmad's verses are quoted, which fit the idiom of sufi poetry. See Shea and Troyer, Vol. 2, pp. 293 ff.
249. Deno J. Geanokoplos, "Pletho, Giorgius Gemistus" (350–1) in *The Encyclopaedia of Philosophy Vol. 6* (1967).
250. B. Carra de Vaux, "La Philosophie illuminative (*Hikmet el-Ichraq*) d'apres Suhrawerdi Meqtoul," *Journal Asiatique* (1902) 19: 63–94, pp. 89 ff., citing Chwolsohn, *op. cit.*, Vol II, p. 701, and drawing a comparison with a work by Rabbi Haja Gaon. Carra de Vaux pertinently stressed the Plotinian ingredient in Maqtul's philosophy, but tended to underestimate certain of the Iranian links.
251. See W. Scott and A.S. Ferguson, *Hermetica Vol. 4* (1936), p. 269, for a translation from Max Horten's version. See note 214 *supra*.
252. Werner Jaeger, *Aristotle* (Oxford University Press, 1948), pp. 50 ff. This subject is not without its importance in classical studies.
253. Scott and Ferguson, *Hermetica Vol. 4*, p. 266 n. 2.
254. David Hume, *Natural history of Religion*, p. 61.
255. Duchesne-Guillemin, *op. cit.*, pp. 14–15. The problem with this otherwise useful survey is its extreme brevity with regard to the sources cited, in some instances assuming a specialist knowledge on the part of the reader. It is not surprising that even Voltaire's article on Zarathushtra in his *Dictionnaire philosophique* is still not well known.
256. *Ibid.*, pp. 21–2, and citing the Insel edn of *Ecce Homo*, p. 117.
257. J.H. Moulton, *The Treasure of the Magi: A Study of Modern Zoroastrianism* (London: Oxford University Press, 1917), p. 252. Duchesne-Guillemin did not neglect to mention this testimony of bias in Iranist studies (*op. cit.*, pp. 26–7), but with a brevity that misses much of the instructional value.
258. T. De Chardin, *The Phenomenon of Man* (1959), p. 323. See also note 103 *supra*. I can offer no apologies for my defence of panpsychism in chapter seven of the present work, particularly in view of the current ideological bias against this subject.

259. J.H. Moulton, *Early Zoroastrianism* (London: Williams & Norgate, 1913), pp. 146–7. This work is now chiefly valuable for its translation of the Gathas (pp. 343–90) based on C. Bartholomae's *Die Gathas des Avesta* (Strasbourg, 1905).
260. See, e.g., Duchesne-Guillemin, *op. cit.*, who has also insisted upon the traditional conservative chronology for Zarathushtra. Duchesne-Guillemin ends his review with a brief paragraph on Sohravardi Maqtul, affirming that for the first time Zoroastrian angelology was united with the Platonic Ideas. This seems an unsatisfactory reference to gnostic elements.
261. A.V. Williams Jackson, *Zoroastrian Studies* (New York: Columbia University Press, 1928), p. 24, which was the conclusion to the abridged version of *id.*, *Zoroaster, the Prophet of Ancient Iran* (1899), a biography which drew uncritically upon Pahlavi texts.
262. H.S. Nyberg, *Die Religionen des alten Iran* (first edn, 1938; second edn, Osnabruck: Zeller, 1966).
263. E.g., W.B. Henning, *Zoroaster, Politician or Witch-Doctor?* (London: Oxford University Press, 1951), who was an advocate of ethical dualism and who adhered to the traditional chronology of *c.* 600 B.C.
264. Duchesne-Guillemin, *op. cit.*, pp. 28–9, citing O. Van Wesendonk, *Das Wesen der Lehre Zarathushtras* (1927), p. 55. For a review of Iranist theories from Nyberg onwards, see Shepherd, *Minds and Sociocultures*, Part Two, and *Ancient Cultures in Flux*, final part.
265. John Wilson, *The Parsi Religion as contained in the Zand-Avasta, and propounded and defended by the Zoroastrians of India and Persia, Unfolded, Refuted, and contrasted with Christianity* (Bombay: American Mission Press, 1843), pp. 147–8, 409–10, 166–8, and citing W. Erskine in *Transactions of the Literary Soc. of Bombay*, Vol. 2, p. 367. For an analysis of Erskine's article, see Appendix 2 of my *From Oppression to Freedom.*
266. See M. Mole, *Culte, mythe et cosmologie* (1963), and note 162 *supra*. Mole devoted much attention to the non-Gathic Avesta. I am unable to agree with his version, but it does effectively demonstrate the variety of interpretations that can be brought to bear upon an enigmatic and obscure subject.
267. Cf. Wilson, *op. cit.*, pp. 411–12. Cf. M. Boyce, *Zoroastrians* (1979), pp. 197–8, who also gives a hostile account of the

*Desatir*, though contrary to Wilson, she is defending the orthodox Parsis. Certain statements which Boyce makes about this treatise are inaccurate; it is not claimed in the *Desatir* that the prophets depicted "had withdrawn from the world as the hidden 'Masters.'" This reflects instead the beliefs of Western Theosophy. In general, Boyce's interpretation is extremely biased against mystical elements in the Iranian tradition.

268. Mulla Firuz Bin Kaus, ed. and trans., *The Desatir Vol. 2* (Bombay: Mulla Firuz Bin Kaus, 1818), pp. 124–5. The story of the Greek philosopher follows immediately after the Alexander anecdote.

269. The manuscript of this was supplied by Anquetil Duperron, who inferred that the treatise derived from Pahlavi sources. The author is named as Zartusht Bahram Pazhdu of Rayy, apparently a Zoroastrian, who is also named as the author of the *Zartusht-Nama*, one of the treatises used by Mobad Shah. The *Zartusht-Nama* is a hagiography of Zarathushtra which locates him and Vishtaspa in Balkh. A trans. of the latter work by E.B. Eastwick was included in Wilson, *op. cit.*, pp. 477–522, which in retrospect is perhaps the sole justification for the evangelical tome.

270. *The Desatir Vol. 2*, pp. 125–6, 143–4. These stories of Hindu sages, and also that of the Greek philosopher, are repeated in the *Dabistan*, which frequently cites the *Desatir*.

271. Cf. A.V. Williams Jackson, *Zoroaster, the Prophet of Ancient Iran* (London: Macmillan, 1899), pp. 85 ff. Jackson was unusual in his references to Sipasi literature, but he merely focussed upon the legends of Zarathushtra in a very literal manner. He refers several times to the *Dabistan*, but did not use the historical material in the Kaivani biographies. Quite unlike Wilson however, he was magnanimous in his appraisal of the *Dabistan*, and in his intro. to the American edn of the Shea-Troyer trans. (New York, 1901), he remarked that the *Dabistan* is "a work by an Oriental and written for Orientals, but we of the West may equally profit by its contents."

272. John Wilson, *op. cit.*, p. 470

273. Cf. R.C. Zaehner, *Zurvan: A Zoroastrian Dilemma* (Oxford: Clarendon Press, 1955), a standard reference work on the subject. It is valuable for its translations of texts, but Zaehner's commentary is next to useless.

274. Cf. R.C. Zaehner, "Our Father Aristotle" (91–122) in *Memo-*

*rial Jean de Menasce* (Louvain: Foundation Culturelle Iranienne, 1974), esp. p. 91.

275. Zaehner, *Zurvan: A Zoroastrian Dilemma*, p. 272.
276. C. Schmitt, *art. cit.*, pp. 505–6, 532.
277. Moni Bagchee, *Ananda Coomaraswamy: A Study* (Varanasi: Bharata Manisha, 1977), p. 110.
278. Roger Lipsey, *Coomaraswamy Vol. 3: his Life and Work* (Princeton, N.J.: Princeton University Press, 1977), pp. 249–50, 219–20.
279. One of the liberal scholars who has expressed a mildly critical tribute to Coomaraswamy is Mircea Eliade in his review of R. Lipsey, ed., *Coomaraswamy* (3 vols, 1977) in *History of Religions* (1979) 19: 167 ff. Eliade expresses a reserve about some features of Coomaraswamy's writings, but observes that unlike Rene Guenon and other contemporary "esotericists," Coomaraswamy exposited his version of the perennial philosophy without surrendering the materials and methods of philology, archaeology, art history, ethnology, and the history of religions (a list to which he adds folklore). Eliade detects a growing influence of Guenon in the theological reflections of Coomaraswamy's last years. (Guenon was a traditionalist who belonged to a dervish order in Egypt).
280. Sripati Chandrasekhar, *Ananda K. Coomaraswamy: A Critical Appreciation* (Bombay: Blackie and Son, 1977), pp. 43, 46–7.
281. On this subject, see my *Minds and Sociocultures*, Part Three.
282. R. Lipsey, ed., *Coomaraswamy Vol. 2: Selected Papers – Metaphysics* (Princeton University Press, 1977), pp. 35, 38–9. Coomaraswamy does not give any detailed attention to Ramakrishna in this article, and tends to abbreviate discernible significances. For instance, he says that *c.*1866, Ramakrishna "surrendered himself to the Islamic way, repeated the name of Allah, wore the costume and ate the food of a Muslim" (p. 34). This misses the significance of the dervish affiliation that was at the crux of this episode.
283. Cf. *ibid.*, pp. 15–16.
284. Cf. *ibid.*, pp. 66 ff.
285. *Meno*, 81 bc.
286. This is Vivekananda's rendering of Hume's well known remark in his essay "The Immortality of the Soul" in *Essays, Moral, Political and Literary* (1741–2). Vivekananda refers

to "the great English philosopher Hume, nihilistic though he was."

287. *The Complete Works of Swami Vivekananda Vol. 4* (eighth edn, Calcutta: Advaita Ashrama, 1962), pp. 257–271, reproducing an article on "Reincarnation" appearing in the *Metaphysical Magazine*, New York, March 1895. Vivekananda later streamlined his evolutionary theory in confrontation with Darwinism. On this, see the intro. to my *A Sufi Matriarch.*
288. For an evaluation of the genetic question, see Shepherd, *Psychology in Science*, pp. 126 ff.
289. Pravrajika Atmaprana, *Sister Nivedita* (second edn, Calcutta: Sister Nivedita Girls' School, 1967), pp. 271 ff. Coomaraswamy expressed the same views at that time as Nivedita and E.B. Havell, an English art connoisseur who was the first foreigner to dispute the Hellenic theory, much to the displeasure of his countrymen. Havell was tutored by Nivedita in Indian aesthetics, though he does not appear to have made this source prominent in his books. Nivedita first met Havell in 1902. Coomaraswamy's first article on art appeared in 1905. For the amplification of Coomaraswamy's art theories, see R. Lipsey, ed., *Coomaraswamy Vol. 1* (Princeton, 1977).
290. *The Life of Swami Vivekananda* (fourth edn, Calcutta: Advaita Ashrama, 1949), pp. 683 ff; *Complete Works Vol. 4*, pp. 422 ff. for a fuller report.
291. Sripati Chandrasekhar, *op. cit.*, p. 48. In this critique of Coomaraswamy's views on the perennial, I do not mean to deny the entire content of his work. For instance, his "RgVeda 10.90.1 *aty atisthad dasangulam*," *Jnl of the American Oriental Society* (1946) 66: 145–61, is of unusual depth in the field of Vedic studies.
292. S.H. Nasr, *Knowledge and the Sacred* (1981), p. 38, whose interpretations follow the explicit precedent of Coomaraswamy, Rene Guenon, and Frithjof Schuon, though most particularly Schuon, whom he acknowledges with high praise (*ibid.*, pp. ix, 107–8).
293. *Ibid.*, and also affirming that Aquinas "was a great philosopher and certainly an outstanding theologian." Others would maintain that only the latter part of this definition is correct.
294. Raymond B. Blakney, *Meister Eckhart: A Modern Translation* (New York: Harper & Row, 1941), p. xv, who attempts

to align radical mysticism with Nazism, a typical recourse of orthodox apologists.

295. Nasr, *op. cit.*, pp. 20 ff., missing the crux of the Eriugenian impact. On this, see my *Minds and Sociocultures*, Part Four.

296. Frithjof Schuon, *The Transcendent Unity of Religions*, trans. P. Townsend (London: Faber, 1953), p. 9.

297. *Ibid.*, p. 11. Such statements are the more remarkable because they accompany the assumption of a prerogative in sufi esotericism. This much abused subject is currently the sport of some very pedestrian exotericists.

298. Cf. F. Schuon, *Spiritual Perspectives and Human Facts*, trans. M. Matheson (London: Faber, 1954), pp. 113–125.

299. In the English trans. of Schuon, the quotation is inaccurate. The complete passage may be found in the original in Vivekananda's *Inspired Talks*, reproduced in *The Complete Works of Swami Vivekananda Vol. 7* (sixth edn, Calcutta: Advaita Ashrama, 1964), pp. 77–8. These talks were given in America in 1895 to Christian pupils at Thousand Island Park. Most of these pupils were women. He was known to speak very highly of the Prophet Muhammad, unusual in a Hindu, but it was difficult for him to convey this perspective to Christians, who had extremely biased views on the subject.

300. Cf. Schuon, *op. cit.*, pp. 124–5. Vivekananda's heresy has also been commented upon by Nasr, *op. cit.*, pp. 111–112, who describes Vivekananda as possessing "a missionary zeal to present a modernized version of the Vedanta to the West," though he magnanimously concedes that Vivekananda "nevertheless remained related" to the teachings of Ramakrishna. In support of this characterization, Nasr cites Schuon's critique as applying to "the enigma of Vivekananda in relation to Ramakrishna." The only enigma is that created by traditionalist heresiographers who demonstrate little or no understanding of cross-cultural factors relating to the perennial philosophy.

301. P.A. Schilpp, ed., *The Philosophy of Sarvepalli Radhakrishnan* (New York: Tudor, 1952, *The Library of Living Philosophers*), p. 80.

302. S. Radhakrishnan, ed., *History of Philosophy, Eastern and Western Vol. 2* (London: George Allen & Unwin, 1953), concluding survey, p. 447.

303. *Ennead* V.1.8, trans. A.H. Armstrong in *Enneads Vol. 5* (Harvard University Press, *Loeb Classical Library*, 1984), p. 41.

304. *The Philosophy of Sarvepalli Radhakrishnan*, p. 80, citing *Librum de vera religione*.
305. For a study of Coptic monasticism, see Shepherd, *Minds and Sociocultures*, Part Five.
306. Evelyn Underhill, *Mysticism* (twelfth edn, London: Methuen, 1930), p. 456, who describes Augustine as one of the "spiritual children" of Plotinus.
307. Ken Wilber, *Up from Eden: A Transpersonal View of Human Evolution* (London: Routledge and Kegan Paul, 1983), pp. 3–4.
308. *Ibid.*, and naming also Einstein, Schrodinger, Eddington, Sir James Jeans, and David Bohm.
309. A.H. Armstrong, trans., *The Enneads Vol. 1* (*Loeb Classical Library*, 1966), pp. 44–5.
310. E.g., Louis H. Gray asserted that Porphyry suppressed the *Chaldean Oracles*, but this supposition is unjustified. Porphyry is only known to have written a critique of pseudo-Zoroastrian writings; it was a much later redaction of fragments which became known as the *Chaldean Oracles*. See Gray's introduction and Greek text in A.V. Williams Jackson, *Zoroaster, the Prophet of Ancient Iran* (1899), pp. 259 ff.
311. The treatise *Against the Gnostics* became *Ennead* II.9. See A.H. Armstrong, trans., *The Enneads Vol. 2* (*Loeb Classical Library*, 1966), pp. 220 ff.
312. *Ennead* II.9.15, trans. Armstrong, *op. cit.*, pp. 283–5.
313. *Ibid.*, p. 279 (*Ennead* II.9.14).
314. R.C. Zaehner, *Hindu and Muslim Mysticism* (London: Athlone Press, 1960), p. 180, and citing H. Corbin, ed., *Opera Metaphysica et Mystica, II* (1952). Corbin's version of Maqtul has been a cause of confusion in some quarters. Corbin's Neoplatonism tended to be in the style of Goethe rather than Porphyry.
315. A.H. Armstrong, trans., *The Enneads Vol. 4* (1984), pp. 396–7. On the gnosticism of Plotinus, see further my *History of Philosophy* (in preparation).
316. Zaehner, *op. cit.*, p. viii. Zaehner's scholarly variant of the Roman Catholic doctrinal perspective is rather easily to be proved inaccurate on scholarly grounds.
317. Zaehner, *op. cit.*, pp. 179–80. On Junayd cf. Shepherd, *Psychology in Science*, pp. 68 ff; on Bistami and Iranian Sufism cf. Shepherd, *Survey of the Sufi Phenomenon*. For aspects of Zurvanism totally neglected by Zaehner cf.

Shepherd, *Sufis, Batinis*, chapter eight, and *id.*, *Ancient Cultures in Flux*.

318. Zaehner, *op. cit.*, p. 180. In general, the literature to be found in Western languages on Ibn Arabi is not particularly clarifying, and despite the enthusiasm of writers other than Zaehner.
319. *Ibid.*, failing to do any justice to Rumi's thought, which Zaehner appears to have found unclassifiable.
320. On Rumi's universalism, see Shepherd, *Psychology in Science*, pp. 63–4; on Shams Tabrizi, see *id.*, *Minds and Sociocultures*, Appendix 1.
321. See Hamid Algar, trans., *The Path of God's Bondsmen from Origin to Return* (New York: Caravan, 1982).
322. Lenn E. Goodman, trans., *Ibn Tufayl's Hayy Ibn Yaqzan* (New York: Twayne, 1972), pp. 95 ff., 102–3.
323. R.C. Zaehner, ed. and trans., *The Bhagavad-Gita* (Oxford: Clarendon Press, 1969), p. 3.
324. S. Radhakrishnan, ed. and trans., *The Bhagavadgita* (London: George Allen & Unwin, 1949), p. 108. Cf. Zaehner, *op. cit.*, p. 133, whose commentary to this verse (2.22) acknowledges the meaning of transmigration, but remarks "perhaps a little illogically." Zaehner insinuates that rebirth is regarded as an automatic progress from a less developed state to a more developed one, but such interpretations are extremely inadequate by comparison with more sophisticated ones.
325. Huxley's introduction to Swami Prabhavananda and Christopher Isherwood, trans., *The Song of God: Bhagavad-Gita* (rev. fifth imp., London: Phoenix House, 1956) pp. 6–7. Huxley was clearly relying upon Coomaraswamy's *Hinduism and Buddhism*, which he quoted as affirming the *Gita* to be "a compendium of the whole Vedic doctrine to be found in the earlier Vedas, Brahmanas and Upanishads."
326. *Ibid.*, pp. 15–16.
327. Radhakrishnan, *op. cit.*, p. 12.
328. *Ibid.*, p. 17.
329. Cf. S. Radhakrishnan, *Indian Philosophy Vol. 2* (second edn, London: George Allen & Unwin, 1931), p. 617. On Shankara's dilemma, see also the intro. to Shepherd, *Vivekananda: his life and teaching*.
330. Louis Fischer, *The Life of Mahatma Gandhi* (1951; repr. London: Granada, 1982), pp. 47–9.
331. *The Complete Works of Swami Vivekananda Vol. 4*,

"Thoughts on the Gita," pp. 102 ff., trans. from Bengali.

332. One Eastern scholar to reach a similar conclusion to Vivekananda, though independently arrived at, is K.N. Upadhyaya, *Early Buddhism and the Bhagavad-Gita* (Delhi: Motilal Banarsidass, 1971), who says that internal references leave little doubt that the *Gita* is an integral part of the *Mahabharata*, despite the scepticism on this point (pp. 6–7), and who concludes that the *Gita* was composed between the fifth and fourth centuries B.C. (p. 29).
333. Zaehner, *op. cit.*, p. 7, and urging that it "seems certain" that the *Gita* was written later than the "classical" Upanishads, and that it is post-Buddhistic. He tentatively dated it to some time between the fifth and second centuries B.C.
334. Cf. Radhakrishnan, *The Bhagavadgita*, pp. 365–7. Cf. Zaehner, *op. cit.*, pp. 21, 393.
335. Zaehner, *Hinduism* (London: Oxford University Press, 1966), p. 168.
336. *Ibid.*, pp. 168–9, 165.
337. Cf. Christopher Isherwood, *Ramakrishna and his Disciples* (London: Methuen, 1965), pp. 75–6. Ramakrishna himself at first condemned the tantric practices implied, and continued to maintain that these practices were dangerous and unsuitable. His main purpose was to emphasize to his disciples that they should not hate the members of tantric cults.
338. Cf. Mircea Eliade, *Autobiography Vol. 1: 1907–1937*, trans. M.L. Ricketts (San Francisco: Harper & Row, 1981), pp. 190–1. One of Eliade's Indian mentors predicted that he was likely to become a second Vivekananda, but Eliade writes that this comparison did not flatter him. He admired Ramakrishna, but not Vivekananda. This relates to Eliade's sojourn at Svarga ashram, near Rishikesh, in the early 1930's. Eliade was not interested in the Vedanta, preferring Tantric yoga. His tantric initiation involved a female at Svarga ashram; it is very probable that any comparison would not have flattered Vivekananda. It seems that some scholarly novelists are a strange mixture of the "sacred and profane," a much abused phrase that appears to be largely meaningless in view of conflations. Eliade's many books and novels clearly reveal a "left hand" (*vamachara*) influence and interpretation, which is apt to be misleading. For a further comment on Eliade's methodology, see my *Minds and Sociocultures*, Appendix 1.
339. Cf. Geoffrey Parrinder, "Robert Charles Zaehner (1913–

1974)", *History of Religions* (1976) 16: 66–74, observing that the subject remained a practising Roman Catholic to the end. Zaehner's general perspective fits that of a Catholic theologian, if with avant garde features of mysticism. He did indeed complain that Christianity had lost its mystical element, but the point is that he did not satisfactorily define the nature of mysticism. Zaehner's *Concordant Discord* (Oxford: Clarendon Press, 1970) was an insidious attempt to implement his theme of theism versus monism. For instance, he compared the Neo-Confucian philosophy of China unfavourably with Roman Catholicism. Neo-Confucianism had expired after six hundred years, he remarked, because Confucianism had ceased to be a religion in any real sense. Whereas Roman Catholicism did not die, its survival being independent of any consideration that Thomism "was never much more than an intellectual game" (*ibid.*, p. 280). Though his attitude to Thomism might be considered contradictory, his adherence to Roman Catholicism was dogmatic enough. Unfortunately for Zaehner's theories, his data is often historically questionable. He still assumed that Zarathushtra had lived immediately prior to the rise of the Achaemenid empire, which suited his belief in a transmission of Zarathushtra's teaching to Israelite religion, and hence to Christianity (thereby rendering Zoroastrianism superfluous). This over-definitive contour was invidiously contrasted with the "timeless revelation of eternal truth" associated with the Hindu scriptures (*ibid.*, p. 26). A desire for historicity is valid enough, but not if it obscures the truth.

340. Zaehner, *Our Savage God* (London: Collins, 1974), p. 16.
341. See Shepherd, *Meaning in Anthropos*, chapter five, note 65.
342. Cf. *Psychology in Science*, pp. 201–2.

# INDEX OF NAMES

*About the Author:*
Kevin R.D. Shepherd was born in 1950, and has been engaged in an extensive private research project since 1977. He is the founder of the Intercultural Research Centre of Anthropography, a non-political educational project which was initiated in November 1984 upon completion of his manuscript *Meaning in Anthropos: Anthropography as an interdisciplinary science of culture*, which now awaits publication. Anthropography is a new science of culture conceived and promoted by the author in a polymathic sense of commitment.

Anthropography covers philosophy, the social sciences, the human sciences, natural science, and the history of religions. It is both scientific and humanistic. Anthropography here extends well beyond current dictionary definitions; the geographical distribution of mankind is given a polymathic focus that does not obscure intrinsic evolutionary dimensions.

Anthropography does not stress mere polymathy as an antidote to over-specialized studies, but is concerned to indicate the priorities that should govern a comprehensive curriculum.

The interdisciplinary strategy of anthropography takes particular account of the heritages of non-Western peoples. The European heritage is also covered, but not at the expense of Asiatic contributions. The author is currently working upon a series of books which has a cross-cultural relevance to Western, Islamic, Jewish, Indian, Chinese, and other culture-groups.

His first book *Psychology in Science* (Cambridge, 1983) was an unusually forthright essay incorporating a support for the ecological and interdisciplinary emphases of the Club of Rome, and a critique of scientific materialism and relativism. His biographies *A Sufi Matriarch: Hazrat Babajan* (Cambridge, 1986) and *Gurus Rediscovered* (Cambridge, 1986) comprise the first two published books in the I.R.S.A. sequence, dealing with Afghan and Indian subjects respectively.